The Enneagram of Death

The Enneagram of Death

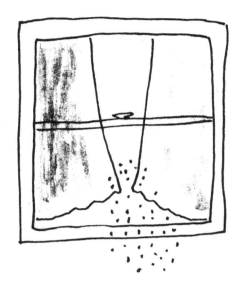

Helpful insights by nine types of people
on grief, fear and dying

Elizabeth Wagele

Published in the United States of America by
International Enneagram Association Publications,
an imprint of the International Enneagram Association.
Registered Offices: 4010 Executive Park Drive, Suite 100
Cincinnati, Ohio 45241 USA

ISBN 978 – 0 – 9857861 – 0 – 6

www.internationalenneagram.org

First Edition

Cover Design: Laura Waters

Book Design: CJ Fitzsimons

Carol Leavenworth's story *Going down to visit the crocodile* is reprinted by permission of Inside Aging Parent Care blog (edited): http://www.desperatecaregivers.com/

Dah's poem is reprinted by permission of the author. It was first published on Page 12 *In Forbidden Language*, Stillpoint Publishing, Spokane WA 2010

"She laughed in the concentration camp" is based on Elizabeth Wagele's November 2010 Psychology Today blog, "The Career Within You."

"Assisted Death" in Chapter 5 is based on E. Wagele's review in the Enneagram Educator, 1997, of "Un Coeur en Hiver," directed by Claude Sautet.

Secrets of the Estate

By Tom Clark

Death may be the side of life's mansion
That's always been turned away from us –
But that hasn't kept us, now and then,
From sneaking around to the other side
Where tall weeds grow over the broken statues,
And peeking in the windows.

From *Paradise Resisted, selected poems 1978-1984*
Black Sparrow Press, Santa Barbara 1984

The fundamental fact about all of us is that we're alive for a while
but will die before long. This fact is the real root cause of all our anger and
pain and despair.
And you can either run from this fact or, by way of love, you can embrace it.

From Jonathan Franzen, "Liking Is for Cowards. Go for What Hurts" May 28, 2011, *New York Times*

Contents

Preface
1

Nine Kinds of Reapers
9

Chapter 1 Perfectionists
11

1. Deaths Inspire Me to Live More Deeply, Expansively, Completely – Katy Taylor
2. Facing the Fear of Death: The Gift of Dying – Jan Conlon
3. Dying on December 27 – A Year to Live – And feeling the serenity of death through meditation – Knute Fisher
4. Valerie's Worm – Elizabeth Wagele
5. Dying Unselfishly – Buddhist Monk – Dharma or the laws of nature vs. modern medicine – Santikaro
6. Dr. Rasmussen's Need to Control Her Life – James Campbell
7. Being Robby – Russell Burck
8. About Perfectionists

Chapter 2 Helpers
31

1. There Is to be No Grieving – Dr. Elayne Savage
2. Death, the Frightening Teacher – Elli Boray
3. Marge's Voice for the Last Time – Elizabeth Wagele
4. "God Makes Your Bed" – as told to Elizabeth Wagele
5. Dixie Reese Couldn't Tell Her Mother How Sick She (Dixie) Was – Elizabeth Wagele
6. Helping Isn't Always Easy – Darlene Yarnelle
7. The Responsible Son – Tom Alexander
8. About Helpers

Chapter 3 Achievers
53

1. Denial of Dying – Manny Glaser
2. A Recovering Achiever and My Asserter Father's Death – Hope Hosier
3. He Keeps His Audience Wanting More – Connie Frecker
4. The Death of Overdoing – Lee Estridge
5. How My Grandfather Influenced My Life – Jeanne St. John
6. Mimi, Dying with Class – Pat Helin
7. When Caretakers Can't Cope – Morgan Silas
8. About Achievers

Chapter 4 Romantics
71

1. Going Down to Visit the Crocodile; Father's Death – Carol Leavenworth
2. Balancing Grief and Celebration – Susanne Arcand-Gawreluk
3. "I Couldn't Tell My Neighbors How You Died." – Elizabeth Wagele
4. Yonderling (a Song) – Rock Ross
5. In Search of a Father – Janet Hartzell
6. Death at the Controls – Courtney Behm
7. My Sister Judy – Dr. James Campbell
8. About Romantics

Chapter 5 Observers
91

1. My Grief Process – Jayne Johnson
2. If You Cry, I Will Never Tell You How I Feel – Charlotte Melleno
3. Three Short Observer Stories – Jaki Girdner and Joan Degiorgio.
4. Letter to His Sister About His Meeting with Pema Chödrön – Dave Scherman
5. Death – David Brooks
6. A Near-Death Experience – Tom L. Clark
7. My Father Had No More Fear – Elizabeth Wagele
8. Symbolic Death and Rebirth: What Dreams Can Do – Elizabeth Wagele
9. Assisted Death, Movie Review – Elizabeth Wagele
10. My Obsession on Death and Dying – Michele Harrison
11. About Observers

Chapter 6 Questioners
119

1. Sorrow and Fear of Living in an Unpredictable World – Dave Hall
2. 1967: Not the Summer of Love – Shelley Berman
3. Accepting Death Without Fear – Georgia Bailey
4. My Father's Death – Mario Sikora
5. Thinking of Death – Marilyn Margulius
     1. What My Near-death Experience Taught Me
     2. Death with Love as Precious and Spiritual
6. "I Was Taught We Don't Have a Body" – Samantha Mercer
7. "Death Will be Graduation Day" – Tom Purcell
8. About Questioners

Chapter 7 Adventurers
137

1. For the Birds – Kathy Heuser
2. Avon Calling – Kathy Heuser
3. I Opened to the Essential Beauty and Awfulness of Loving Someone Deeply – Catherine Williams
4. My Happy Reactions to Death – John Stabb

5. Uncle Wayne – Jaki Girdner
6. Evidence: Clarity – Poem by Dah
7. She Laughed in the Concentration Camp – Elizabeth Wagele
8. Party Girl Too Young to Die – Pat Helin
9. Dying Having a Good Time – Valentine Illidge
10. A Reason for Urgency – Harriet Berman Glaser
11. Victor the Adventurer – Vicki Zenoff
12. About Adventurers

Chapter 8 Asserters
155

1. "If you don't give me the time I'm requesting, I'll push you out forever." – Helen Clarkson
2. Two Guns – Mario Sikora
3. Lester – Jan Conlon
4. Two Hospice Stories – Pat Helin
5. Martin – Judy Meyer
6. Death by Assassination – Elizabeth Wagele
7. Bolu Bauri is Dead – Tom Rosin
8. Killer: Jim Schnobrich – Elizabeth Wagele
9. Death of a Drug Dealer – Jaki Girdner
10. About Asserters

Chapter 9 Peace Seekers
179

1. Breast Cancer – Mary Bast
2. Death is Going Home – Tom Purcell
3. The Miracle of Life – Tom Rosin
4. Real: Significant Other – Dr. Jim Campbell
5. My Buddy Karl Kresge: Peace at Last – Elizabeth Wagele
6. Belaram Bulai Was Dying – Tom Rosin
7. My Father: "Can't We Have Some Peace?" – James Campbell
8. Very Quiet Man – Jill Fanning
9. Love in Passing – Bertha Reilly
10. Dying of Picks (Almost) – Joyce Dowling
11. About Peace Seekers

Afterword
203

About the Author
205

About the IEA
206

Preface

The purpose of this book is to soothe and inspire anyone who is dying or close to someone who is dying, or grieving, or afraid of death.

The key to becoming less frightened of death is to let yourself feel deeply. While it's practical at times for some feelings to remain unexpressed, more often than necessary they remain hidden in the unconscious. One tool for enhancing your awareness of these repressed feelings is a system of personality built around nine types of people, the Enneagram. Each chapter of *The Enneagram of Death* features stories, poems, and essays I have chosen and lightly edited about one of these Enneagram types.

Many of us are afraid of our own demise and the loss of loved ones, though some of us may not realize it because we avoid thinking about the end of life. But neither fear nor avoidance changes death's reality. A third relationship to death, however, exemplified in many of the contributions in this book, is to engage with it to the extent we overcome the fear. Then a precious new beginning is possible and we can release the energy previously held back by fear.

Why are these stories organized around the Enneagram personality system and not another, for example the respected MBTI™ (Myers Briggs Typology Inventory)? Because these nine personalities are archetypes and they are immediately accessible to our emotions. We're all familiar with characters such as the powerful Asserter, the skeptical Questioner, and the ever-harmonizing Helper.

You'll distinguish how people with characteristics similar to and different from yours cope with their fear of death, the prospect of their own death, the shock of a loved one's death, end-of-life care giving situations, near death experiences, and more. You'll see how some other cultures deal with death. You'll especially resonate with your own type. *The Enneagram of Death* is an individualized way of looking at death and dying. Stories of types different from yours will offer you new perspectives.

Experiencing these stories offers an opportunity to uncover some of your previously unacknowledged cache of feelings; you can use the passion stored there to power the process of liberation. When you lose fear, life, vitality, and joy rush in to fill the gap.

The stories in this book may awaken your own unknown. I hope these stories and the Enneagram system will provide you with tools, models, soothing, and inspiration for what you are dealing with.

From defenses to authenticity

It's possible you unknowingly delay, camouflage, or deny your deepest feelings when consumed by fear of death or shocked by grief. These defenses are often necessary, yet sometimes they signify trouble. Some signs you may be resisting your true feelings are:

- spacing out (taking drugs, excessive drinking, eating, TV, etc., so as to not feel anything),
- restlessness of the mind (distracting oneself by excessive worrying, fretting, pessimism, or inner torment), and
- excessive doing (keeping busy to avoid pain).

Some of these stories may open your heart and inspire you directly, while others may give you the door to your emotional center by showing how your defenses operate. You learn from those who didn't conquer their fear as well as from those who did.

When you become aware of your defense mechanisms (see the three corners of the triangle, below), you can change direction by centering yourself and making room for your true feelings to flower. Authentic feelings take time to emerge out of the murkiness, symbolized by the lotus rising out of the mud.

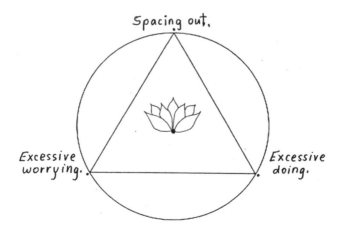

More about the Nine Personalities

The Enneagram personality system can increase your ability to observe yourself. It can also teach you to identify defenses you use along with strengths and strategies to keep your balance. Please read the sections *About [Each Type]* at the end of each chapter to learn about Enneagram theory and individual type characteristics.

The nine types and how they are connected

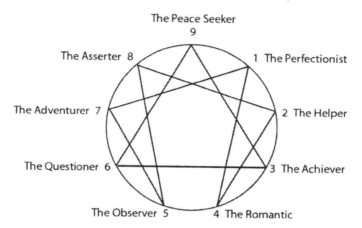

Enneagram means a drawing with nine points. *Ennea* means nine; *gram* means a drawing. The centuries-old symbol was developed as a personality system by psychiatrists Oscar Ichazo and Claudio Naranjo in the 1970s; it is used worldwide in such facets of life as personal growth, parenting, teaching, relationships, business, careers, and spirituality. The theory states that you embody one main type, which does not change, and the other eight types to a lesser degree. The two types on either side of your type, called its wings, may exert an influence on your type. Your type is also connected to the types at each end of the lines that emanate from it, called arrows. (If you are an Observer, for example, your wings are the Romantic and the Questioner. Your arrows are the Adventurer and the Asserter.) The goals of studying the Enneagram begin with learning who you are; you find your type. You continue to expand your self-acceptance and your acceptance of others as you become more familiar with the types and the theory.

You might think the Enneagram limits you by putting you in a box. The reverse is true: continually reviewing all nine personalities by studying the Enneagram can expand your vision and range of behavior. You learn to see yourself and the world from many points of view.

Subtypes or Instincts

The stories in *The Enneagram of Death* refer to the Enneagram subtypes or instincts from time to time:

- The *self-preservation subtype* refers to a person's natural instinct for protection. People of this subtype tend to keep their house full of provisions and may keep extra clothes and food in their car or extras of what they need in their purse.
- The *one-to-one subtype* is based on the in-born desire or instinct to attract a partner. People of this subtype tend to draw attention to themselves—sometimes seductively—and have dynamic personalities.
- People of the *social subtype* have an instinct for communicating and are community-oriented. They might spend time on social media, keep abreast of the news, and relay information to friends, family, and business associates.

While each person usually favors one subtype over the others, the subtypes can also be fluid and shift according to circumstances.

Death as Shadow

Ego and Shadow locked in a tango.

Your shadow includes beliefs you have about yourself that are untrue. You may think of it as negative—things you don't like to admit—however, it also consists of positive qualities you don't take credit for. Naturally, you're not fully aware of your shadow, but you can glimpse it in dreams, fantasies, and other ways. You may sometimes feel tension between your persona (the image you present to the outside world) and your shadow, similar to the tension between right and wrong, good and bad, full and empty. Part of growing is to learn how to contain this tension between opposites, for example, the tension between knowing you love your friend at the same time you are angry with her. Another important goal is to reconcile the co-existence of life and death.

The Enneagram can help you become aware of shadow elements. You'll probably dare to face your own type's shadow material first (of course, we can never uncover it all). Little by little you'll learn how some shadow elements reflect the other eight types within us and how they get along together. For example, the lion of your inner Asserter and the lamb of your inner Peace Seeker may conflict. Or your inner Adventurer with its devil-may-care attitude may war with your inner Perfectionist insisting on following rules.

Integrating shadow images into your personality by recognizing and taking responsibility for them is part of the process of becoming whole. If you reject your shadow, you're likely to project it onto others unconsciously. Without knowing it, you see in them the quality you reject in yourself, so you also reject it in them. In doing this, you're not seeing others for who they are.

Each shadow issue you reclaim is one less to project onto another person, nationality, or race.

Death lurks in the shadow of most Western cultures, which tend to deny and sanitize death, and it hides in our individual shadows, too. The thought of death—whether our own or someone else's—can bring up painful feelings, from loss to anger to fear, and even hatred. It's natural to shield ourselves from feelings that hurt. Hiding them, however, doesn't work for two reasons: first, keeping them hidden robs us of energy. Second, they continue to fester and will eventually erupt.

Everyone has the problem of facing death. This is a standard mystery.
– Joseph Campbell

Joseph Campbell and the Conquest of Fear

Bill Moyers: Which stories from mythology help us understand death?

Joseph Campbell: You don't understand death, you learn to acquiesce in death... The Sphinx in the Oedipus story is not the Egyptian Sphinx, but a female form with the wings of a bird, the body of an animal, and the breast, neck, and face of a woman. What she represents is the destiny of all life. She has sent a plague over the land, and to lift the plague, the hero has to answer the riddle that she presents: "What is it that walks on four legs, then on two legs, and then on three?" The answer is "Man. The child creeps about on four legs, the adult walks on two, and the aged walk with a cane."

The riddle of the Sphinx is the image of life itself through time—childhood, maturity, age, and death. When without fear you have faced and accepted the riddle of the Sphinx, death has no further hold on you, and the curse of the Sphinx disappears. The conquest of the fear of death is the recovery of life's joy. One can experience an unconditional affirmation of life only when one has accepted death, not as contrary to life but as an aspect of life. Life in its becoming is always shedding death and on the point of death. The conquest of fear yields the courage of life. That is the cardinal initiation of every heroic adventure—fearlessness and achievement.

I remember reading as a boy of the war cry of the Indian braves riding into battle against the rain of bullets of Custer's men. "What a wonderful day to die!" There was no hanging on there to life. That is one of the great messages of mythology. I, as I now know myself, am not the final form of my being. We must constantly die one way or another to the selfhood already achieved.

From "The Power of Myth" by Joseph Campbell; Doubleday 1988

How does one go about dying? Who on Earth is going to teach me—the world is filled with people who have never died. – Franz Wright

This book is meant for caregivers, hospice workers, counselors, grief counselors, psychologists, coaches, anyone suffering from the fear of death, loss, or complicated grief, and anyone interested in the ways death impacts the way we live.

My deepest gratitude to this book's editor, designer, and senior diplomat, CJ Fitzsimons, who has seen this book through as Jack of All Trades from almost the beginning to the very end. He has volunteered remarkably long hours, fitting them into his already busy and full life. I value his wisdom and hard work more than I can say.

Many thanks to those whose contributions have made this book possible:

Hap Allen, Tom Alexander, Susanne Arcand-Gawreluk, Georgia Bailey, Mary Bast, Courtney Behm, David Bennett, Shelley Berman, Elli Boray, David Lincoln Brooks, Dr. J. Russell Burck, Dr. James Campbell, Tom L. Clark, Helen Clarkson, Jan Conlon, Dah, Joan Degiorgio, Joyce Dowling, Lee Estridge, Jill Fanning, Knute Fisher, Connie Frecker, Harry Gans, Melanie Gerlich, Jaki Girdner, Harriet (Happy) Berman Glaser, Manny Glaser, Ted Grabowski, Dave Hall, Michele Harrison, Janet Hartzell, Pat Helin, Kathy Heuser, Theresa Hoang, Hope Hosier, Valentine Illidge, Jayne Johnson, Carol Leavenworth, Marilyn Margulius, Peter McNab, Rev. Vernon McNear (BCC), Charlotte Melleno, Judy Meyer, Tom Purcell, Bertha Reilly, Dr. Thomas Rosin, Rock Ross, Jeanne St. John, Santikiro, Dr. Elayne Savage, Daphne Schicketanz, Jim Schnobrich, Mario Sikora, John Stabb, Katy Taylor, Nigel Thompson, Clarence Thomson, Gus Wagele, Catherine Williams, Darlene Yarnelle, and Vicki Zenoff.

It's a gift for us to speak together and talk about our shared awakening consciousness at this time, on this planet. – David Bennett

We are like children building a sand castle. We embellish it with beautiful shells, bits of driftwood, and pieces of colored glass. The castle is ours, off-limits to others. We're willing to attack if others threaten to hurt it. Yet despite all our attachment, we know that the tide will inevitably come in and sweep the sand castle away. The trick is to enjoy it fully but without clinging, and when the time comes, let it dissolve back into the sea. – Pema Chödrön

NINE KINDS OF REAPERS

Contents

1. Deaths Inspire Me to Live More Deeply, Expansively, Completely – Katy Taylor
    (Becomes aware that doing what's right could be a way of covering up her grief.)

2. Facing the Fear of Death: The Gift of Dying – Jan Conlon
    (She collected bones and skeletons to fight her fear of death.)

3. Dying on December 27 – A Year to Live – And feeling the serenity of death through meditation – Knute Fisher
    (Prepares to die in a year and loses his fear of death.)

4. Valerie's Worm – Elizabeth Wagele
    (An event from almost 60 years ago torments her friend who is dying from a paralyzing disease.)

5. Dying Unselfishly – Buddhist Monk – Dharma or the laws of nature vs. modern medicine – Santikaro
    (Famous Thai monk, a Perfectionist, wants to remain in the forest, but doctors take him to the hospital to maintain control.)

6. Dr. Rasmussen's Need to Control Her Life – James Campbell
    (His mother, also a doctor, commits suicide after dementia sets in.)

7. Being Robby – Russell Burck
    (The bottom falls out when a respected older student dies.)

8. About Perfectionists

Chapter One - Perfectionists

My job is to not be easy on people.
My job is to make them better. – Steve Jobs

Chop your own wood, and it will warm you twice. – Henry Ford

What sets the principal characters of the stories in this chapter apart from the characters in the other chapters is the degree to which they try to do what's right.

Writing styles

Perfectionists try to explain things carefully and logically. Even when they write with humor or with a light touch, the reader can sense serious intent due to their adherence to principles. Note: Perfectionist Jan Conlon also wrote *Lester* in Chapter 8.

1 Deaths Inspire Me to Live More Deeply, Expansively, Completely

By Katy Taylor, Perfectionist/Reformer, Helper wing

In this story, Katy's conscience telling her she's not doing enough fights with her feelings for her sick friend.

I have a friend diagnosed with a brain tumor. It all happened quickly, from a seizure at the end of May 2010, to stage IV (spreading to at least one other organ) that November, and now, in May of 2011, he is in his last days.

Before I tell my story, I'd like to explain that I prefer to describe myself as a Reformer rather than a Perfectionist. I love to improve things and reform people and gardens in order to make them "right," but I have no sense of making them perfect.

As a Reformer leaning toward the Helper personality, my response to my friend's condition has varied. Sadness wells up when I think he may disappear from this earth. I desire for him to feel loved and cared for by his friends; am I doing enough—sending enough cards, communicating my love? Should my partner and I take a day trip to see him—six hours each way? In our crazy life-schedule we don't have enough time together to even make dates with nearby friends. I want to see him again before he dies, to help him feel better, to let him know we care about and miss him. I'm afraid if I follow my human heart-desire for contact with him while he is still here and fully feel the sadness and fear of losing him, these feelings will take over my life, and I won't be able to function well, to take care of the things I need to do and the needs of those around me.

However, when I feel this sadness, how it *really* affects me is to make me more human, more able to be touched, more open to life. My heart is sensitive and tender; my senses are more attuned to connection and contact. My typical Reformer way, however, is to close my heart down a bit so that I can focus on getting things done well.

I had a similar experience earlier this year. Just before my friend was diagnosed, an acquaintance from my Unitarian Church died of cancer. I felt called to be of service to her during her end-months, even though I did not know her well. Her death opened me to a deep experience of the mystery and preciousness of life, of life's beauty and aliveness *right now.* It inspired me to live more deeply, more expansively, more completely.

This year I also lost my sweet old dog, Teddy Bear. Losing him showed me

how much I relied on him to hold parts of myself that my identity as a Reformer did not allow. He slowed me down, brought me into my body, into my senses, into the now. He reminded me of my Being—my living presence-full connection with True Nature. He encouraged me to listen and to "Be" with him. I miss that reminder and encouragement since he died. I dealt with the same mix of motivations in his dying-process, too: wanting to care for him in the right way, so attuned to his every need that I wasn't sleeping well; and loving him. I miss him.

Death wakes me up to life. At the same time, death shows me the many ways I'm not awake to life and I push life away. It shows me how I close life down in myself. Can I allow life to crack me open and invite me to participate more in *all* its aspects? Even this desire is mixed with my Reformer desire to

improve. It's also linked to a deeper desire to reunite with my True Nature that is welcoming and loving and expansive enough to hold all things, death and life.

Katy Taylor is the partner of Dave Hall, who writes about the same friend in the first story in the chapter on Questioners.

When we recognize the genuine from within, the right action flows naturally.
– David Bennett

2 Facing the Fear of Death: The Gift of Dying

By Jan Conlon, Perfectionist, Peace Seeker wing

In this story, fearing she's not good enough to deserve a positive afterlife, Jan becomes so anxious she has no choice but to confront her fear of death head-on.

Death and Dying terrified me for most of my life. Not only was I afraid of the possible physical pain, but also the deeper issue that I was afraid of being bad—not good enough to merit a positive afterlife. Since I didn't know when I was going to die, I felt immense pressure to be perfect, so that at the requisite moment I would be prepared to meet my Maker and be found worthy. The pressure manifested itself through my gut, often causing digestive upsets. I have always held tension throughout my body. Old photos from my youth show I held myself rigidly, as if constricting my muscles would control my bad impulses. I feared if I didn't take the time to sugar coat my truth in politeness, I would not be seen as a good person. My tension held in decades of pent-up anger and I felt guilty about harboring anger. I believed if I relaxed my body, I might unleash that rage, lashing out and hurting others in the process.

Even now, my inner dialogue goes like this: "That person made me mad! Uh, oh, don't get angry! Hold your feelings in. Stiffen your body. Tighten your shoulders even more. Smile! Be nice! Control yourself! Oooh, feel the hurt. Don't feel it! What's wrong with you?"

My body then constricts even more as my fears of not being good prove to be true. I will lose my connection with my inner wisdom and my inner logic, and feel like I am in a downward spiraling vortex. Often, the only experience that is powerful enough to shock me out of it and take me to a healthier place is to be in the presence of someone who is dying. When that happens, I find myself in a situation beyond good or bad. In other situations I feel responsible for everything around me, but I cannot control the inevitability of death. I feel I have been jettisoned out of my anxiety and into a place of peace. I have no need to do anything or become anything but simply to be present.

I feel I'm being held in the arms of a mother, allowing me to let go and give myself over to something bigger and more powerful than I could ever be. My spinning cycle relaxes and a sense of safety enables me to open my mind. My Inner Critic stops judging me, others, or any part of the process. Inner peace leads to a simple state of being. I gradually realize I am not responsible for, nor do I have any power over, most things that happen around me. I begin to breathe deeply and fall into a serene acceptance of life, with all of its beauty and all of its pain.

How did I get from being terrified of Death and Dying to this better place?

One day, in my own personal consciousness-training work, I realized how much my fears, especially of death, were affecting my entire being. I

made a decision to fight against them. I started collecting skulls and skeletons, and surrounded myself with them in my bedroom. It gave me almost a sick pleasure to have these stark examples of death and dying in front of me. I jumped into this collection. What a relief to stop fighting this real part of life, accept it— and eventually embrace it.

As I became more comfortable with the presence of death around me, I found myself drawn to it even more deeply. It called to my center because death is real and genuine. As I studied more about the subject, I felt called to the study of grief and loss, and eventually became a Grief Counselor.

The gifts of doing counseling work have been immense. Working with clients I am in the presence of truth. As I support others in this work, I also remind myself of the gifts of surrendering, of there being no right or wrong, just intense presence to the moment. My Inner Critic is mostly silent, and I feel free. The reality of death is so clearly beyond my control that it is a relief to give up to something bigger; truly, this has been a pathway to surrendering and letting go.

Chapter 1

3 Dying on December 27 – A Year to Live – And feeling the serenity of death through meditation

By Knute Fisher, Perfectionist, Helper wing, Social subtype

I was one of his friends when Knute said he might not be around after the first of the year. What should I do—call suicide prevention? Talk him out of it? Play it cool? Tell him how much his friendship meant to me (as if he didn't already know)? What if he saw what I did as manipulative and not real?

A man should not leave this earth with unfinished business.
He should live each day as if it was a pre-flight check.
He should ask each morning, am I prepared to lift-off?
– Diane Frolov and Andrew Schneider, Northern Exposure, All is Vanity, 1991

It was January 7, 1999, and we were seated in a circle around a burning candle giving our check-ins. These brief stories consistently followed a period of physical centering and an opening of sacred space. The twelve men in our group had been performing this ritual every Thursday night since 1993. But tonight was a bit different. We were asked to check-in as though it were January 7th, 2000. In other words, to tell our new year's resolutions as though we'd already lived them. As the other men told their stories, I had a strange feeling. And when my turn came, I said, with hair standing up on the nape of my neck, "I won't be here in January 2000. I will die on December 27th." With the sense that I really would die in December, I described how I intended to live my last year on the planet. And that began my process of a year to live.

Interestingly, when I had the initial premonition that I would die on December 27, I was unaware of Stephen Levine's book *A Year to Live*. And when, after a few months, I read it, I was amazed at the parallels of process and perceptions. For example, I had begun journaling about the same time in my process as did Stephen, starting with a life review and identifying and forgiving old baggage. I became more and more accepting of *what is* as the year and my awareness progressed.

During check-in, when I described how I had lived 1999, it became immediately clear that I was describing my deepest values and the core of my being. I was crystal clear about what I needed to fulfill in the year I had left before death overtook me.

Part of my January 7 awareness was that friendships were incredibly important to me, and that I wanted to deepen them. So I reached out to get together for coffee, walks, and talks. I found quickly that our fast-paced society made it difficult for most folks to make the time for such leisure activities. But I valued those who made the effort to find the time. And our conversations were often of substantive topics related to an intensifying awareness of the beauty, fragility and impermanence of life.

I also knew that I needed to end the long-distance romantic relationship that I was in. I had involved myself with a woman and her two boys who needed far more than I could give. After I had spent several days in their home, I always felt emotionally, physically, and spiritually drained. I would need to return to my own home to regain my spent soul. In the men's group circle I described how I would end the relationship, which I did.

I also strongly felt that I needed to forgive myself and former loves for betrayals given and received. For example, I made a special trip to Portland to leave a letter of forgiveness to one of the most important loves and soul mates in my life, who had left me almost a decade before for another man.

I also had felt emotionally distant from my only son, and before I died I wanted to feel closer to him and to participate in his life. On January 7 I wasn't sure how that might come about. My son was a corporate pilot and flight instructor, and in April at age fifty-eight, I began taking flying lessons from him. Since he lived 250 miles away, this involved getting up at 4 a.m. to drive down highway 101. As I drove, I would listen to his voice on instructional tapes I'd made from the previous week. I'd usually arrive in time for a bagel breakfast and catch up on his life and relationships. And I always left feeling increasing love and admiration for the young man.

My mother had severe alcoholic dementia. For several years I had been managing all of her affairs, including her properties. The time and energy drain of those duties had been increasing significantly. I realized that for my last year of life I wanted to rid myself of as many of these responsibilities and burdens as possible, especially since I didn't want my son to inherit them. I wanted Mother's business to be on automatic pilot after I had gone. I contacted a property management firm to handle her properties, and I put her accounts on automatic deposit and payment schedules.

For several years I had an increasing interest in human temperament and typology. I had studied the Enneagram system but had felt I couldn't afford the training with respected lecturers and authors Helen Palmer and David Daniels. With time running out, it was now or never, so I signed up for the first of the three-year training course, realizing I might not complete it. The friendships made there have lasted to this day and the work has deepened all my relationships.

Another value that was immediately clear to me was stewardship of the planet. I love the ancient redwood trees, so I volunteered to be an interpretive ranger at Muir Woods National Monument in Marin County, California. My duties included giving talks about the old-growth forest there and helping promote an understanding and love of nature. I finally felt that my thirty years of university teaching and research in the sciences were actually being used for a good cause.

A further pull was to give back to those parts of my life that had meant a great deal. For example, I had been a member of the local public radio station KQED for many years. So I volunteered to help staff the early morning phones on their pledge drives. I would get up at 5 a.m. to drive into San Francisco and enjoy the company of other like-minded souls.

I made a firm commitment to begin each day of my last year with jogging and my spiritual meditation practice. As I extended my sitting sessions, my meditative experiences included feeling the serenity of death. Those experiences obliterated my previous fear of death. Exercise included contra dancing, which meant fully experiencing joie de vivre. I love to dance. And the dance community in the Bay Area involves superb musicians and delightful dancers and events. So I resolved to dance at least once every week and kept that promise during the year.

As the year wore on I became increasingly compelled to get my own house in order to pass on to my son. I wrote a will and living trust, transferred property to that trust, and set up appropriate accounts. I created detailed spreadsheets and put all pertinent estate information in clearly labeled files. I wrote my eulogy and obituary. I described how I wished to be cremated and to have my son fly over the redwoods to disseminate my ashes.

I was blessed to have the support of friends and my men's group throughout my year to live. As each week passed the men were both interested in and nonjudgmental of my process. In early December the group had a special evening for me. They placed me on the ground covered with a shroud and talked about me as though I had died. They spoke of my unfulfilled potential, of my joie de vivre, my chanting and dancing, my struggles with relationships, and my participation in the group. I felt deeply seen and known by these men.

Shortly before December 27 I realized that I needed to visit Death Valley. I drove down and stayed just outside the valley on the 26th, and on the 27th hiked the canyons there. Blue sky. I was deeply grateful that my body could still climb the rocks in Mosaic Canyon. I explored Bad Water and Artist's Drive, but as the day wore on, I realized that what I wanted most was to die in my own bed at home. Strangely enough, though it was late in the day and late in

December, there was no snow over Tioga Pass to slow my progress back to the San Francisco Bay Area. I arrived home around 11:30 p.m. and went to bed, not knowing if I would awake in the morning.

When I opened my eyes on December 28, I felt physically light and incredibly happy and grateful to be alive. I'd survived a *year to live* and survived it pain-free. Many lessons learned that year have become integrated into my life: omnipresent awareness without fear that death is a breath away, deep gratitude without attachment for being alive, delight in the smorgasbord that is our existence, trusting my heart and intuition, appreciation and love for fellow human travelers, and compassion for our suffering.

Of course, some days still are just pure shit.

We are reminded not to grasp onto the moment, but just live within it & allow the flow of the universe to unfold. – David Bennett

4 Valerie's Worm

By Elizabeth Wagele, Observer, Romantic wing

One of the things we learn from this story is that Perfectionists dread making even tiny errors because they can haunt them for a lifetime.

Valerie, a highly principled Perfectionist in her sixties, was several years into her illness. She made a goodbye video for her adult children in which she pledged she would never become a burden to them. Before she would become bedridden, she said, she would kill herself.

Energetic and gregarious, with a rich laugh, Val led a busy life. A social subtype, she volunteered to help with the finances of her church and was a successful Certified Public Accountant. At the time she had a high-powered job traveling around the country teaching other CPAs, she was diagnosed with Parkinson's. The doctor told her she should remain active, so she did what he said and regularly took long walks. Her disease didn't bother her much for about eight years.

Cooking and entertaining were a big part of Valerie's life. One morning she was making breakfast for houseguests, and she couldn't turn the hotcakes over. Her tremors had begun a few months before but until now had not been a big problem. Soon after this morning, however, she quit her job and quit driving. She made the video a year or so later.

As a Perfectionist, Val had no doubt about what to do—she was determined to keep trying. She was also determined to be a good example. At meal times, she insisted on reaching for her own china cups and saucers, which were kept on a high shelf. It was a slow process. They wobbled and shook on the way down, while friends or relatives who were watching held their breath. Anyone would do this, you say? Yes, but not to such an extreme, perhaps. The time it took her stretched out teas and mealtimes interminably and food got cold. She guilt-tripped anyone who tried to talk her into letting them help her. Undertaking a simple task, she forgot what she was doing.

Getting dressed to go somewhere took her two or three hours. She didn't allow any assistance with the complicated fastenings on her sophisticated clothes, so everyone rejoiced when she finally gave in and let her daughter buy her pull-on pants and loose tops she could put on easily. Aides hired to help commented that Val was one of their most exacting clients, especially when it came to executing the menus. Val periodically published rules for the household.

I met Val when I was thirteen and she was a bright, vivacious, and popular high school girl of seventeen. I only knew her casually then because of our age difference. Her sparkling brown eyes contrasted with her fashionably styled taffy-colored hair and she had a grown-up voice. She married at nineteen, became a competent mother of four, divorced while her children were young, finished college, and rose to a high position in her company. She enjoyed dancing, attending operas, working for causes, and traveling.

We'd meet at reunions over the years but we didn't get to know each other well until I published my first book. She invited me to lunch to celebrate—to let me know she was proud of my accomplishment, I think—and we began a tradition of going for long walks together. Our relationship became closer during her illness. I talked to family members when problems arose, organized her friends to take turns visiting her, and visited her often myself.

Sometimes she asked me to look up something on her computer. I had never seen such organized files in my life! I brought her music CDs and offered to play the piano for her, but she preferred playing board games. Val expressed her appreciation of my caring for her, and I appreciated her sense of humor and her friendship. We confided in each other, but when I had helped other friends who were dying, we had shared more of an inner world together.

Near the end she had some bedsores, but for the most part she had little physical pain. The stages of Val's illness lasted several times longer than predicted by the doctors. Sometimes Parkinson's turns into All Systems Atrophy, a paralyzing disease that lasts an average of eighteen months and resembles Lou Gehrig's disease. It lasted several years with Val. When she became bedridden with this, she didn't mention her vow to kill herself.

Those of us who helped Val suffered from watching her abilities wither away. During the last year of her life she was so weak she would sometimes faint when nurses took her out of bed and put her into the wheelchair, but she kept striving to live. For many months she was almost completely paralyzed and couldn't speak, so she spelled what she wanted to say by pointing to a large alphabet board. Her hand shook so much we had difficulty determining which letters she was pointing to.

The Enneagram of Death by Elizabeth Wagele

On one visit, she gestured that she had something important to tell me. By this time I had become fairly good at guessing the words as she pointed to them on the alphabet board:

"When I was sixteen, I was invited to dinner at my friend Susie's house. Before dinner, Susie's mother, Marion, talked about the importance of finishing every morsel of one's meal."

"During dinner a small green worm appeared on my plate."

At this point in her story, Valerie began to sob uncontrollably. When she calmed down I asked her what she did with the worm (thinking if it had been me I would have pushed it onto the floor when no one was looking). Her solution, however, had been to cut a piece of B-R-O-C-C-O-L-I (Val pointed to the letters) slightly bigger than the worm and leave the worm underneath.

Then she began to sob again. "I'm crying and I don't know why," she wrote, adding, "I have thought about this incident, which happened close to sixty years ago, many, many times."

"Maybe it's because you were given conflicting rules: 'eat all the food on your plate' and 'always be polite' and you couldn't do both," I offered. "Why didn't you toss it on the floor?"

Val didn't think that had been an option—someone might see her scoop it off her plate. "I just didn't want to embarrass Marion," she wrote. And more tears.

It was time for me to leave, but Val still had something on her mind, so I stayed until her nurse finished giving her some medicine. Then she spelled, "On January 7 there will be no more eating." It was now early December. She had chosen this date to begin starving herself because it was her father's birthday.

On my next visit, twelve days before January 7, I found Val peaceful, as I had never seen her. She looked relieved to have made her decision. I had brought her two kinds of ice cream. She wanted me to feed her a big bowl of each. I talked about movies that featured food: *Babette's Feast, The Wedding Banquet,* and *Like Water for Chocolate.* She lit up the way she had before she was paralyzed, when she would leaf through pictures of food in the grocery supplements of the newspaper.

As I left I felt certain that Val would keep her vow this time, though death could not have been far off in any case.

I've often wondered about the significance of Val telling me about the worm incident. I think her strong emotions indicated she was coming to terms with dying. She hadn't killed herself when she had promised her children she would because her habit as a lifelong Perfectionist to work hard and strive was so strong. She wasn't ready to give in.

I believe Val's psyche used the worm incident as a symbol to help her wrap up her life and acquiesce to death. Val needed to cry over her cruelty to herself of struggling to be perfect, symbolized by her reaction of burying the worm and feeling guilty on behalf of Marion. Val needed to cry over the stress that had eaten away at her for most of her life. Susie's mother was also a Perfectionist and represented the rules that are so important to Perfectionists. The worm itself was a symbol for decay, a message that her death was near. Val needed to cry her sadness and anger away and to have someone witness her grief. Then she could live the remainder of her life in peace.

5 Dying Unselfishly – Buddhist Monk – Dharma or the laws of nature vs. modern medicine

By Santikaro, Perfectionist, as told to Elizabeth Wagele

Both Santikaro and Buddhadasa are Perfectionists. Buddhadasa was controversial for his purist attempts to examine Buddhist scripture's roots.

I am an American Buddhist monk who lived in Thailand from 1980 to 2000. My teacher, Buddhadasa ("servant of the Buddha"), a Perfectionist, died there on his eighty-seventh birthday, in 1993. He was influential in the West and a creative, innovative, and controversial reformer in Thailand. Conservatives considered him a heretic because he didn't represent the status quo. He criticized how out of date the monastic leadership was and how many Buddhist traditions had lost their meaning. The orthodox were upset about his fresh examination of the teachings. By shifting emphasis to *this* life from past and future lives, he reframed the understanding of Buddhist scriptures. He was considered radical, but his radicalism represented going back to the roots.

I lived in his monastery when Buddhadasa was in his mid-seventies. He said he would only live to eighty because the Buddha only lived to be eighty, but suicide wasn't an option. When his eightieth birthday came, he expressed embarrassment that he was still around. This was a self-deprecating way of expressing himself, not guilt. The concept was, "If the Buddha lived eighty years, that should be enough for me." In Thailand there was no desperation to live longer than necessary. Buddhadasa's actual death in 1993 was significant in Thai history. The body of a senior monk is kept a year in Thailand, and the monasteries use this occasion to make money. Monks normally act somewhat like royalty, but he turned his back on that, saying a monk has no business doing that sort of thing. (Thailand was a monarchy until 1932. It's a constitutional monarchy now, like England.) Some years before he died, he talked about just wanting his body put in an inexpensive concrete crypt he had made and covered up with sand. It would be cheap—a Buddha image could be put on top. But when he told a few of his students about this, someone told the newspapers, and it became a big stink—so he dropped that idea. But after he died, some of the bones eventually made it there.

In the last few years, Buddhadasa had some strokes, heart problems, and diabetes. The doctors wanted to take him to the hospital so they could be in control. He politely declined all such offers as long as he was conscious. When much younger, he went to the hospital to have a burst appendix removed without anesthetic. Otherwise, he didn't believe in spending a lot of money to keep him alive. In his eighties he wanted no resources wasted on him. He spoke of nature healing us.

Dharma means, roughly, the Buddhist equivalent of god, the Buddhist teachings, nature, or the law of nature. Dharma is how everything—physical, mental, and spiritual—operates. Buddhadasa's point was that dharma or nature has ways to heal itself, and that the best medicine cooperates with dharma. It's not just physical, chemical, and mechanical. The health of our mind plays a big role. From the Buddhist perspective, mental/spiritual health depends on dharma. He was wary of expensive, high tech medicine that takes control and may not cooperate with dharma.

To remain connected with nature was therapeutic for Buddhadasa. He preferred to take what the doctors could do at the monastery and live in the woods where he had been for over fifty years rather than to live in a high-tech, stressful setting that his body was completely unfamiliar with. Hearing birds, lizards, even mosquitoes, and the monks and nuns chanting—that was his ecology. His personal doctor understood all this. Later, problems occurred because high-powered doctors from Bangkok became involved and for the most part didn't understand. They sent specialists down to the forest. The respiratory specialist, especially, spent a lot of time at the monastery, discussed dharma, came to understand, and was an important ally. But then the medical system kidnapped the body.

For institutional reasons within the Thai medical elite, his comatose body was flown to the government's leading hospital in Bangkok. A few influential doctors gave distorted information and lied to us so that we would acquiesce to their wishes. A few monks, including me, and lay supporters, accompanied the body. Within the hospital itself, there was much controversy as to how to treat him, but the more powerful doctors, who preferred a lot of interventions, tended to win out. We, of course, were barred from the meeting where these issues were discussed, even though some of us were MDs. As this was going on, his illness was front-page news in the major papers for a two-week period. During that time many people came to the hospital to pay respect.

Thai Culture

We heard many stories of grandmothers and grandfathers or mothers and fathers who had chosen to die simply and quietly at home. It seems that in Thai culture there was an acceptance of death as part of life, so people would recognize when their time had come, refuse food, and ask for their children to come and say goodbye. Usually, they would die within a couple of days. Not eating food would make the process less uncomfortable. Usually they would refuse water at the end. This was a part of the culture until more aggressive technology came along in around 1980. (Whether Thais really benefited was uncertain, since their mortality rates in the last one hundred years had been better than in Europe.) At the same time, we were hearing stories of families that were torn apart because they were arguing about whether to subject their loved ones to surgery or let them die at home. Hospitals are scary if you're not familiar with them. They were told the hospitals were safer, but they were the source of many infections.

Buddhadasa was in a coma for six weeks, which would not have been necessary if he had been allowed to die in the customary way. We knew if he were conscious, he wouldn't want to be here. The doctors—most of whom were decent people trying to do their jobs—became increasingly demoralized after futile attempts to resuscitate him. Many told us there was no way he was going to recover. The director of the hospital and the neurologist in charge of the case, however, insisted on never giving up. Buddhadasa's body continued to fall apart. He caught pneumonia a couple of times. The second time the antibiotics didn't work, but they had already ruined his kidneys so they did dialysis (these were broken promises). This wouldn't have happened had he been an ordinary monk.

I would ponder when sitting near his body, now attached to a machine breathing for it, and I could see no sign of consciousness or awareness or wisdom or intellect that made him one of the most important teachers of the last century in Thailand. I saw a leftover body the doctors were doing their rituals with.

Sixteen specialists came to check their particular organ every day, such as the heart. After the antibiotics caused bad diarrhea, and there were other mishaps, eventually he got septicemia (infection of the blood stream). The army transport plane that had brought him to Bangkok was lined up and we flew him back to the monastery. He died within a half hour, as the doctors were trying to hook up breathing equipment.

About a year before he died, Buddhadasa had made a will that specified certain things about his cremation, including that it be done simply, at the monastery. The body was burned on a pyre of wood in a very moving ceremony.

Buddhadasa's death was not what he wanted and caused much suffering. Because of all the controversy about his hospitalization, however, much debate in the media followed, seminars were held, and books were published. Some of the good that came out of the unfortunate part of his death was to inspire a discussion on the right to choose how one dies. Thai society was ripe for this.

6 Dr Rasmussen's Need to Control Her Own Life

October 28, 1903 – August 23, 1984

By James Campbell, Observer

Ruth's life is based largely on hard work and staying in control. When these are no longer possible, it appears living has lost its meaning.

Nobody ever drowned in [her] own sweat. – Ann Landers

My mother, Ruth Rasmussen Campbell, a Perfectionist, was born on a farm in Minnesota. Her parents had emigrated from Denmark twenty-five to thirty years previously. She was always ambitious, worked hard, and excelled in school. She worked her way through medical school, graduating around 1931, and married my father, nineteen years her senior, in 1933. After having two children (in 1934 and 1936), she interrupted her medical career for a few years. In 1942 she became affiliated with the South Bend Medical Clinic as a clinical pathologist and retired at age seventy-five in 1979.

Ruth had control of everything and everyone in her life—her husband, children, household help, and laboratory employees. The only thing she couldn't control was her anger. She was almost always composed at work and in social situations, but not at home. She described herself as systematic and practical. Everything was in its place. She was deft with her hands and liked doing carpentry work, refinishing antiques, and remodeling our house and the tenant house. I worked in her laboratory one summer when I was majoring in chemistry at college. We got along well because I could advise her on theory and she helped me with technique.

Chapter 1

Our father (her husband) died in 1972. She seemed to mellow a bit after that. She had always had 4.5 ounces of dry martini per day. No more. No less. She started drinking at 5:00 p.m. and ended at 6:15 p.m. when dinner would be served. After she retired in 1979, she started taking a few more liberties, maybe a beer for lunch and a nightcap. One day around that time she informed me that she had been collecting sleeping pills for several months (or years), pointing to a secret place in her closet where she kept them. She said she would take them if she ever developed an incurable illness or severe disability. As I said, she wanted to be in control. She warned me against heroic life-saving measures and definitely didn't want to be in a nursing home. Also no autopsies. She felt all this was undignified.

By 1981, I and my sister, who was a bit more alarmed than I was, noticed that she was having a few "senior moments." My mother was making out her will and had provided a trust fund for my sister, while I would inherit money outright. This ended their relationship. Up until then they fought a great deal. My mother said she missed the fighting. She was rapidly losing control.

In 1983 (my sister had been dead for one year), I met Mother in the Copenhagen Airport with the intention of visiting our Danish relatives. I asked her if she had brought her address book. She said she hadn't, but thought we could find them in the telephone directory. The cousin's name was Eric Andersen. There were fifty such names in the directory. She thought she could remember the street name—Vangejvej or something like that. I went down the list of fifty names; the second one lived on that street, answered the phone, and was the cousin. We had a great time visiting him and others whom he was connected with.

In early July 1984, I was to meet her in the Minneapolis Airport; my mother said she wanted to say goodbye to relatives. I reminded her to bring her address book. Not surprisingly, she forgot it again. We managed to contact one relative who had the phone numbers for the others. Ruth seemed intermittently confused during that trip. Although she could drive short distances at home, I needed to do all the driving. I last saw her at the Rochester MN Airport. She was quite confused.

On August 23 I was on vacation visiting my cousins in Los Angeles. One of them gave me the message that she had died on Thursday, her housekeeper's day off. The housekeeper found her on the floor in the kitchen the next day. Burnt food was on the stove. She said she had been acting very strangely Thursday morning. One of her doctor colleagues came to the house to pronounce her. He signed the death certificate as "Acute Myocardial Infarction: This was the coroner's examination."

I came home the next day and arranged for the funeral. It was assumed that she died of natural causes, but no one knows.

7 Being Robby

By Russell Burck, Ph.D., Perfectionist, Peace Seeker wing

For Russell, as with many Perfectionists, control is a major theme in his life. He realizes he has a tendency to be responsible for things that aren't his to control, however, and pledges to try harder to just be himself.

I was at home between semesters in my sophomore year at Princeton and had had my twentieth birthday less than a month before. Early Saturday evening, I got a call from Gary, a student a year ahead of me. He said, "Robby is dead." I said, "Robby? Not Robby." I started crying. My mother got a chair for me to sit down while I asked what happened.

Robby was John Robinson, the star among Christians at Princeton, or at least among the ones I knew. He was the student commander of Navy ROTC and an honors student in the English department.

What mattered to me was that Robby was one of two people who could take me aside privately and say, "Russ, what you're doing isn't the way to do things. It's not the way we as Christians live." I trusted him because he was able to talk to me gently and firmly.

"Oh, no," I thought as I felt the bottom fall out. "What will I do without him?" I hadn't had a serious conversation with Robby in some time, but I still hung on to him as one who could help me stabilize my chaotic life. I was bouncing among various ways of trying to control the world: Carrying a chip on my shoulder and putting it back whenever I thought it got knocked off, taking just about anything as an affront, bursting out in anger, trying to charm my way along, improving the hell out of every paper I wrote until I'd lost sight of the point of the assignment, and grimly plodding ahead to who knows where.

My family ridiculed mental health professions, so I didn't even think about getting professional help. I didn't even think of talking to my minister. In those days, my repertoire for seeking help from my minister consisted of my Protestant version of confession; "Rev. ___, I'm a sinner and I don't know what to do about it." All I could think after Robby died was, "There's no one else I can turn to."

Gary said that Robby and two other Princeton students had driven to a conference at Asbury Seminary. On the way home, their car had crossed three lanes and collided with an oncoming car. Robby was killed instantly. The other two were severely injured, but they survived, and as far as I know, are still alive today.

I can't recall any of the rest of that weekend, but the world was bleaker when I got back on campus. I wanted to look for Robby, but didn't know where to find him. Sometimes bereaved people think that their loved one isn't dead when they see another person who resembles their loved one when seen from the back or the side. I don't remember mistaking anyone else for Robby.

Somehow I decided that I couldn't live in a world without Robby. The only thing to do was to just take his place. I'd have to become Robby. No, not "become Robby." I'd be Robby.

Being Robby was an understandable choice for me to make. My father was away from home a great deal from the time I was 2½ until I was fourteen. In 1947 he went to Saudi Arabia to work as an agricultural consultant. When he left, he told me I was going to be "man of the house." MOTH, I called it. I'd already been MOTH, so why not be Robby? The choice was so obvious that I don't remember thinking that as pseudo-man-of-the-house, I'd already been a pretender to a significant role. I didn't remember that that experience of pretending hadn't worked.

In May 2010, however, I learned that I wasn't the only one who decided to do something like "being Robby." For my senior year I had asked George Hutchinson, then a junior, to be my roommate for the next year. At his fiftieth reunion in 2010, George told me, chuckling as he said it, "You know when Robby died, I decided that I'd just have to take his place."

Through my work with the Enneagram, I have learned that I take on responsibility that isn't mine. I assume that something is my responsibility, and I act on that assumption. In 2007, I wrote some columns for *Talk Journal*, the publication of the Association of Enneagram Teachers in the Narrative Tradition, about the importance of having a code of ethics for teachers who

work in the mode taught by Helen Palmer and David Daniels. Peter O'Hanrahan pushed back about those columns. Later, the association of Enneagram teachers roundly rejected any proposal for such a code. l didn't have the responsibility to "help" the organization in that way. But somehow I concluded that I did.

Over the last twelve to eighteen months, I've been learning that when I feel that I have a responsibility for something, I have to double-check: "Do I have responsibility for this?"

How I learned that my responsibility was not to be Robby, I don't remember. I don't remember ever concluding back then that I had gone down that path by mistake. I think I just continued not being mindful.

Over half a century passed before I began to see that my responsibility is to be myself. As often as not, I feel habit about to take over before I notice that I'm at another choice-point between my felt responsibility and my actual responsibility. Sometimes, I catch myself in mid-sentence and say, "Oh, I'm not going to finish that sentence." When I'm lucky, I catch myself before I open my mouth.

There are probably some connections between not being MOTH and not being Robby. But what they are I don't know. I'll be asking about that in the future.

8 About Perfectionists

A good example is the best sermon. – Benjamin Franklin

The truth that death is near can be the gift that drives some people to surrender to the moment and accept what-is. The desire of some Perfectionists to strive, persevere, and be in control is often so strong, however, it trumps their desire for inner calm.

Perfectionists place importance on being logical, dignified, and disciplined and guide their lives by ideals and principles. Knute Fisher methodically wraps up the details of his life and shows how well organized, good, and responsible Perfectionists can be. They try to follow rules and like to improve themselves and/or others: Russell Burck admits that he tried to improve every paper he wrote so much, he lost sight of the point of the assignment.

Many Perfectionists alleviate the stress of trying not to make any mistakes by emulating their *Adventurer arrow* (Valerie Wolf and Knute Fisher have fun by taking trips and dancing, for example). Perfectionists' *Romantic arrow* models gravitas, melancholy, and the artistic and spiritual side of life (Jan Conlon becomes a grief counselor; Santikiro and Buddhadasa are monks).

Their agenda of trying to live the right way (according to tradition, usually) can distract Perfectionists from their authentic feelings (Katy Taylor's story). They often worry excessively, feel angry about the imperfections in the world, and almost always suffer from guilt. They easily feel they or others aren't doing a good enough job, or even feel guilty for others' mistakes, as in Valerie's case. Jan Conlon worries she's not polite enough and expresses rage. Logical and competent Dr. Ruth Rasmussen goes to the greatest possible lengths to control her own life by killing herself.

Grieving

Facing one's grief or the fear of death can bring the gift of a precious peace, as Katy Taylor and Jan Conlon found out. Sometimes Perfectionists become so worn out from their self-criticism and internal pressure (similar to the *Inner Critic's* voice Jan Conlon describes), they have no choice but to go through a process of healing. Some find this reward relatively early in their lives. Others worry throughout life and may have more difficulty recovering from grief.

Shadow

Avoiding the reality of death—keeping the truth from consciousness—belongs to the shadow. For those who are idealistic, the shadow figure has no principles or the "wrong" principles. For those who are especially neat or clean, the shadow figure is messy or dirty. Some Perfectionists act out their repressed shadows when they're away from their usual environment by doing naughty things they normally wouldn't do. Puritanical Perfectionists sometimes act out their shadows by volunteering to censor risqué movies and magazines.

Shadow elements show up in the arrows. Among other things, the Adventurer arrow represents breaking loose and having fun and the Romantic arrow represents taking artistic liberties and looking at the dark side of life. These behaviors don't seem right to many Perfectionists, but Perfectionists benefit when they're able to bring them into their consciousness.

Nine types of people

Learning the nine types' points of view helps individuals find balance, acceptance, and wholeness. The Enneagram is valuable both in facing an immediate crisis and in long-range growth.

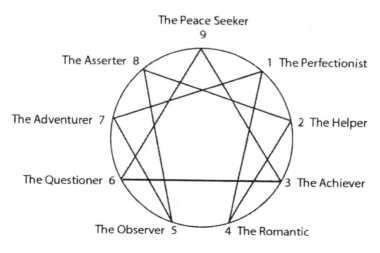

Contents

1. There Is to be No Grieving – Dr. Elayne Savage
(Therapist, who writes a blog called "Queen of Rejection," recounts the death of her mother and grandmother in airplane accident.)

2. Death, the Frightening Teacher – Elli Boray
(Uprooted in Europe by World War II, death is all around her.)

3. Marge's Voice for the Last Time – Elizabeth Wagele
(At 89, Marge's health is poor and she is tired so she decides to stop eating.)

4. "God Makes Your Bed" – as told to Elizabeth Wagele
(Health care giver knows how to treat an angry dying woman.)

5. Dixie Reese Couldn't Tell Her Mother How Sick She (Dixie) Was – Elizabeth Wagele
(Telling her mother she had terminal cancer was too painful.)

6. Helping Isn't Always Easy – Darlene Yarnelle
(Dynamics of a Helper nurse taking care of an ill Romantic mother.)

7. The Responsible Son – Tom Alexander
(Takes care of his mean father, later his suffering mother.)

8. About Helpers

Chapter Two - Helpers

How we interact with others is much more important than what we perceive as our great accomplishments in life. – David Bennett

What sets the principal characters of the stories in this chapter apart from the other chapters more than anything is their seemingly inborn ability and desire to care lovingly for other people. This chapter has few stories contributed by authors of this type.

Writing style

Helpers tend to write in a feel-good style, using adjectives freely to create colorful descriptions. Their intention in their writing, as in their behavior, is to create harmony and warm feelings. Note: Valentine Illidge, a Helper, wrote *Dying Having a Good Time* in Chapter 7.

Helper bumper sticker: I ♥ ♥

1 There Is to be No Grieving

By Elayne Savage, PhD. Helper, Achiever wing

In this story, we follow Elayne from experiencing tragedy as a child to her choice of a helping career. She uses her life experience, including her innovative method of healing her grief, to help others.

On August 22, 1954 my mother was accompanying my grandmother to the Mayo Clinic in Rochester, MN. They never arrived.

During the long layover in Des Moines, my mom learned a Braniff flight would depart earlier than her scheduled flight. What she didn't know was the Braniff flight was a "puddle jumper," stopping at every city *en route,* and a fierce storm was approaching. The Mason City flight controller instructed the pilot not to land. He decided to try anyway.

The plane with sixteen passengers and three crewmembers on board crashed into a cornfield in Swaledale, Iowa, just south of Mason City. The pilot and co-pilot died. The flight hostess and six passengers survived. Debris from the crash was spread along a line of more than 500 feet.

I was twelve years old. My brother Lee was nine.

The Long Wait for News

We waited into the evening for my mom to signal us from Rochester saying they had arrived safely. I was looking forward to our little phone company trick where she'd place a person-to-person call for "Aloysius." We'd say, "Sorry, Aloysius is not here," then we'd giggle about how we got away with something.

But the call never came.

I was absorbed in the sewing project on my lap, not paying much attention to the TV news. I had just returned from overnight camp where all the girls except me were wearing embroidered cutoffs. My dad said they cost too much to buy, so I was embroidering my own.

I heard the announcer's ominous voice; "A Braniff DC-3 went down during a storm ... on a farm ... near Mason City, Iowa." My dad jumped up, muttering something about Braniff not being the right airline. Then he was on the phone for a long time.

I just sat there, stitching. And thinking about that morning when I had acted badly toward my mother. Overnight camp was my first time away from home. I'd missed my mom terribly and couldn't wait to tell her about my experiences.

As soon as I arrived home she announced she'd be leaving on a plane the next day with my grandmother. So what if my grandmother needed medical tests at the Mayo Clinic? Why did it have to be my mother who took her? I wanted to hug my mom and say, "I need you, please don't go." Instead, as they

were leaving for the airport I screamed, "I hate you—I wish you were dead."

Poof. They Were Gone.

So I was sitting cross-legged in the overstuffed chair, staring at the cutoffs in my hands. I forced myself to concentrate on pulling the needle and embroidery thread through the thick denim. In and out, making those tiny stitches, repeating to myself, "Dad said that wasn't the right plane." Out of the corner of my eye I could see he was still in the kitchen on the phone.

I'll never forget the slump of his shoulders and that awful look on his face as he walked back into the living room. "Their plane crashed. Your mother is dead. So is your grandmother." I couldn't believe his words. I could only stammer, "You're kidding, aren't you? Tell me you're kidding."

My uncles arrived. Uncle Joe had a handkerchief tied around his neck that smelled of Ben-Gay. Uncle Max kept repeating the story of the drive to the airport. My mother and grandmother almost didn't take the flight because my mother left her purse at home. Uncle Max gave her a wad of cash and they boarded the plane. No wonder my dad had been so long on the phone—since my mother had no purse, she had no I.D. Finally the temporary morgue was able to identify her from the inscription in her wedding band.

My nine-year-old brother, Lee, was still sleeping. "Tomorrow will be soon enough to tell him," the adults decided. "Let him sleep."

The next morning Dad told Lee about the crash urging, "You have to be a brave soldier." Then Dad bundled us off to my aunt and uncle's. I wanted to talk to Lee about the crash, but I didn't know how. The three of us rode across town in silence. "There are only three of us now," kept repeating in my head.

Later that morning, we were eating pancakes at my aunt's kitchen table. The radio was on: "Two Omaha residents were killed yesterday in a Braniff Airlines crash—Goldie Raskin and her mother, Sarah Wolfson."

"They're dead?" my brother gasped. "Dead?" He ran out of the kitchen, sobbing.

Lee and I didn't go to the double funeral. Dad thought it best we stay home. "The biggest funeral Omaha has ever seen," people bragged. "There was even a police escort!"

Nothing seemed real. There was the shock of the newspaper headlines. I was embarrassed to see my mother's picture on the front page. I wished they'd used a better photo. It was so blurry I could hardly tell it was my mom. The TV and newspaper reporters were angling for an interview with Lee and me. Thank goodness my family kept them away.

After the funeral, big-bosomed women, smelling of talc, pulled me close, clucking, "Oh, you poor baby." I couldn't breathe. I overheard wisps of speculations about the cause of the crash, the condition of the bodies. I learned some new information: almost half of the passengers survived the crash! I had thought everyone died.

That's when my mind began playing tricks. "Maybe there's a big mistake and they didn't die after all," would alternate with, "Why did *they* have to be the ones to die?" In the middle of this confusion, my camp counselor phoned me saying how sorry she was. Maybe she wasn't upset with me anymore about the trouble I caused in the cabin. Camp seemed like a very long time ago.

Things stayed surreal for many years. My dad removed all photos of my mother. Lee and I thought he'd thrown them out, but when he died thirty years later, Lee found the albums hidden in the back of the highest shelf of his closet. He had moved with them four times, yet we never knew they existed. Shortly after she died he sold his business, took a job traveling, and hired a housekeeper. So we lost him much of the time as well.

The unspoken family rule was: There is to be no grieving. Our grief was to remain wrapped in silence.

There was no place to have feelings. It didn't cross anyone's mind that Lee and I would benefit from seeing a counselor or therapist. In those days it just wasn't done. I was doing a lot of acting out—mostly getting kicked out of class and study hall for talking.

My middle school principal, Dr. Brown, tried to counsel me but I completely shut down. My high school English teacher, Marcia Blacker, tried as well, asking "Is everything okay at home?" I said, "Just fine," but it wasn't. (Years later I actually searched for and located Ms. Blacker and thanked her for caring.) I threw

myself into schoolwork, socializing, school clubs and cheerleading so I didn't have to feel the sadness or spend time in a lonely house.

For many decades I lived with this tender, unhealed wound. Every year I dreaded the arrival of August 22. I felt different from friends and professional colleagues. It has always been awkward to explain that my mother and grandmother died in a plane crash. People didn't know how to respond. I couldn't talk about it. I couldn't cry about it.

Thank goodness I was required to start therapy as part of my Psychology Master's program in my mid thirties. Luckily I found a therapist who understood unresolved grief and abandonment fears.

I worked for many years to move past this childhood double loss.

I began to recognize my feelings of sadness and hurt and anger. I began to understand I don't have to be a scared child any longer.

Yet something more needed to be done. Fortunately a grief counselor reminded me: in order to grieve a loss and move on we need to make it real. You'd think as a psychotherapist and relationship coach I would have known that. But we so often miss our own issues and solutions until someone else points them out.

I woke up one morning knowing the best way to make this loss real would be to arrange a private visit to the kind of plane my mother and grandmother died in—a DC-3.

Becoming a DC-3 Groupie

Finally, I gathered the courage to track one down and found a DC-3 in pristine condition in Van Nuys: the private plane of Clay Lacy, a major aviation figure. I flew from Berkeley to Los Angeles for the adventure, taking along my yellowing newspaper clippings of the crash, and brought photos of Lee, me, and our children. I carried two long-stemmed coral roses.

DC-3's are really quite adorable. The plane was waiting for me on the tarmac, it's nose high in the air and it's tail almost touching the ground. When the door swings down it reveals the steps on its backside. I was so excited as I climbed the steps and peered into the plane. Then my heart sank: "What happened? This is *not* the passenger plane I was expecting." I had no idea many DC-3's were built solely as executive planes. This one was built for the president of United Airlines and later used by Governor Jimmy Carter. There were large, comfy chairs, burl wood cocktail tables, a sofa, and a long open bar. I thought: "Well here I am. I'll just make the most of it."

I ended up spending most of the time in the cockpit because I knew it would be identical to the one on the plane my mother and grandmother were on.

Their plane would have had two rows of seats on one side of the narrow aisle, and one row on the other. What a narrow, confined space it is! I understood for the first time how difficult that flight must have been for my claustrophobic mom. Taking off and landing several times along the route must have been miserable for her.

I could sense the essences of my mother and grandmother. I imagined tucking these essences into the blue pouch I brought with me. I had never used the pouch before. Now I know it was waiting for just the right time to be the guardian of something precious. I could feel my mother's presence. We could laugh together, sharing memories.

I got up the courage to talk with her about her experience of the plane falling from the sky. I imagined her telling me her last thoughts before she died.

As I was sitting on the plane the shackles that had confined me for so many years fell away. I could feel myself rebalancing and realigning. I experienced the healing and liberation that had eluded me for so long.

I guess you could say I'm becoming a DC-3 groupie! Jason Gore, a colleague and executive coach located another DC-3 for me to visit. He brought his camcorder and videotaped me as we sat on the plane. Thanks to Jason's sensitive coaching I had a long talk with my mother that day. We were able to say things to each other that we could not say when she was alive and I was twelve years old.

I told her how her death influenced both Lee and me in the paths our lives have taken; how much I miss her and what I appreciate about her. She told me about her dreams for us and how proud she was of our successes. She assured me she would always be present in our lives, watching over us . . . and our children . . . and our grandchildren.

My visits to the DC-3s have been life changing. The best part is how this profound experience has been captured on video to share with others who are grieving.

My college roommate has reminded me over the years of my inability to grieve in those days. She thought it odd how I never talked about my mother dying in a plane crash. Recently we watched the DC-3 video together. Bette made a powerful observation: how much I've matured in my ability to grieve and how I have allowed my mother to mature as well. My mother and I were having an adult-to-adult conversation on the DC-3!

Out of the Ashes — A Community of Survivors

Truth be told, each time I've told my story, I've fantasized someone will recognize the circumstances of the crash and contact me: "I knew someone who survived that crash" or "I know a family who lost someone on that plane."

And then it happened. The editor of the Mason City Globe Gazette interviewed Lee and me. One by one, members of the Swaledale community stepped forward to share their stories and to describe how deeply affected they are by memories of the day the DC-3 crashed in the cornfield. How neighbors volunteered for search and rescue to save the injured and protect the dead. How their farm tractors pulled ambulances through muddy fields. How they pulled down barn doors to use as stretchers.

I was stunned to learn how this community has been dealing with their own unresolved grief all these years. Just like us! Even the newspaper editor wrote, "Thank you for the opportunity to tell your story and to open another door in my life." He reflected how our reminiscences are a reminder that people heal at different speeds.

Passing Down Fears

For some of us it is a struggle to move on. And some of us pass our unresolved grief along to our children. I had developed massive fears that loved ones might die and I'd be left alone. And I was passing these fears along to my daughter.

One Mother's Day brunch when Jocelyn was about twenty-one, we were recalling how she would sob uncontrollably whenever her dad or I were late picking her up from after-school care. She remembers how she agonized that we had died in an accident.

Jocelyn and I made an amazing discovery that day. She remembers outgrowing her fears about death when she was around nine years old. I'd been working on my own abandonment fears in therapy for two years! I don't think it's a coincidence that once my anxiety abated, her fears lessened as well.

My fear of abandonment affected my daughter in another way: I sometimes held back from showing my love for her. I guess I felt if I showed too much love I might lose her, just as I had lost my mother and grandmother.

Overcoming Fears

Now I'm the grandmother, Jocelyn is the mother and Cora is the child.

I've been working hard to create in my life what I lost in that Iowa cornfield. I've been trying to do for my family what my father could not do for his—searching for ways to address our fears and overcome them together.

Because we live so many miles apart, we have created the ritual of "The Three-Girl-Photos." Ever since Cora was born I insist on taking a photo of the three of us when we are together. After all, we are the surviving women of the family now! The photos are a reminder that each of us has an inherited potential that is unimpeded by the tragedies and limitations of the past.

We *can* fly—even soar. And carry our dreams into the world.

2 Death, the Frightening Teacher

By Ellie Boray, Helper, Achiever wing, One-To-One subtype

Ellie tells of living in through World War II. Her story includes terror, anger, sleep, pain, beauty, gratitude, and appreciation of the mystery of life.

I was born into a Catholic family in Rumania. We also lived in Hungary and Austria, moving around a lot, according to the whims of World War II. By the time I was six we were living in Graz, Austria, in war-torn Central Europe, and bombs were our daily bread.

The vicious intruder

We all acted "normal," going to school, not knowing if we would survive the morning air raid, if our house would be standing by lunchtime, if our mother would survive, or if our father in the war was still alive.

On the way home from school we saw bodies or body parts pulled out of the wrecked houses. I always stopped at the point were I almost could see the house we lived in. Taking the next step and looking took courage. It was all accepted: that is life.

Slowly I suppressed all fearful or painful feelings.

I marched through my life smiling.

Slowly it dawned on me that God had failed miserably, human beings prayed on both sides for peace and God would not listen and do something. **If there was going to be anything good done, any loving and helping, it had to be done by me** – and individuals like me.

By the end of the war I was totally free and fearless (I thought).

At night the sky would light up with "Christmas trees" (fire works to show where the planes were). I could not be held back in the cellars where we tried to protect ourselves, but ran outside to collect anti-aircraft guns' shrapnel.

I lost all memories from our refugee trek: the snail pace at which we crawled along in a cloud of dust, the whole world fleeing west ahead of the Russian army. The column of Jews was dragging along beside us. Each person who collapsed was pulled out of the line and brought to a pile of corpses where they were first shot and then thrown on the pile. No time for burial.

I was about fifty years old when the memories returned and I could see it all again: the pile of corpses with one arm waving from the middle. And my mother bending over me, saying, "Ellichen, don't worry, soon he will be dead."

For the rest of my life I have not been able to feel negative and destructive feelings, until they come out as sickness.

I had become proud: I was a survivor. I was doing God's work where God had failed.

And I felt I had to unravel the mystery of death.

The war was over. We were starving but surviving.

I did not need to be vigilant any more and collapsed into sleep. Sleeping at school and home, everywhere, and I could not be woken up.

When I was fourteen, a teacher who had become a friend and healer, literally loving me back into life, died at age thirty. I thought that this was the end for me, too. But strangely her faith in me and her love for me carried me on.

Now I started to haunt funeral homes. In those days in Austria, the open caskets were lined up arranged in rows, like hospital beds. Each casket had a big sign in front of it: Name... Age... Time of funeral...

I stared over and over into dead faces, trying to force them to reveal their secret.

No answer.

Consequences

I surrounded myself with helpless people.

Often these people seemed strong, but I sensed their terror inside.

I married a Questioner. Not an easy combination. But in the end it worked out very well.

He was seventy when I realized that we were dealing with serious dementia.

Now my Helper status, my negation of negative feelings, always joyful, smiling, passionate, and getting things done, came in handy.

As he deteriorated he became the sweet man I had met when I was fifteen and whom I married at twenty, who waited for me to grow up.

His gentler loving ways returned, his macho side forgotten (*the bully who is afraid*), and he became his true self. I fell in love again and in a way these were the easiest and best years of our marriage.

He died at age eighty-two, two years ago, and I have not cried yet.

In my younger years I thought I was always well-intentioned. It took a long time to see how my behavior served me. I called my shadow side my rotten apple side and struggled to accept it. What a kick to my pride. I could see manipulating people as "helping" and what good positions it brought me.

Now I'm volunteering at the dementia ward where my husband died. I am happy there. I just seem to belong. I serve all the people at recreation time, but I also have my special friend, Kathleen, whom I adopted. We are gifts to one another. She does not know my name, but we both love one another. No blindness, no thinking that I am the Helper and Giver. No more one-way street. I need her as much as she needs me.

Somehow, over the years, *death became a friend and a teacher.* Death brought necessary endings. Death also brought a huge measure of full, living gratitude. I have to live fully and love fully because tomorrow is very iffy.

Whenever I come home now and see my house around the corner, I say, "The house is still standing." My kids used to tease me about this, so now I say it under my breath. But I feel grateful saying it.

Ann Mortifee, the Canadian singer, wrote a beautiful book called *Loving the Mystery*. We don't know what waits for us when we die, but we trust in the mystery. I sing in the Threshold Choir now, and in the care facility where I volunteer in Canada. Death is a regular companion. I feel so peaceful and grateful if I can share my peace with my dying friends. It isn't that I am less selfish than before, I am just aware of how much all this blesses me.

Somewhere along my life I received so much love and care, and still do in full measure, that I started to trust God and can accept what is. I pray that all the unexpressed fear, pain, and anger over a lifetime will somehow be healed.

His gentle loving way.

3 Marge's Voice for the Last Time

By Elizabeth Wagele, Observer, Romantic wing.

Marge was a kind and helpful person whose personality was characterized by the connection to her Asserter arrow.

All the world is written in our hearts. Love is Everything & Everything is Love
♥=∞ & ∞=♥ – David Bennett

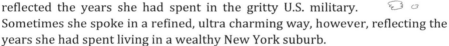

I met Marge in a Greek language class (taught by a man named Thanasis, which signifies death). She was an intelligent, classy lady of sixty-one, beautiful and sophisticated, tall, with stylish satin white hair. And she had a gift for buying fashionable clothes (often soft grayish blues) and accessories that suited her. Some Helpers project an extra-feminine image, but not Marge. Her normally matter-of-fact manner could turn gruff in an instant and she would speak with a husky voice that reflected the years she had spent in the gritty U.S. military. Sometimes she spoke in a refined, ultra charming way, however, reflecting the years she had spent living in a wealthy New York suburb.

I watched strangers pursue Marge for advice, attracted by her open, motherly face and her crystal blue eyes. These admirers annoyed her, however, because as an incorrigible Helper she couldn't refuse them. She didn't want new friends—she had plenty—and she especially didn't want anyone needy pestering her. So she would give them a tidbit—some information or a referral—and let them know this was all they could expect from her. Then she'd send them on their merry way.

In her early twenties, Marge joined the military to get away from home. Later, she became a fabric designer in New York City. Her first husband didn't have much push, so Marge got behind him and helped him find the power to create and market one of the first computer languages, which brought him a fortune. After a few years she left him and their upscale lifestyle on the East Coast and moved to Berkeley California with their young daughters. Marge taught second grade and started a private learning center. Soon she met Hack, a likable man who worked for the state government, was interested in Cuba, and liked to hike in the Caucasus and other interesting places.

Marge supported me enthusiastically whenever I played the piano someplace or gave a book talk. We took frequent long walks together where she amused me with her humor and her imitations of people. She found my husband Gus irresistible because he was newly suffering from a painful back ailment, ankylosing spondylitis. She made us dinner often and pampered him, insisting he lie on her sofa to eat.

Once when she and Hack went out to lunch in San Francisco for their anniversary, Gus and I happened to be in the same restaurant. After they were seated, long, gangly Hack spotted us and bounced over to our table to say hello. I expected Marge to come over, too, but she remained at their table looking uncharacteristically stiff. I wanted to go over and say hi to her, but the chill emanating from her table kept me back. I sensed her agenda didn't include running into anyone she knew. Not even us.

Right then she screamed at Hack, "I thought you were MY date!"

Hack scurried off to his place at her table. Gus and I, both Observer types, didn't know what to make of this until we learned the Enneagram years later. Helpers probably take anniversaries more seriously than Observers do. It's

Marge in her eighties.

likely that Marge had really been counting on this *private* romantic lunch, with Hack giving her 100% of his attention.

Late in life Marge and Hack moved to Ashland Oregon where they took classes, met new friends, and became involved in peace activities. Osteoporosis was impinging on her lungs and she contracted pneumonia repeatedly. Hack died and she began to tire easily and need daily help. I talked to her on the phone two or three times a year.

Eighteen months ago, I answered my phone:

"I called to tell you I'm going to die."

I didn't want to believe it, but it had to be true. Marge told me her body hurt so much she didn't want to keep going, so at age eighty-seven she decided to stop eating.

I felt grief-stricken about Marge's life coming to an end and about my future without her; thoughts of past and present whirled in my mind. Where would I find the words for what I wanted to tell her? I only had this one chance to express myself one last time to my precious friend. The me who interacted a certain way with Marge-and-only-Marge would cease to exist when this conversation was over.

We talked and reminisced for half an hour. Finally, we told each other *I love you* and I had the presence of mind to say, "I'll be thinking of you," instead of, "I'll talk to you later."

And "I'll be hearing from Paula, then."

A little over a month later, her daughter Paula called me and told me in the gentlest way that her mother had died. She had cherished spending the last month with her.

I miss Marge, but she was such a positive force, I feel happy when I think of her.

4 "God Makes Your Bed."

By Yolanda, Helper, Perfectionist wing, as told to Elizabeth Wagele

Yolanda is a caregiver with the appropriate loving instincts to go with her occupation as a hospice nurse.

We need to permeate our being with positive loving energy, as much as we can take, as often as we can. – David Bennett

I am a hospice nurse from El Salvador. I've seen many people through their deaths. Death, like birth, is the most private moment of your life. You retreat into yourself. If you say *thank you*, and you mean it, your eyes will show it. It's a mystery: if someone is angry and decides to starve herself, she will suffer and not die if she's not ready. For example, I worked for a seventy-year-old woman who was bitter because she felt she was too young to die. She hadn't stopped smoking when she knew it was bad for her, and now she had lung cancer.

This woman wouldn't let anyone near her. Instead of enjoying the last days of her life with her family, she was being mean to herself. When I realized what was happening with her, I started making nice food and she could smell it cooking. After two weeks of sitting in a chair, rocking and holding her stomach from hunger pains, her mood turned around and she decided it was possible to accept my offer to nurture her. "Okay, make me some scrambled eggs."

God didn't have the bed made for her yet. In the meanwhile, he wanted her to relax and have a smoothie. She began to eat and was soon visiting with her family and having a good time living again in the moment. The cancer would take her appetite away in its own time.

5 Dixie Reese Couldn't Tell Her Mother How Sick She (Dixie) Was

By Elizabeth Wagele, Observer, Romantic wing

Dixie's type was reflected in her careers in the healing professions. Her interest in a spiritual life and in art indicate her leaning toward her Romantic arrow.

Dixie was a pretty little blond girl with curly hair whose parents owned a casino in Reno, then Las Vegas. Their only child. After college, Dixie joined a cult in the Utah desert, where she lived until its leader ran off with the money. Back home in Las Vegas a few years later, she was moving out of an apartment

after breaking up with a boyfriend. When she went back to get something, he held a gun to her head, then shot and killed himself.

Dixie earned her living as a dental hygienist until, in her forties, she decided to follow a Catholic priest to Berkeley to study at the Jesuit seminary. Several times a year, she'd fly back to Las Vegas to check on her widowed mother and take her out to dinner at her mother's favorite casino on the Strip. After Dixie graduated from the seminary, she took classes in bodywork and began to build a career as a physical fitness teacher and massage therapist. In her early fifties, about a year after having chemotherapy and radiation for breast cancer, she developed ovarian cancer.

Dixie included me and a few other close friends in the spiritual and physical journey of her illness. She consulted us about decisions and sought soothing from us. She decorated her house with special tokens, flowers, paintings, and fabrics. Some of the paintings she had created herself in the style of Georgia O'Keefe. She liked honoring women and women's sexuality. Dixie filled her bedroom with soft welcoming pillows and cozy quilts, completing the atmosphere with recordings of Irish nuns singing.

As an outgoing Helper type, Dixie had strong opinions about how people dressed. Once, early in the morning on her way to work as a popular fitness class teacher in the Hotel Claremont Spa, she saw a man walking in front of her in the hotel's garden. "I can't let this guy continue through his day without letting him know how ugly the pants he's wearing are," she thought. So she ran to catch up to him and said, "Excuse me, sir, but those pants don't work for you." Then quickly continued on her way.

Dixie was like family. We phoned each other almost every day. About once a week, we'd take a walk, then make dinner with my husband, Gus. She liked to keep up on the latest styles, so I'd pay attention to how I looked, too. We'd use our best linen, decorate the dining room with candles, and include wine. When we finished talking over tea, we'd watch a movie on DVD. One of those evenings, she told us about the guy's ugly pants and asked if we thought she'd been too bold. She was allegedly asking our opinions, but knowing Dixie, if we had told her she'd been rude it wouldn't have made any difference. I think she still would have spoken her mind the next time someone made a serious fashion mistake.

Dixie was so gregarious I worried about her safety. She'd meet strangers at farmers' markets, on the train, anywhere, and fearlessly go home with them. She wanted to trust everybody.

Mabel, Dixie's mother, was frail and used a walker with oxygen. Dixie couldn't bring herself to tell her she had cancer. So when she visited or phoned Las Vegas she pretended she felt fine.

One evening about a week before she died, another close friend of Dixie and I spent an evening with her in her bedroom. She asked us to play her favorite CD of Irish nuns singing as we sat on her handmade bedspread with a bright flower pattern on it. When she got hungry, the friend and I brought home some of her favorite food. Dixie got cozy in her bed and we talked about important events in Dixie's spiritual life while we ate. Suddenly Dixie's mood changed. She became anxious and said she felt the presence of death. We stayed with her for several hours until her fear and shaking subsided. She'd sent to China for a special kind of healing coal, which she soaked in water. She'd had operations, chemotherapies, and other painful medical procedures. She'd been to healing meditation retreats and experienced hope, denial, and tonight what seemed like a spiritual transformation. Death was close at hand.

I spent Dixie's last day with her in the hospital. In the morning we made a list of who would get her most valued clothes and jewelry. I believe she left her mother out except for a ring. Her bank account went to an old friend from the cult days who had helped her with her computer. She wanted him to be able to buy a house. Around noon she fell asleep.

Friends, doctors, and associates from work stopped by and shed tears. One young nurse cheerfully remarked what a perfect body Dixie had, which made her death seem all the more unfair. I phoned Dixie's mother in Las Vegas around 1 p.m. to tell her that Dixie had terminal cancer. That left her only a few hours to prepare for the news that Dixie had died. Dixie took her last breath around 5:30 p.m.

I had encouraged Dixie to tell Mabel she was dying. Sometimes she'd seem determined to go through with it but she couldn't get the words out. Dixie told me her father repeatedly sexually abused her on the way to nursery school. She never fully recovered from the trauma. I wondered if Dixie was unable to confide in her mother because she harbored anger toward her (possibly unconsciously) for not protecting her.

It was not at all surprising that Dixie's mother felt bitter after Dixie died. Much of her attention went to trying to reclaim objects she thought should have been left to her.

6 Helping Isn't Always Easy

By Darlene Yarnelle, Helper

In this story about a caregiver, we see the conflict between two Enneagram types, the Helper wanting approval, and the Romantic wanting to be understood.

I discovered how strong the connection to the mother energy is during the illness and death of my mother, Rose Ann.

My mom had developed rheumatic fever as a child, which left her health compromised. Although she needed my help as a nurse, I struggled with feeling I never measured up to her expectations. She was mysterious. I was always trying to figure her out and look for a way to let her know I understood her difficulties. She let me know in some fashion that I most certainly did *not*, could not understand her. We did an interesting dance as a Romantic mother and a Helper daughter.

The Enneagram was a huge gift to me in helping me perceive that I was running after ways to help her and she was running away just fast enough to keep me at a close distance. When I realized it's impossible to understand someone who is determined to be unique, I stopped making myself crazy trying to do so. I believe she had a lot going on in her interior but she did not, could not, share it. I think she held on to it so it would stay mysterious/unique. My struggle with our relationship was that I could never read her and she never told me straight up what was going on for her. Sometimes I hit the right chord and did what I thought she meant and other times—no. So being part of her caretaking team was hard for me. I was devoted to being part of it but worried always that it wasn't what she really wanted.

In time, my ability to understand her improved and I relaxed more in the way I communicated with her. I became interested in looking at her more objectively and in watching my own reactions to her. I learned to appreciate her giftedness—her flair for fashion and decorating, which are different from my gift for being a good nurse.

When my mother's health seriously declined, I found myself worrying about whether I was doing enough or doing the right thing. My sisters, her main caretakers, did a good job. As the *nurse*, it was my responsibility to talk with the doctors and staff about her care and how to proceed. She had strong ideas about some things, such as wanting to die at home, but many other things, she wanted me to decide or figure out. I was always searching for signs that the choices I made met her expectations. She seemed to retreat inside herself and I needed approval. I wonder if I was too overbearing for her. She was ill, trying to deal with her own impending death and whatever process she was going through; we couldn't communicate.

One thing I have learned is that sometimes the process of dying is beautiful and enlightened but just as often it's difficult work. The ones who care suffer from watching and feeling helpless and the one dying feels the pain of letting go. Mother's process was not beautiful. She had to work hard and I wanted desperately to make it easier, but it was her process. I think she was surprised that it was as hard as it was. She didn't just go to sleep and not wake up. She had pain and impairment, and she couldn't move much. As a Helper, I wanted to make it better. I wanted it to be an enlightening experience for her and for me.

I was getting ready to serve Christmas dinner to my family when my sisters called and said my mother's breathing was becoming irregular. She had been comatose all day and showed no signs of pain until the early evening. I left dinner and went over to the house. We all spoke to her, tried to comfort her, and told her we loved her. My children came in and spoke to her. It was as if she had waited to see everyone. Shortly after they left, mother's breathing changed and I knew it was close to the end. I began to pray out loud and told her to go to the light. I believe she let go and did just that. The moment she passed turned out to be a beautiful moment—a peaceful ending to a very difficult week. We will never forget the anniversary of the death because it was on Christmas. We giggled as we wondered if she planned it that way!

We were stunned afterwards. It is hard to believe that your mother can actually die. I was numb for several months. I cried easily over little things that would remind me of her and things I thought I should have done and didn't feel like I did. It has been over a year now and I'm better than I was. I miss her and I always will. My faith and knowing she is not in pain and is in a wonderful place helps me a lot. A gift I got from the experience is that I can relate better to people who have lost their mother and I can *help* them with their pain. My mom reminded me that death is truly a personal experience. We can support people as they move through the process, but it does belong to that person. I feel blessed that I was there at the end as she made her passing. It will always be a sacred time in my memory.

Our dance is over for now. I hope we dance again someday...

7 The Responsible Son

By Tom Alexander, Helper, Self-Preservation subtype

In being conscientious, caring, and the oldest son, Tom repeatedly finds himself in responsible roles: school principal and caretaker for his parents.

My father died in 1973 at the age of seventy-five. He left my mother and three adult children; I had an older sister and a younger brother, who has since died.

My father had been ill for some time with congestive heart failure and developed a strangulated hernia, which necessitated going to the hospital by ambulance. The doctors told the family the hernia would become gangrenous without treatment.

Being the oldest son of a self-preservation Asserter father who was quite unkind to me all of my life, I had to make the decision to take over or bow out. Being born in this country, yet the oldest son of a family from the Middle East, the pressure was on me to take over, which I did.

The operation was done and on the third day in intensive care the sides of the bed were left down and my father rolled out of bed. He hit his head on the floor, the bottle of liquid hooked to the stand fell on his head and he went into a coma for three days. He came out of the coma but it took its toll on him. He needed medical as well as custodial care after that.

My father would be allowed to stay in the hospital until his strength was built up, and then assigned to the hospital floor of a nursing hospital facility for up to nineteen days. Then the family would be financially responsible. My sister and brother were married and I did not want my mother, who was on a limited retirement income, to be financially responsible. So being the oldest son and single, I signed the papers that I would be financially responsible, even though my father was unkind to me all of my life. I am a Helper!

All of us made daily visits to the hospital and hospital facility as he lost strength in the nursing facility and would be sent back to the hospital to build up his strength, then back to the hospital floor of the nursing facility again. This went on for six months.

The last night of his life he was in the hospital. I went there after work as usual, but I had a strange feeling during and after the visit, so I went back to the hospital around 11:00 p.m. during nurse shift change. When I looked at him, his oxygen tube was on the floor disconnected. I reported it to the

nursing station and was told that was impossible. After pressure from me, the nurse checked and found the oxygen tube disconnected from the wall. I went home and at 1:20 a.m. the hospital called and said he had died.

Again, being the older son, I had to take over and make the funeral arrangements. With the help of my sister, we picked out a cemetery plot, selected a casket, and attended to other funeral related tasks. I gave information to the minister for the funeral service and planned the reception after the service. I had to thank everyone for attending the service and invite him or her to the reception.

It was a long six months and a long final day, but being the older son and a Helper on the Enneagram, I felt good about what I had to do and did.

She Never Complained

My "self-preservation subtype" mother died eleven years later in 1988 at the age of seventy-seven of an extremely long and painful illness—multiple myeloma. When she was diagnosed, she was given two years to live at the most. They did not perform stem cell harvesting or transplants for this illness.

During the eighteen months she suffered she never complained. She had a strong desire to be independent and live life to the fullest. At first she could do all the daily tasks of shopping, getting her meals ready, and caring for herself. As the disease progressed she slowed down. Blood transfusions became necessary every two weeks; they'd provide a temporary uplift of energy but she'd quickly wear down until the next series of transfusions.

During the progression of the disease, the pain became more and more acute and her ability to do things for herself lessened. She made numerous trips to the hospital and at one point the hospital social worker said there was little that could be done for her and we should begin to look for nursing home placement. Since both my sister and I are Helpers, we decided we couldn't do that so we cared for her in our own home. Since we both worked, we hired a nice lady to care for her at home during the day. She would take our mother to the doctor as needed and get her breakfast and lunch ready. We'd get her dinner ready, help her eat, and provide personal care.

As her pain increased, it became necessary to get her a hospital bed and a wheel chair. Being a person of strong faith, our mother faced each day with a quiet strength and dignity.

One evening at 8:50 p.m. I picked her up from her bed to place her in her wheelchair and she died at that moment in my arms. I placed her back on her bed and called my brother who lived in another city to let him know what had happened. Since my mother's doctor knew the end was near, he told us to call him when she died, but my brother directed us to call 911. The scene at home when the responders arrived was not pleasant.

My sister and I went to the funeral home and made all necessary arrangements. Since my mother was an active person all of her life and well connected with friends both inside and outside of the church, several hundred people attended her funeral and there were more flowers than there was room to place all of them. As the older son, I had to speak and thank everyone for attending the funeral and invite everyone to the reception.

The lengthy illness was a difficult time and my sister and I somehow got through the funeral reception that followed.

8 About Helpers

Helpers belong to the Heart or Image Center of the Enneagram, which also includes Achievers and Romantics. People from this Center are concerned with how they appear to others. Helpers strive to be good, which is related to their Perfectionist neighbor's desire to do things the right way.

Helpers tune in to others' needs, enjoy giving, and are natural harmonizers. Typical of Helpers, Tom Alexander's self-image is of a good person. He doesn't like to express his negative thoughts or feelings and takes care of his teachers, students, and parents dutifully and, especially in the case of his mother, lovingly. Darlene Yarnelle and Yolanda are professional nurses. Dixie Reese was a dental hygienist and massage therapist.

Some Helpers believe they can do things for people that no one else can do. Some feel they deserve extra attention after all the care giving they've done. Many are truly selfless and do good deeds because it's right or for the pleasure it brings them. Helpers often bring out the good in others. Yolanda is able to convince a client to be kind to herself by her good-natured demeanor and by cooking food the client can't resist. Elayne Savage becomes a psychotherapist in order to help people.

When Helpers access their Romantic arrow they often spend more time alone immersed in a creative project. This helps them get in touch with who they are instead of being caught up in others' needs. Dixie created art, Elayne writes books, and Elli Boray sings and uses her compassion to help Alzheimer's patients. Accessing their Asserter arrow encourages Helpers to be more decisive and protective, as Tom Alexander was in his role as school principal. It also helped him deal with his parents. Marge was courageous and strong to seek independence and resettle across the country with her two children, not knowing what she would find. She also accessed the Asserter when she became angry with Hack for leaving her at their romantic anniversary lunch.

Needing to be needed and codependence are dangers for Helpers. Some (Elli Boray) become indispensible to someone weak. Helpers need to be careful not to overdo by volunteering too much, which can wear them out and lead to illness.

Grieving

Ellie Boray's defense mechanism of narcotizing through sleep protected her when she was traumatized from the grief of war as a young girl. In time she woke up and accepted love, beauty, reality, and a spiritual life.

Helpers frequently become exhausted from overdoing helping when there's a loss in their family or among friends. Their own wants and needs may take a back seat to giving loved ones advice, physical help, or a shoulder to lean on. Helpers also need to take time to recognize and process their own feelings and memories. What they usually do for others may be what they need for themselves when they are grieving a death or suffering from their own illness.

Shadow

The Helper might say, "I help *others*. I don't need help myself," but Helpers are as much in need as anyone. They often hide their neediness from themselves in order to support their ability to give. They become more realistic when they bring this secret out of the shadows. When they aren't direct about what they want, they risk becoming manipulative, often without knowing it. Elli eventually saw that what she called helping was manipulating.

Shadow elements show up in the arrows. Among other things, the Romantic arrow can represent the pain the Helper doesn't want to recognize. The Asserter arrow represents confidence and strength. Helpers consciously want to be good. Sometimes, however, their shadow gets the upper hand and they become bossy and overpower, thinking they know what others need. They can learn to distinguish whether they're working on behalf of the others' or their own interest.

Nine types of people

Learning the nine types' points of view helps individuals find balance, acceptance, and wholeness. The Enneagram is valuable both in facing an immediate crisis and in long-range growth.

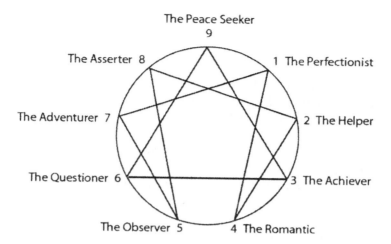

Contents

1. Denial of Dying – Manny Glaser
   (Worries he made a mistake by making himself essential for his family's well-being and happiness.)

2. A Recovering Achiever and My Asserter Father's Death – Hope Hosier
   (Stays on task doing jobs when her father dies instead of grieving.}

3. He Keeps His Audience Wanting More – Connie Frecker
   (Consummate Achiever loves the limelight.)

4. The Death of Overdoing – Lee Estridge
   (Learned to smell the flowers when she had to stop doing because of an operation.)

5. How My Grandfather Influenced My Life – Jeanne St. John
   (Her father transformed his own father's legacy of anger into working for peace.)

6. Mimi, Dying with Class – Pat Helin
   (While dying, Mimi's appearance is uppermost in her mind.)

7. When Caretakers Can't Cope – Morgan Silas
   (Maldoon's anxiety and need to present a self-sacrificing image are a problem for this family in crisis.)

8. About Achievers

Chapter Three – Achievers

If I work hard enough, there will be things I can do tomorrow
that I can't do today. – Randy Pausch

What sets the principal characters of the stories in this chapter apart from the other chapters more than anything is their ability to act in the world with confidence and energy.

Writing Styles

Achievers' writing tends to range from efficient and to the point to flamboyant (e.g. story #1). These extremes reflect their no-nonsense work habits and their attention to the image they present.

1 Denial of Dying

By Manny Glaser, Achiever, Romantic wing

In this story, Manny expresses his love for his family and literature and his need to control his life.

What is stronger, fear or hope? – Lance Armstrong

As I drive down the divided parkway, I glance at the majestic trees, which recently have been trimmed or pruned with the delicacy of a Rembrandt painting; these mammoth spectacles of nature in their most glorious way of stretching to the Gods in the heavens deserve a special moment and appreciation for the traveler to marvel at their magnificence. They existed before I was born, and no doubt will still thrill the spectator after I am gone. I then wonder whether or not those who follow me will take their time from their busy travels to notice what lies before them in their absolute sublimity.

I then arrive at my destination at the ocean bluffs overlooking the majesty of the Pacific Ocean. The gentility of the soft surf that licks the sand pebbles on the beach, as if two lovers would greet each other with their fond embrace. The foam the surf generates appears like a welcome refreshing top of a beer mug. The views of the waves undulating towards the beach are a breathless sight and can occupy one's thoughts for hours. Do I bequeath all this to my progeny? One can stare at the ocean's surf endlessly, watching for its pattern of licking the rocks and embracing the sand, welcoming the sun-bathed beach dwellers and beckoning them to enter the softness of its refreshing liquids.

All this wonder seems as if the heavens have provided a roof or a blanket for the animals of the deep sea. The miracle of the ocean, which harbors so much life and tranquility, is one of man's greatest future challenges. My interrogation of these wonders will no doubt be discovered after I am gone, but I want to know these secrets now. Will I die before I learn them? Will the secrets of the deep bottom ever be disclosed? Is it like the search for the Holy Grail? I will fight for my longevity. I want to hang around long enough so my

many questions will find resolution.

Now to the topic that really makes me crazy—what about those who I will leave behind? I cannot imagine the life of my family, wife, children, and grandchildren without me. I am their anchor—their support mechanism. The tears moisten my eyes when I ponder what their future will be. I am responsible for their life's philosophies, their wellbeing—their sense of charity and spiritual kindness to others. How can they manage without me? I cannot die; I must always be here for them. Perhaps I made serious mistakes in my life, by making myself so essential for their wellbeing and happiness. I might have provided too much ease in their lives not understanding how many pitfalls life can hand out. Who will they search for in cases of calamity when I am gone? I cannot bear the thought of it. I must always be here for them.

Do I have to face reality that nobody lives forever? In the face of actuaries, I don't have much time left. I must fight statistics and survive—everything depends on it. When the time comes, will their grief be overwhelming? Will it last in their memories throughout their lives? Or will they be content to forget their dear old dad, when they count their share of the assets I will have left them? Will their mercenary character come out and fight for every dollar? Or will they be thankful that in my life I was able to make their future a bit more comfortable? I want an answer to all these questions, but how can I know after I'm gone?

I am afraid to die, because my curiosity is so great as to what the future will be for my family. How can I prepare them for the inevitable? Can I make arrangements that I can control from the grave? In the final analysis, I must trust to their good judgment—their love for the siblings—their sense of fair play, or am I being too optimistic? Since I am afraid to die, what can I do? I know—I must keep myself alive as long as possible, and take care of my health.

Eventually, I must depend on the good work I have done in bringing them up to do all the right things. If this is possible, my death won't be too traumatic. If I am wrong, lying in the grave my pain will tell me that I didn't do enough. I can search the world for some magic elixir to extend my years, or perhaps I can do what Ted Williams' family did when he died, and send my body to Arizona for freezing so as to wake up at some future time to see what developed during those absent years. In the meantime, I need to make whatever arrangements I can, that when the grim reaper will no longer be denied, that all my best wishes are carried out. Certainly at this point, I am in denial of dying, but I must count and enjoy every moment that I have left.

Know what our purpose is and trust. In this space there is no need to strive for tomorrow, the miracle is today. Always was. – David Bennett

2 A Recovering Achiever & My Asserter Father's Death

By Hope Hosier, Achiever, probably a Romantic wing

Hope stays busy both from habit and in order to deny her grief, then realizes it's important to experience her feelings to achieve balance.

You're never ready for what you have to do. You just do it.
That makes you ready. – Flora Rheta Schreiber

I'm a performing arts teacher. My name is Hope Hosier and I am a recovering Achiever. It sounds a bit like an AA meeting, however I would like to tell you how I, a definite Achiever, and my father, an Asserter, approached his death in 1997. I didn't truly understood the realities in my story until 2002, when I learned about the Enneagram by taking a course titled *Why We Communicate*

Stay on Task!

One Less Task At a Time!

Fighting It Out

the Way We Do from Diane Morrison through Adams State College in Colorado. The Enneagram is intrinsic. In times of crisis, I believe our true personalities shine more brightly than at any other time.

I decided to go to the free University Health Center counseling to see if I needed some help to get through three major issues:

- My father had been diagnosed with lung cancer in October of 1996 and would pass away.
- I was about to graduate from college that December.
- I knew that within the next three months my four-year relationship would either end or move on to marriage.

I had listed these issues efficiently on paper with all the possible conclusions and repercussions. After hearing my statements and looking through the paper, the counselor stated the following: "Um, I am not sure what to do here. You have already come to the possible conclusions for all issues. Do you need any emotional support? If not, I think you have done a great job on your own of listing of the facts..."

December came and I did graduate and I did end the relationship with the guy. However, the next big issue would be my father's death. Starting in January, I began calling the list of local funeral planning companies and gathered as much information as possible. I chose a mortuary and wrote the number in my "death notebook" along with the phone numbers of important family members and non-immediate family/friends. I purchased *Death Rehearsal* by Doug Porposki, a step-by-step guidebook for preparing for the inevitable. I gave my friend a list to call when she got the news so that I would not have to deal with any extraneous calling. Then I sat down with my dad and asked him about music, officiates, and any details that he would want. I gathered the sheet music and had everything ready to go.

My father, the Asserter, prepared for this day by making sure that all his life insurance policies were up to date and buying me a new truck on a loan that was secured by a life insurance policy. He made sure his life insurance would cover all my mom's expenses for the rest of her life. I started dating a man my father had respected throughout my college career. Dad said, "Now I know that you and your mom will be cared for." At work my father was a PhD in Zoology and a successful member of the USDA (United States Department of Agriculture). At home he did his job and took care of his wife and daughter.

When I got the terrible call that my father had died, I went on auto pilot, as I had expected, and put my "death notebook" plans in action by coordinating food and making trips to the airport, grocery store, and plant nurseries. I was extremely efficient and his funeral was a great success. Now, 13 years and an Enneagram class later, I wonder... did I grieve? The answer is no. Not then. I couldn't grieve. I had to just keep going, keep coordinating, and keep organizing. In Spanish the verb that means "I will stay on" is *mantenganse*. My aunt and I kept saying over and over, "Mantenganse task. Mantenganse task." "Stay on task. Stay on task." If I could just stay on task, I wouldn't realize the horrible thing that had happened. For the first four months after his death, I just kept staying on task. There were piles of lists and always something that needed to be done.

I ignored the emotional side. But I realized it later and went through a huge grief breakdown. Then thanks to the class I have found a balance in my life.

My mother is a PhD as well and a straight up Observer. Holy cow. My parents were married for 34 years. When my father died, I never saw my mother cry. In fact, I saw neither emotion nor tasks. She just quietly sat. My mother has never been an emotional person, wife, or mother though I know in my heart that she loves me. So it was not a surprise to see zero emotion in this situation. She dealt only with the details that she needed to. Her response after the paramedics left our house was facts only. "Well it must have been a heart attack. The timeline doesn't make sense with anything else."

Here is one more short story from my world. My husband and I were going to see his grandmother who had just been moved into a hospice and was nearing the end of her magnificent life. (I helped coordinate all of the food for this event in my super-Achiever fashion as well.) When my husband called in to his work, he told his boss, an Adventurer, of the situation. His boss's response? Remember... an Adventurer. "Well, let me know the silver lining!" We were grateful for the Enneagram because, although it didn't excuse the statement, we at least understood where it was coming from.

3 He Keeps His Audience Wanting More

By Connie Frecker, his Questioner daughter

This story describes a sociable concert pianist and music professor who is proud of his accomplishments and of the important musicians he and his teachers have studied with.

*Hard work is never an option but a mandatory exercise
to achieve your dreams. – Sonu Sood*

My father was the quintessential social subtype Achiever. Befitting a concert pianist he had a Romantic wing. Hired as a full professor, he was the Artist-in-Residence at Ohio State University. He would question workers who came to the house about what they loved about their jobs because he loved individuals as well as the limelight; he always made the person he was speaking with feel important.

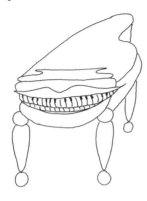

His accolades were numerous and his pedagogical lineage (whom he studied with) dated four generations back to Beethoven! The teachers he studied with were Theodore Leschetizky who studied with Carl Czerney who studied with Beethoven. He also studied with Nadia Boulanger who studied with Gabriel Faure who studied with Camille Saint Seans! And he loved for people to know that he played three concerts in Europe on the same day.

His adored mother lived to be 104 and he was proud of his ability to age gracefully. He loved being told he looked 20 years younger than he was. He worked out at the gym regularly as an octogenarian, determined to maintain his health. As he aged, he vacillated between being stoic and overly focused on his health. Instead of being clandestine about how old he was, he decided at one point to revel in how well he was aging. Appearances were important; all along the way he maintained a concern about his hair—even if he was in the hospital. He was driven and energetic nearly up to the point when he stopped teaching private piano lessons the week before he died at the age of 92.

My father, always a pragmatist and a humanist, didn't give much concern about what would come next. I did notice him cautiously inquiring of others who had had close family members pass on as to what they had recalled of the experience, however. He never let on that he was worried or afraid, but he became more and more pensive. In the eight or nine months leading up to his "transition," he began to develop some melancholy along with his reflecting.

My father displayed an incredible professionalism and an unparalleled zest for life. Ironically, however, since he was always looking for things in his house, he left all of his financial matters in impeccable order. His Achiever *can do* attitude had always attracted hosts of friends and admirers.

My sisters and I planned his service to be fitting for the Achiever that he was—lots of tribute and adoration, music he had loved and music he had written, eulogies depicting his humanity and his artistry, many remarkable photographs. The bookmarks had a professional photograph of his hands on a score of music. He had frequently remarked that fame was fleeting; however, he also said to always keep your audience wanting more. And he sure did.

4 The Death of Overdoing

By Lee Estridge, Achiever, Helper wing, One-to-one subtype

Lee works as hard as several people put together, typical of many Achievers. When she becomes ill she decides to completely change her life to improve her health and relationships.

 My husband wrote *Do Be Do Be Do Be Do* on our refrigerator door when he first met me in 1991. He had to keep reminding me life was to be lived fully in the moment. *Done is Beautiful* was not an optimum philosophy to live by. When we met, I was in *Do* mode most of the time, focusing on tasks. I was a successful sales executive with two sales people working for me. We serviced 2000 accounts and were always on the go. We participated in ten conferences a year and I was on the Board of Directors of several trade associations as an active contributor. The awards and medals I had received were testimony to the hard work that had become my trademark. Everyone knew they could count on me to get things done.

I had always been a high achiever, busy all the time accomplishing goals. Between work and personal life, there was never a moment when I could rest because my to-do list never ended. For many years, I was a single mom putting a daughter through college. I became a leader in my industry with too many things to do and never enough time.

Waking up is hard to do. For years I had studied the Enneagram and I knew that I was a Performer/Achiever. It took getting sick to take a look at how the pattern that helped me to become successful professionally and financially was costing me my health and adversely affecting the length and quality of my life and relationships. Intellectually, I understood that I needed to change, but breaking a pattern that is so rewarded in the American culture was one of the hardest things I have ever done.

In 1994, surgery on my abdomen forced me to slow down for several months. I remember the beautiful fall day in New England my inner voice spoke to me as though it was yesterday. I loved the sound and the smell of the leaves crunching under my feet as I walked along the road and the smoke from wood-burning fireplaces in the air. Time stood still for a few moments.

Then a voice from the depth of my soul said to me, "How many falls have come and gone that you did not experience? Do you want the rest of your life to be this way?" Then another voice quickly answered "NO!" I knew that this moment was a wake-up call to rethink how I was living my life.

To my surprise, as I was forced to slow down my pace in life, I had glimpses of the benefits of living in a new way. I could take the time to sit, have a cup of fine tea and watch the sunrise. I could taste and enjoy a meal. I could be present for other people rather than thinking about what I had to do next. I began to see what my fast pace had been costing me. My health was in jeopardy and I had gone through two divorces. Constant doing had cost me dearly.

Despite this inner awakening, it was hard for me to slow down while working in my job. As soon as I recovered from my surgery, I got back in the fast lane. It took me until 1996 to really listen to my inner wisdom. I couldn't change as long as I was in my current job. So I decided to retire and take time off to re-think how I wanted to live my life. I stopped doing everything for a while to create a new rhythm for myself. I went to Maui for the winter to exercise, enjoy the sun, and hang out with people who were into personal growth. After taking time off and studying things that interested me, I decided to become a life coach and help other people live a well-balanced and purposeful life. I guess we teach what we most need to learn.

My next big wake-up call was breast cancer. This chapter of my story provided me with another opportunity to evaluate the quality of my life. I kept hearing the message *slow down and stop overdoing* loudly and clearly. Deep in my heart, I knew it was not my time to die and that the cancer was yet another lesson. Indeed, this event was life changing. I was getting larger and larger glimpses of enjoying the most important things in my life. I made more changes that slowed me down. I could sustain *being* for long periods of time— long enough to see that I wanted to live a balanced life for whatever time I had left on the planet.

Today, I can accomplish plenty in a day but I always take the time to enjoy the little things along with the larger things. I spend quality time with the people I love. I am selective about the clients I work with. And I organize my life to have time to play and exercise, eat healthy and fully live. I listen to my body when it tells me to slow down. I realize I would have had an early death if I had not learned the lesson of overdoing.

*I want to sing like the birds sing, not worrying about who hears
or what they think.* – Rumi

5 How My Grandfather Influenced My Life

By Jeanne St. John, Achiever with a strong Helper wing, Social subtype

Jeanne's grandfather's violent death influenced her father's career. When she was almost fifty years old, she realized her grandfather's life also influenced her and her father to work for peace.

Growing up in a small town in the Colorado Mountains, I lived with death on a daily basis. My father was a mortician and we lived above his business. When I was four, my best friend's father was killed in an icy truck rollover. She was sad and I was happy that my Dad was okay.

We lived above a mortuary, and later next door to another, which took from death the mystery it obviously held for others. I often read to my sister from the encyclopedias Mom bought when I had learned to read at three. In one vivid memory my sister and I sit quietly on the scratchy nylon sofa during funerals so we don't un-nerve the mourners downstairs. During high school I played for funerals when the regular organist was "under the weather"—unavailable due to a slight drinking problem. My sister learned to do hair and make-up for the deceased—and the rest of us. When she permed my hair, she always started by saying, "Okay, lie down."

Life on the Brown Ranch north of Denver was hard but good in 1932. My father, Howard, an Adventurer with a Questioner wing, was sixteen and ready to start his junior year in high school. He had been anticipating a road trip with his twenty-six year-old sister and her husband all summer. In the depths of the Depression his father, Walter, was the ranch manager, which gave the family a secure income, a place to live, and even a little prestige. His mother, Helen, cooked for the crew, raised a huge vegetable garden, kept chickens, and made her own butter. She had saved butter and egg money to buy him the trombone he played in the high school band. (Actually the trombone was the result of a mix-up—when he first heard the haunting wail of a saxophone, he had mistakenly identified that magical sound with the trombone.)

Walter, an Asserter, was a demanding, hard, and angry man who had driven away Howard's much older brother in his teens. Walter was feared more than respected. He was rough on his ranch hands as well as his family—Helen, Howard, and his older sister's out-of-wedlock child they were raising as his younger sister.

That late August morning was filled with anticipation and joy—Howard's first real trip away from the ranch and time with his beloved older sister were here at last. Then, the unthinkable happened—the scrawny boy found his dad, nearly dead, in the field where the bull had gored and rolled him again and again, then finally wandered away. The trip back to the house was almost unbearable. He was sickened and frightened, and totally exhausted from the nearly lifeless weight he carried.

Walter died hours later at home and the horror of his death settled on the family, deepening their grief and guilt. The Funeral Home took the battered body and transformed it into the person they remembered. The almost-magical process of cosmetic restoration returned Walter to his normal appearance and gave the family a final image that helped to lessen the trauma.

This experience had a profound effect on Howard. He resolved to learn how to do cosmetic restoration and to make his living helping other families in this way. He asked the Funeral Director about the education and training needed and turned his life toward that distant goal.

The path from the Brown Ranch through mortuary school was daunting. They had to leave the ranch—the boy, his mom and ten-year-old "sister." They moved to southern Colorado to be near his two older siblings and their families and ran a boardinghouse where Howard cleaned, helped with the cooking, and did other odd jobs to keep the family together. He missed much of his senior year, confined to bed-rest with rheumatoid arthritis (frequently a result of trauma and grief). With a little help from a Sunday school teacher and the pastor, he accumulated enough credits to graduate in 1934.

After a year in college, he moved to Kansas City and the closest mortuary school and dedicated himself to the work. To pay for his education, he worked in local mortuaries, and played his trombone in jazz bands on weekends.

At twenty-one, he bought a small-town mortuary in southern Colorado with a loan from a family friend. For many years his skills were in great demand and he traveled to nearby towns, restoring the appearance of hundreds of victims of accidental and traumatic deaths. Families were deeply comforted and expressed their gratitude in heart-felt letters to him.

I didn't fully appreciate the impact of my grandfather's death on our family until I was nearly fifty and took courses in *Grief and Loss* to lead crisis response teams for the school system. As part of the training, we examined our own grief history, beginning with the deaths we remembered from childhood. After processing several deaths—my childhood friend LeeAnn's father, my other grandfather, and my mother—I began to see that my entire childhood was colored by the death of someone I had never met.

Because this death influenced my father so deeply and inspired his life's work, our entire family has lived in the wake of the violent death of Walter Burress—and the transforming effect it had on his youngest son. In addition to his choice of a profession, Howard consciously chose to tame and manage his own anger. He became a model of humane and loving relationships with family, friends, and employees. Leadership in Rotary International and its programs for peace, good will, and worldwide understanding has been his primary avocation for over seventy years. He was named the Johnny Appleseed of Rotary—he started eight new chapters, was a District Governor, and led a six-week tour for young Rotarians to India when he was seventy. He drove Meals on Wheels and worked at a church storehouse until he was ninety, then retired from volunteering!

While that long-ago August day was the last day of life as my father knew it, a door opened and opportunities for growth, change and transformation appeared. My life has been profoundly affected by my father's dedication to international understanding and modeling of compassionate service.

When I finished my PhD before age thirty, I had already taught English in middle and high schools for almost ten years. I spent the next thirty years as a district curriculum director, professor of education, and educational innovator. Some achievements included bringing together childcare, primary education, and family support systems; demonstrating that acupressure was an effective tool for improving student performance in physical, academic and emotional strands; introducing the Enneagram to public school teachers and students; and organizing Crisis Response Teams to help schools deal with the death of a member of their community.

Although retired for ten years, I'm still up to my ears in Peace and Justice work, Bully Prevention projects with schools, and supporting LGBT (lesbian, gay, bi-sexual, trans-sexual) kids in rural areas. I've taught workshops at International Enneagram Conferences and in the community, published an education article in the Enneagram Monthly, and still volunteer with the school district's Crisis Response Team where I wrote a script for their recently completed training film.

Death is busy now. Last week it took the daughter of one friend and the father of another. At seventy I'm acutely aware of the finiteness of our time on earth, and preparing for the loss of my own father, Howard. He's ninety-five and healthy but fading, and is well past his "three score and ten."

6 Mimi, Dying with Class

By Pat Helin, Adventurer

Achievers are known for their interest in their image or how they appear to others. Mimi also took great interest in her image after life.

Mimi, a former kindergarten teacher, was in her late seventies, but you'd never know it. Propped up in a hospital room, wearing beautiful orange satin nighties with spaghetti straps, hair perfect, pure red wig, she could see the world going on outside her window. She had intestinal or colon cancer and was Miss Hospitality. One day she asked the nurse to go to her house and get a shoebox off the floor of her closet. "I'm committing these love letters to you," she told her. "My husband doesn't know." (Her husband was a car salesman.) "This has been going on for years. I need them out of the there."

I visited Mimi in my role as hospital Chaplain and asked how I could help with her memorial service. The music was bothering her but she had decided the first song would be *Somewhere Over the Rainbow*, then *When You Wish Upon a Star*. She knew what kind of cookies to serve. She needed an urn for her ashes, but she didn't like any in the catalogue from the mortuary. They didn't match the décor of her living room where she was going to be on her piano. She was the chairman.

Done is better than perfect – An Achiever

7 When Caretakers Can't Cope

By Morgan Silas, Questioner, Observer wing

Speaking of questions of image, this unhealthy example of an Achiever tries to pass himself off as a caring husband. Morgan Silas sees him differently.

Hell for an extravert from *The Happy Introvert* by Elizabeth Wagele,
Ulysses Press, Berkeley CA.

Maldoon couldn't admit he wasn't up to the job of taking care of his dying wife. He already lacked sensitivity, but when his wife's illness struck he became vindictive and would treat Cameron cruelly. Except when they had visitors, then he'd turn into Sir Laurence Olivier going after another Oscar as a loving, self-sacrificing husband.

Maldoon was an unhealthy Achiever type with a dramatic Romantic wing. A few months after I met him in a men's group, I joined his wife's support group. I had recently retired and this was my second time trying my hand at volunteer care giving. My first experience had been one of the spiritual high points of my life and I was hoping for a repeat.

One Monday I arrived at their home at 10 a.m. to keep seventy-one-year-old Cameron company and give her husband a break. We had just settled down to tea and conversation when Maldoon came into the kitchenette zipping up his green jacket and looking for his keys. "Every morning I wake my beloved up by gently rubbing her eyes with a warm wash-cloth," he said glancing toward me. "She loves the sweet things I murmur in her ear." After adding a couple of stories about his navy experiences I'd heard many times before, he went off to do errands. Cameron looked a little puzzled and said, "I don't know why he said that. He never wakes me up that way."

When I had first arrived, with Cameron within hearing distance, he had announced in a loud voice she had urinated on the floor earlier that morning and he'd had to clean it up. (Her disease caused her to have occasional accidents). Boy, was I pissed at him for humiliating her! I wanted to either turn around and go home or smack him one, but I controlled myself and concentrated on what I was there for: to entertain and help Cameron for two hours.

As the weeks went by, I realized that Maldoon's image of himself as a heroic, saintly guy who could take care of his ailing lady all by himself wasn't going to change, even as conditions got rougher. Well into his eighties he was ailing himself, mentally and physically. As a younger man, he had been a practical and resourceful mechanical engineer. Those skills wouldn't work for the problems at hand, however. If he had ever had a knack for care giving, those days were over. But he insisted he could do it and nobody could convince him otherwise.

Cameron's adult children wanted to help take care of her, but Maldoon took their offers as doubting his competence. He accused them of insulting him. Hiring full-time nursing helped, but led to conflicts over what to feed her and when to give her which medication and how much. Cameron and Maldoon had opposite diets—he could eat no fat, she was trying to gain weight. At least one of Cameron's nurses quit, citing his cruelty to Cameron.

Cameron complained to me frequently about Maldoon's frantic behavior and refusal to lessen his load. He would go shopping to many stores for food instead of one, for example, and wear himself out. Then he'd tackle a gardening job that didn't need to be done and exhaust himself. She wanted him to move out but bringing that up to him would be like starting World War Three. Plus where would the money come from to support two households?

When Cameron became bedridden, he set up a hospital bed in the living room so she would be more easily accessible. The disadvantage was if he made any noise in the night she would wake up and ask for something that could take forty-five minutes out of his sleep. So he got the idea to sleep downstairs in the basement and moved many of his activities down there where she couldn't hear him. There were two sets of stairs to the basement. When he told me he took the set of stairs that went the long way around to check on Cameron every night so the floorboards wouldn't squeak and "wake his darling up" I blew up. I'd had enough of his bullshitting. I pointed out the real reason he didn't want to wake her was that she'd want something from him. I shouldn't have, but I did. Since I had challenged his altruism, he screamed at me for fifteen minutes. The nurse on duty heard him rage and gave me a thumbs-up as he stormed out of the house.

Maldoon made a lot of bookkeeping mistakes and flew off the handle trying to figure out the nurses' taxes. Cameron began to plot behind his back to get her needs met. For example, she'd ask me to make a phone call for her, not telling me she'd already asked Maldoon to do it and he'd refused. That made me angry because they both knew I didn't want to be put in the middle of their disagreements.

Maldoon's behavior kept getting worse, with his anger coming out as insults. He mentioned to her friends—in front of her—that Cameron was drooling more. Cameron tried to seek help from her social worker, but she was no help. Our support group got so frustrated, we started having meetings to help each other. I wrote notes to myself: "I often witness Maldoon complain to Cameron of taking care of her. He doesn't understand that frightening her is abusive." A few days later I vented: "I perceive fear between family members largely based on Maldoon's rage. He's confused, overwrought, and can't stop talking. This is not to lose sight of the fact that he has worked tirelessly taking care of Cameron for years. His severe hearing loss and her nearly inaudible voice add to the chaos." And: "Cameron is frightened of Maldoon. She tells me he rages at her, insults her, and has shaken her by the shoulders."

Her children and Cameron tried to get Maldoon to go to a support group for caregivers but he didn't see the value in it until years had gone by. He felt some relief when he did go. Cameron died soon after.

The family arranged a big funeral at which Maldoon cried and spoke poetically of the love of his life. Everyone involved with Cameron's dying process was beyond frazzled.

8 About Achievers

We should be going the distance for each other, helping each other become all that we are capable of. – Anonymous

Achievers are usually positive, charming, energetic extraverts who work hard and set high goals for themselves. They are most comfortable competing, performing, and *doing* (Connie Frecker's pianist father, Hope Hosier, and Lee Estridge). A minority of Achievers is introverted and works behind the scenes. Many Achievers are relatively out of touch with their feelings and tend to act more because of the responses they and their work receive than from inner motivations.

Achievers excel at selling things and themselves; they can often convince themselves and others of what they can do whether they have the adequate experience or training to do so or not. They can also play roles as needed. Since they are often useful to others for getting things accomplished, some doubt they are loved for who they are and have a secret desire to *feel* loved for who they are.

As an Achiever, Manny Glaser is partially afraid to die because he feels responsible for his family and doesn't want to give up control. We see the influence of his Peace Seeker arrow in his desire to hold onto the status quo—the family traditions—and the influence of his Questioner arrow in his fears about what will happen to his family without him.

Grieving

Achievers may be so rushed they don't have a chance to grieve or to complete the process of grieving. At first, Hope Hosier is too busy *doing* to grieve for her father, an example of how type structure can serve to cover up painful feelings: "For the first four months after his death, I just kept staying on task. There was always something that needed to be done. I just ignored the emotional side."

Counseling, attending grief groups and reading books on grieving can help Achievers to slow down and process their grief.

Shadow

Some Achievers keep the possibility of failure in the shadow and don't let it enter their conscious minds, yet it's natural in everyone's life to both succeed and fail. Lee Estridge begins to integrate the non-achieving, *simply being*, side of life after she has an operation and begins to question if being driven made her ill.

Exploring their feelings helps Achievers find out who they are and discover things they've been hiding from themselves. Illness and death can be particularly frightening for them. Manny admits he's in denial of dying, and then tells himself to count and enjoy every moment he has left—so he does accept his death on some level.

Shadow elements show up in the arrows. Among other things, the Questioner arrow represents looking for what might go wrong. The Achiever tends to forge ahead and not dwell on the negative, but finding and admitting mistakes is often beneficial. The Peace Seeker arrow represents calmness and lack of conflict. Achievers think they must keep going and stay on their toes if they are to get ahead, but this keeps their stress level high. If they don't take a little time off to relax they're in danger of breaking down.

Nine Types of People

Learning the nine types' points of view helps individuals find balance, acceptance, and wholeness. The Enneagram is valuable both in facing an immediate crisis and in long-range growth.

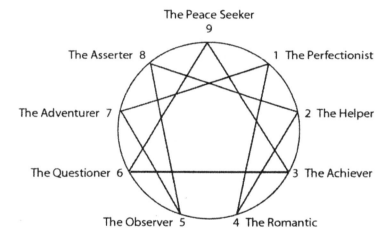

Contents

1. Going Down to Visit the Crocodile; Father's Death – Carol Leavenworth
    (Her dream calls her to face painful feelings and memories, which leads to healing.)

2. Balancing Grief and Celebration – Susanne Arcand-Gawreluk
    (Raised to be a Helper, she knew she was a Romantic from an early age. She becomes a hospice worker.)

3. "I Couldn't Tell My Neighbors How You Died." – Elizabeth Wagele
    (His experience with AIDS became another way to explore the truth.)

4. Yonderling (a Song) – Rock Ross
    ("When I go I want to explode into total oblivion.")

5. In Search of a Father – Janet Hartzell
    (When her mother dies, she reads letters that fill in information she has yearned for.)

6. Death at the Controls – Courtney Behm
    (The importance of believing death is inevitable. And her fear of dying in a plane crash.)

7. My Sister Judy – Dr. James Campbell
    (Medications for bipolar disorder interferes with her creativity and she has melanoma.)

8. About Romantics

Chapter Four – Romantics

Within us is the ability to represent our deep truths in a way that allows them to be heard. – David Bennett

What sets apart the principle characters of the stories in this group more than anything is their intense involvement with the emotional, searching side of life.

Writing Styles

The writing style of Romantics is usually expressive and distinctive. It ranges from flamboyant (Achiever wing) to intellectual (Observer wing). Note: Besides these stories, Romantics Charlotte Melleno wrote *"If You Cry I'll Never Tell You How I Feel"* in Chapter 5 and Judy Meyer wrote *"Martin"* in Chapter 8.

1 Going Down to Visit the Crocodile

By Carol Leavenworth, Romantic

In this story, Carol is so upset by her father's death she has trouble functioning until a dream reminds her to embrace her painful feeling and memories rather than avoiding them. The gift of Romantics is their capacity to open their hearts to human sorrow. Their reward is to feel deeply.

Immediately after my ninety-one year-old father died last month I felt numb and shocked. Then I began to experience symptoms of grief: waves of sadness, deep fatigue, lack of focus, physical clumsiness, and diminished ability to solve

complex problems. I found myself staring into space, wondering what to do next. At the same time I felt overwhelming pressure to accomplish the many tasks that accompany the death of a parent. I had trouble sleeping, and when I did drop off, my sleep was disturbed by vaguely threatening dreams that I could not recall.

Then I had a dream I did remember:

I walk down a hill to the edge of the water where I encounter a crocodile. I am captivated by her, and return to visit her several times. On my last visit, her nest is filled with baby crocodiles—thirteen in all.

Before I had this dream, painful feelings and memories would immediately arise whenever I closed my eyes to try to sleep. I'd try to lull myself to sleep by listening to recorded books, but being alone in the dark with the contents of my mind was too painful.

I felt the dream was calling me to face the painful feelings and memories that came up each night instead of attempting to avoid them. It was a reminder of the creativity that can emerge out of embracing a threatening or dangerous energy in the psyche.

Working with the Crocodile

Now at night when I close my eyes I imagine I am going down to visit the crocodile. Sometimes she welcomes me with a difficult image, sometimes with a sorrowful feeling or even twitchy feet. Sometimes I fall asleep easily, but wake up in the early morning hours with distressing thoughts or difficult memories that I need to welcome and accept. These nights I am often conscious of dreams where I am working hard to solve a problem or finish a project.

But overall I am sleeping better. And my intuition tells me that not only is this approach to grieving healthier, but that the promise of the thirteen baby crocodiles is a gift of acceptance and of renewal that awaits me.

2 Balancing Grief and Celebration

By Susanne Arcand-Gawreluk, Romantic, strong Achiever wing, One-to-One subtype

Romantics, in general, are probably the most comfortable with death and the thought of death of all the Enneagram types, as this story demonstrates.

Everyone agrees that we all come and we all go, however I feel there is more to the going process than what Western society focuses on. The grieving process offers depth and beauty as well as the opportunity to revel in the celebration for a life well lived. Death and dying to me are fascinating, comforting, and dear subjects to me.

As an Enneagram Romantic that grew up a socialized Helper in our household of ten, I ranked second oldest surrounded by five brothers and two little sisters, nine and sixteen years younger than me. Obviously, my Helper qualities were more needed and more socially accepted within our home than the sensitive and emotional qualities of an authentic Romantic, and so Helper it was.

As a child, I was confused by the hushed whispers surrounding the dying process and the immense sorrow around a person's death. Yes, I do understand and respect the loss for those left behind—but I am referring to the lack of honoring the person who has just graduated from Earth school; couldn't we celebrate a job completed and well done, according to the dead person's own standards?

On the way to my first funeral, my mother instructed me to say, "I am sorry for your loss," to our dear neighbor's wife. My eyebrows shot up and I felt outrage in my chest and throat at the thought that I'd lie to our sweet neighbor lady! My childhood Romantic perspective was, "What a lucky duck. He's done and outta here, so how about, 'Congratulations on your husband's success, Mrs. Nelson!'" This was my beginning to struggle out of the grips of being a socialized Helper and finding my true essence as a Romantic.

Understand, I am not unfamiliar with the dark side of death. I have experienced: (1) the unexplainable pain of being pregnant on bed rest and witnessing a friend lose her unborn child after months together in the hospital. I was left to mourn her unborn baby and wrestle with the uncertain fate of my own child for weeks. (2) the horror of witnessing a young girl get hit by a car, holding her in my arms, unable to feel her breathing. (3) a fun evening with a group of friends, only to have one go home and commit suicide.

Most of us know the hollow feeling of missing a relative or friend who left too soon. With every birthday, anniversary, or another death, that basic lesson of death resurfaces, brushes against our heart, and haunts our mind over and over until it's our turn. Death is an impressive invisible force that deeply affects everyone, even those who pretend to ignore it.

I have had the opportunity to celebrate with some amazing people as a hospice volunteer for the past thirteen years. One of my hospice friends was Will, who led a simple life doing maintenance work. He never graduated high school and decided not to marry after retiring from the Navy. Will was dying alone in a nursing home. Hospice honored his meager request to provide someone to come visit and play cribbage with him. Sure, we played cribbage, but my real work was in listening to his life stories. Don't tell the nurses, but there was one more private request—to roll him outside for "a breath of fresh air," also known as a cigarette. To witness him draw in hard and deep on those hand-rolled cancer sticks and release the smoke with slow, exquisite reverence was one of those humbling moments volunteers experience doing God's work. He was dying of chronic pulmonary edema so he would basically drown in his own lung liquid, if pneumonia didn't get him first. That's how he saw it, anyway.

One visit, he sheepishly asked me to help him "gussy up" before I left. I apprehensively said, "Sure thing, Will." I explained that when it came to shaving I usually nick my own smooth-surfaced legs, so I couldn't guarantee the outcome of this venture through his beautiful wrinkly face! We laughed and I cautiously proceeded. I felt humbled to be the one to shave him and comb his hair just right. Even more so looking back, when I found out he had slipped away peacefully that very night. I believe he knew something was up and wanted to be properly prepared. What a neat and concise ending to an unassuming man's life; just like he'd have wanted it, I believe. Was I sad to see him go? Absolutely! But I was just as jubilant to have him leave having celebrated his history over afternoon chats and a cribbage board. As simply as this man lived, I was honored to be his witness as friend and family on his final afternoon on earth with us. Job well done, Will!

We all will journey down the sacred path to death's door. So from a Romantic's perspective, let's embrace the path with courage and celebrate the destination with faith, right? Roosevelt was quoted as always trying to balance the ideal and the practical. I feel the

Romantic can grip the practical harsh reality of dying and death and continue to be ideally awed at its celebratory mystery. This balances our outlook on life and our well being as a society. I enjoy the soul-searching roller coaster ride of a Romantic's path, which is introspective, rich, and requires finesse at navigating the pitfalls of emotional excess.

As a Romantic, I feel death and dying require a balance of grief and celebration and I embrace this divine paradox whole-heartedly.

3 "I couldn't tell my neighbors how you died."

By Elizabeth Wagele, Observer, Romantic wing

John's mother was widowed when he was a child. He had tried to tell her he was gay several times and failed. Then he got AIDS. Now what should he do?

On a vacation trip to Hawaii in the mid-1980s, John Herlin had night sweats and thought he had the flu. He cut his trip short, returned to Berkeley CA, entered the hospital, and almost died of pneumonia. Doctors thought it was AIDS. Then they told him he didn't have AIDS. A few days later he received a definitive diagnosis of pneumocystus pneumonia, meaning he had contracted AIDS at the age of forty-five. The next eighteen months he spent helping with the early AIDS epidemic, educating other AIDS patients and high school students. He also self-published books of his poems and short stories. As one of his best friends, I accompanied him through his illness. Ironically, were it not for AIDS we wouldn't have become nearly as close.

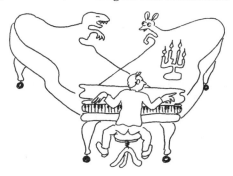

John Herlin was a popular and creative high school English teacher I had met in a piano jazz improvisation and barrelhouse blues class in 1980. I stood up for him when the teacher forgot he'd promised he'd play us some music John had recorded at home: John had worked out a relationship with a lover on the piano. John was too shy to stand up for himself concerning his music, though he was assertive in other situations. My help in this vulnerable area made me his instant friend. Part way through the classes he asked me if he could study classical piano with me. We also spent occasional evenings together where he introduced me to recordings I wasn't familiar with on the sound system he had mortgaged his house to buy. He remained somewhat standoffish, however, until he became sick.

He lost 60% of his good friends, he estimated, when he had AIDS, but not because they had contracted the disease. Coming down with AIDS was a death sentence in those days and John reasoned that his gay friends didn't want to be reminded it could happen to them.

A probing, funny, quirky, thoughtful, writer, photographer, and poet, John expressed himself with passion as he searched for the truth. He said the intensity of his AIDS experience was so valuable, even with all the pain and suffering, he wouldn't trade it for anything.

Times do change... sometimes.

John's sister, who lived in Wisconsin as did his mother, came to visit and to support him emotionally. He often debated whether to tell his mother he had AIDS, however. Close to the end of his life, when he finally did tell her, she reacted the way he had feared she would.

We had a support group for him of around fifteen people, which he named the Herlinettes: fellow teachers, nurses, old friends, an AIDS volunteer, and John's next-door neighbor. I was designated the person to take him on outings. We went on day trips, took nature classes, and deliberately scared ourselves by going to places like the halls of the Transamerica skyscraper building and back alleys in San Francisco's Chinatown. On one of these trips he extracted a promise from me that I would let him die alone.

About a week before he died in 1988 he demanded I take him out for a drive, against doctor's orders. The nurse who came to his house every day to give him an IV wore red high heels and tiptoed around his room, driving him nuts by being overly polite. He couldn't wait to get away from her and see some real life. As I drove on an overpass on our way to 4th street, he ranted about how he craved the truth. His voice became serious and gruff. "Elizabeth! Tell me something you don't like about me!" I recoiled from the thought. But this being John's possible last request and such a fervent one, I felt I had no choice but to squeeze an answer out of myself. "You're too opinionated sometimes, John... And what don't you like about *me*?" I asked quickly to change the subject.

"You're too naturally conciliatory," he said. "I can't get you to argue with me."

That stung. Since it was exactly what I most didn't like about myself in 1988, I started wondering why nobody had ever said it to me before. I was grateful for John's honesty, painful as it was. It meant he really saw me. Damn! The one person who perceived my private hell was going to die any minute.

I parked the car. We sat near it on the sidewalk leaning against a building for about twenty minutes while he gathered his strength. Crossing the road to reach the café, he took the most agonizing steps of his life, he said, but he insisted on fetching his own coffee. He was exhilarated to be out one last time.

I've heard that those who are sure there is a god and those who are sure there isn't accept death more easily than those who are not sure, like John. The next few days he was mostly unconscious and struggling violently, whether because of the illness or his beliefs there's no way to know.

We Herlinettes kept vigil at his bedside, taking turns holding his shaking body and trying to calm him. He seemed to be in pain, yelling and groaning. We'd tell him everything was taken care of, that it was okay for him to go. Who was I to tell anyone it was okay—or not okay—to die? But I'd try anything that might diminish his suffering.

One morning, at about 4:30 a.m., the nurse at his house called me to say he had died.

He was alone.

We Herlinettes had a lovely dinner together at one of John's best friend's house a couple of nights later. I played Chopin at his funeral at his request. And we Herlinettes made a quilt in his memory and gave it to the AIDS Quilt Project. I helped get his house ready to sell and found a ladder to help paint his bedroom in his basement. It looked strange to me. I set it up. I put the full gallon of paint on top and started to climb up to paint the ceiling. When my foot hit the second rung, the ladder turned inside out and the can tossed and turned all around the room, landing upside down on John's wooden floor, the paint can having splashed its contents all over me. I don't remember getting there, but I was hurled backwards onto the floor. John would have laughed so hard. He would have run out of the house all doubled over and continued around the block three or four times laughing out of his mind until he dropped. I was alone in the house. There were no rags. It was a nightmare. Intense, dramatic, and funny—like John.

4 Yonderling (a song)

By Rock Ross, possibly a Romantic type

Romantics often suffer because they feel misunderstood, life is too difficult emotionally, and because others have what they don't have. In this song, Rock dreams of being free of pain and "eternal yearning."

When I go
I want to explode
Beyond all hope of retrieval...

Expand and release,
Disperse and blend
Into total oblivion.

Bye bye... to harps and wings!
Bye bye... to pain and burning!
Away, away yonder!
Make me a Yonderling!

That vanishes... in the light.
That swirls... through the stream
That joins... the graceful current
That flows through everything.

Just, a breath of air... singing!
Just, a grain of sand... gleaming!
Just, a drop of water...
Just the astonishing.., seen and unseen

Fly!... without time,
Drift.., without desire,
Wander.., through splendor,
Swim.., the ocean of fire,
And, sail away, sail away, sail away, y'all,
Away, further, yonder.., sail away...

Bye bye to harps and wings!
Bye bye to endless burning!
Away, away yonder!
Make me a Yonderling!

Bye bye to crowns and kings
Bye bye to eternal yearning
Away away yonder!

5 In Search of a Father

By Janet Hartzell, Romantic, strong Observer wing, Social subtype

In this story, Janet loses her father too soon and is haunted by not having had an opportunity to get to know him as an adult and feeling abandoned. Many years later something unexpected happens that helps recover him.

In August of 1974, complete with an M.A. in English and a teaching certificate, I made the decision to teach for two years in Australia— where there was a shortage of qualified teachers. My Peace Seeker father was excited for me; my

Questioner mother, who had always encouraged my two younger sisters and me to travel, was worried. My Observer boy friend supported this decision because he was trying to decide what he wanted to do with his life and both of us believed this separation would clarify our relationship. Ironically, one of the books I began reading during the long flight from San Francisco to Melbourne was Elizabeth Kubler-Ross's book, *On Death and Dying*. I thought this was a fascinating topic and saw nothing unusual in my choice of reading material. It turned out to be a foreshadowing of what was ahead.

My world turned upside down with a letter from my mother, which arrived some two months after I had been in Australia. My father had suffered a major heart attack and was hospitalized. Disbelieving that my father was so ill *and* that my mother had written to me rather than calling, I immediately checked on his progress. I also made the decision that rather than staying in Australia during the upcoming holidays, I would fly back to the States for Christmas and the new year.

While I was home, my father had tests that revealed his heart muscle had been severely damaged and he was living on borrowed time. Although I returned to Australia in January 1975, some seven months later when I was summoned from a portable classroom for a "trunk line call" (i.e. long distance), I knew immediately that my father had had another heart attack and this time it was fatal.

As a Romantic, I had always been prepared for this loss. Most of my life had been measured by the death of important people: my maternal grandmother, a childless neighbor who had "adopted" my sisters and me, the elementary school teacher who had given me special attention without alienating my classmates, and so on. The numbness that initially set in with the news was helpful in getting me through the ordeal of the thirty-six hours it took to get from my apartment in Australia to my home in the States. But almost immediately I became fixated on all the auxiliary losses connected with my father's death: he would never get to see any grandchildren that might come along; those grandchildren would miss knowing their grandfather; how would my mother, sisters and I cope without his mediating presence? Most of all, however, there was a sense always lurking in my Romantic-style mind, that I had been abandoned. There was nothing rational about this—it was, and still is thirty-six years later, a feeling that I cannot shake.

My boyfriend called as soon as he heard the news of my father's death. Because he had just started a vacation several hundred miles away, he asked if I wanted him to come back. In one of those moments that I understand only now looking back, I said, "No, you just arrived at your destination. I have family and friends here; I'll be fine." I wanted to be selfless about this and I thought I believed what I had just told him. However, after the funeral was over and everyone else returned to their lives while I waited for clearance to get back into Australia, I began to brood about the fact that (1) he had even asked me this question and (2) he didn't override my response and return to me anyway. Finally, I wrote a letter to him terminating the relationship. I regretted the letter immediately, but the genie was out of the bottle.

Part of my grief about my father's sudden death at sixty-two was also the realization that, having left home at eighteen for college, I would never get to know him as one adult knows another adult. That knowledge haunted me. I had not only lost my father in the physical sense, but I also felt grieved that I had trouble remembering the essence of who he was. I'm still puzzling about why we rarely spoke of my father in my immediate family because he was a loving and beloved man. (It was clear that even shortly before my mother's death in December 2010, after having lived thirty-five years without her husband, she was still missing him.)

But as my sisters and I began clearing out the detritus of the ninety-three years of my mother's life, I rediscovered my father. Among the voluminous boxes of Christmas cards and letters that Mother had collected was a box of love letters that my father had written to her while he was in the army during World War II. There were at least seven hundred letters covering a span of about three years, which marked when they first starting dating through the time he was released from service and they could plan on marrying. At first, I felt it would be an intrusion somehow for me to read these letters, but as I started to read, I could hear my father talking; that connection I thought I would never have with him as an adult emerged. True, I couldn't ask him questions, but all sorts of memories about him flooded back—things that I would now be able to share with my nephews and niece about the Grandfather they never knew. With her death, my mother had given me back my father.

6 Death at the Controls

By Courtney Behm, Romantic, Achiever wing, One-to-one subtype

Courtney describes coping mechanisms that help control her unexplained fear of airplane crashes and death. She realizes if she fails to accept death as inevitable, she cannot be fully alive and pledges to work on accepting what is.

Airplanes may kill you, but they ain't likely to hurt you. – Satchel Paige

When I was young, I didn't think much about death. People in my family lived long, and no one close to me died until I was far into adulthood. There were no funerals, no ailing relatives, just people living their lives, day after day. My goldfish had a high mortality rate, being unable to survive the chemicals in our softened water, but though I got a pang when I came down in the morning and saw them floating on top of the water, I just got another fish and life went on. So I can't explain why, at sixteen, I suddenly became paralyzingly afraid I would die in an airplane crash. I had flown since I was a baby, and had been comfortable—even exhilarated—by the prospect of a trip to see relatives or friends, but suddenly, on the eve of a flight, I would be

81

tormented by vivid images of falling from the sky, and spend the night fretting and sleepless. I wasn't actually afraid of flying, I was afraid of dying when something went wrong. I read up on crashes—takeoffs and landings were usually the dangerous times. So once in the air, I would relax, and start to enjoy being in the airplane bubble with my book and my thoughts, but every bump and shudder and unexpected sound put me on high alert, listening hard, looking for the nearest exit. My imagination churned out water landing scenarios, and fire scenarios, and plummeting toward the earth scenarios. I envisioned myself alternately terrified and gibbering in my seat, or helpful, brave and selfless in the face of disaster. I would put children on the slide ahead of me. I would scramble to be the first out of the plane. I would be calm and Buddha-like—fearless in the face of destiny. I would be sobbing hysterically, begging to be saved. Sometimes I saw myself surviving to tell the tale, brave and bruised in front of the TV cameras, but at the end of most stories I would be very, very dead.

I'd like to say that I grew out of that fear as a normal part of maturing and becoming more sensible, but that would be a lie. It seemed lodged in my psyche, firmly placed in how I viewed the world. Rocks were hard, water was wet, and I was going to die in a plane crash. I flew when I had to, but not happily, and I avoided it when I could. Finally, in my early forties, I felt so limited by my reluctance to fly that I took a job that required me to fly coast to coast on a monthly basis, in hopes that I would somehow just get over it. And it mostly worked. I am now a competent flyer, but the fear scenarios still lurk at the edges of my awareness, and before I leave for the airport, I call or email everyone I love so I don't regret not having a last word with them; I leave all my important paperwork and the phone numbers and addresses of my family in a manila envelope on the kitchen counter so that people will know who to contact; and I make copies of the photos I took while visiting and distribute them before my return trip just in case I die before I get a chance to mail them from home.

Though I can usually shake my head and laugh at my own absurdity, I have also promised myself that if I get really, really scared, and my visions get really, really specific, I'll treat them as a premonition and I just won't fly. I confess there have been a few times when the darkness has descended so swiftly and pervasively in my mind and my thoughts are so graphically threatening that I have almost backed out of the trip. It's a delicate sorting process—do I really think I'm going to die, or is this just that old tape? And how will I know for sure, except that one day I will talk myself into getting on the plane and I really, really should have stayed on the ground. Oops! My bad!

I've spent a lot of time examining and dissecting and trying to understand what it is about airplanes that convinces me I will die. It certainly isn't the statistics. The numbers tell me that driving, which I do with great enthusiasm in trips short and long, is much more likely to kill me than airplane travel. But though I know it's possible I could die in a car crash, there's this belief, illusion, delusion—whatever you want to call it—that my skill and my quick wits will give me an edge, that I have control. I can turn the wheel this way or that, slam on the brakes, and veer around the pothole. Better yet, I'm on the ground, not suspended in midair, trusting my life to a pilot who may have had too little sleep, or has a secret drinking problem, and to a plane that may malfunction in some permanent and deadly way I'm powerless to prevent.

So, yes, a big issue in my dysfunctional relationship with Death involves giving up control. I've read "The Appointment in Samarra," and I know how useless it is to flee to another city when Death shows up in your hometown. Death is an inevitable part of life, and one of the things we all have in common. Everyone, everywhere, at any minute in time, has a terminal illness called Life, from which no one escapes alive. I'm OK with that, really. I don't fear being dead, I just don't like the prospect of being taken off the board without having some say in the matter.

And then there's the suffering thing. Falling from the sky would involve suffering. Dying painfully from a vicious illness would involve suffering. Being beaten or tortured to death would certainly involve suffering. Shoot me quickly, give me a nice heart failure or catastrophic stroke, let me die in my sleep, but don't make me suffer. I'm afraid to suffer. I know, I know, Romantics are supposed to be in love with their suffering. And, I will admit, I certainly used to be. A therapist friend once told me I was always rehearsing the drama of the trauma of my life. But something happens when you become aware of your own personality mechanisms; it's harder to let them run amok. One side effect is that suffering and I haven't been on all that good terms lately. It can really take the pleasure out of living; you're hearing this from an expert.

So I not only want to control the time and manner of my death, I also want to control how much I suffer, and by extension, how much the people I love suffer. My son, my grandchildren—my heart is so open to them that I often feel their senseless, painful deaths would be an experience I could not survive, would not want to survive. Even as I write this, I know I would most likely find resources unknown to me that would allow me to cope, but I will never know for sure until the time comes. Maybe we will all die peacefully, and my fearful thoughts are just that—thoughts. But when I imagine myself or my loved ones in agony or terror, my heart stutters and it suddenly becomes very difficult to breathe.

In the face of a losing, but tenacious, strategy, I've had to develop some robust coping mechanisms. The first step is to identify where the real problem lies: all my stories, the twisting and struggling to maintain control, to see into the future, to program my life; it's my personality in overdrive. Over time, my ability to manage my affect in the world has become a work of art, but my inner landscape is still a lot like a 24/7 showing of the Lord of the Rings. My emotions get tangled up with my thoughts, and my emotions still like to think they describe my reality, so when I'm afraid, there's something to be afraid of and when I'm grieving a potential loss, it's because I need to be prepared to grieve. There's probably nothing that could happen to me that I haven't already dreamed up in some form. I've gone through all the phases and stages of shock and grief and pain and recovery without leaving the comfort of my home.

In a way, it's like a dress rehearsal for the tragedy my personality is sure will happen. I'm preparing so I'm not helpless in the face of loss. In some societies, this preparation for death would be woven into everyday life, as a natural manifestation of being human. But we live in a death-denying culture, and dying is something that happens off-stage, hopefully quietly, but isn't to be discussed, acknowledged, honored or accepted. We fight it with surgeries and life support machinery and chemicals. There are few rituals to ease someone's passing from this life, but there are many machinations to stave off the inevitable. Death is treated as an enemy that must be defeated and we use heroic means to keep people alive at all costs. Even when they've had enough, our system has a hard time allowing them to holler "uncle." Life has become a fight against death, instead of death being an organic part of life.

To me, this is unacceptable. Way down deep, underneath my fear, is a hunger for the natural rhythms of life, for birth and life and death to be a continuum that I acknowledge and celebrate. For if I fail to accept death as inevitable, I cannot be fully alive; to be fully alive I need to acknowledge the impermanence of everything around me. Every moment, every experience, every living thing vanishes and cannot be replaced, and that's just the way it is. The universe is indifferent to my desire to be in control. But I still need to foster enough wisdom to help me through the dark nights, to help me calm my fears, and to help me be alive to what is good now, instead of fearing some future hell.

I have many allies in this struggle to face death, suffering, and the great unknown with equanimity, but one of the most powerful is the Buddhist meditation called the Five Remembrances. The words are sometimes hard to read, and even harder to accept, but they are so undeniably true that they settle my mind and allow me to open my hands, release my fear, and return to being fully alive. I will leave them here for you, just in case you could also use some support in forging a new relationship with the fragile nature of life, and the inevitability of death.

The Five Remembrances

I am of the nature to grow old.
There is no way to escape growing old.

I am of the nature to have ill health.
There is no way to escape having ill health.

I am of the nature to die.
There is no way to escape death.

All that is dear to me and everyone I love is of the nature to change.
There is no way to escape being separated from them.

My actions are my only true belongings.
I cannot escape the consequences of my actions.
My actions are the ground on which I stand.

7 My Sister Judy – July 27, 1934 – August 31, 1982

By Dr. James Campbell, Observer, Social subtype

Judy was an artist. This is the anatomy of her cancer as told by her Observer brother, a doctor.

Musicians must make music, artists must paint, poets must write
if they are to be ultimately at peace with themselves. – Abraham Maslow

My older sister Judy was a Romantic with an Achiever wing and a One-to-one subtype. She had a full, accomplished life as a young person, having graduated Phi Beta Kappa from DePauw University in 1956 with a major in art. She was outgoing, creative, quite popular, and could be moody at times. As children we fought quite a bit because I didn't feel she had the authority to tell me what to do. After college graduation, she went to Paris and Florence to study art. While in Florence, she met an Italian man, Piero, whom she married five years later (1962). Meanwhile, she moved to New York, where I was attending medical school, and became quite a successful freelance illustrator. We actually got along very well during those three years. She married Piero in our garden in Indiana in July 1962. After six weeks of travel in western U.S., they returned to Florence to set up housekeeping. Her three children were born in 1963, 1965, and 1967. Most summers she and the children went to Indiana to be with my parents.

In March 1972 she returned to Indiana to visit because my father had become ill. My mother, an M.D., noticed a spot on Judy's lower leg, which had apparently been there about six months. A colleague surgeon removed it. Diagnosis was melanoma, but it was felt that it was fairly superficial and not likely to cause future problems. Judy left for Italy the day my father died at eighty-seven.

She visited me in San Francisco about three times in the next ten years; I also would visit her in South Bend for a few days in the summer when she was visiting my mother. I never knew if she would be down or up. She fought a great deal with our mother and expected me to mediate.

Judy, her son, and my mother spent Christmas 1981 at my house. She had become very heavy, had a big belly, and was drinking heavily. Four months later she phoned me from Italy to say that she had been ill much of the winter, had stopped drinking, and was seeing doctors who couldn't diagnose her problem. I suggested that she come to UCSF (the hospital at the University of California in San Francisco) for consultation. She arrived in early May 1982 looking quite ill. My at-home physical examination revealed that she had ascites (fluid in abdominal cavity) and a pleural effusion. We thought it might be alcoholic cirrhosis. I referred her to a colleague who performed a liver biopsy, which revealed melanoma cells. I informed her of the diagnosis. She was furious. From there she went to an oncologist whom she liked very much.

Her mood was very labile the whole time she was in San Francisco. She stayed in my bedroom but was able to go out with me at times. She took chemotherapy, but the disease only worsened. I became concerned that she wouldn't be well enough to return home to spend her last days with her family, but she didn't want to leave until there was evidence of improvement. Our mother wanted her to come to Indiana to spend some time with her, but my sister refused. Fortunately, some of my friends kept her company, she visited some friends of her own in the Bay Area, and a couple of other friends visited here from back East. This made life much easier for me, because I was working full time and feeling overwhelmed.

I had a new friend by then. My sister hated him and requested that he not visit me while she was there.

Finally, her oncologist convinced her to return to Italy. She left San Francisco in late June 1982. Though she was separated from her husband, he returned to care for her during the final weeks in Florence. I told Mother on the phone that if she was going to visit her she must do so by mid-August. Judy told her not to come until September. Mother did take my advice and visited her in Florence in mid-August. Judy died on August 31, about four days after my mother's departure.

I suspected that the melanoma was in someway related to her poorly controlled bipolar mood disorder. In those days, lithium was the only option. She had many side effects from this drug, mainly

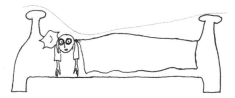

tremors and lessening of her creativity. Consequently, her compliance was poor.

8 About Romantics

Romantics' gifts include potentially recognizing the deep human truth that death is a part of life and the ability to express the transcendent qualities of the human spirit through art and beauty. Romantic composers, such as Gustav Mahler, Tchaikovsky, and Beethoven, excelled at expressing grief, though expressing grief is not limited to one type.

Among the Romantics featured in this chapter, Judy was an artist, John Herlin wrote poetry and fiction, played the piano, and was a photographer, Courtney Behm is a singer, and Rock Ross writes and performs songs. Carol Leavenworth puts creative energy into working with her dreams. Romantics often become therapists, which calls on their creativity.

Romantics' Perfectionist arrow can be seen in Courtney Behm's desire to control her own and her loved ones' suffering and in John Herlin's Puritan ethic. Suzanne Arcand-Gawreluk uses her Helper arrow to assist her large family.

Romantics with an Achiever wing tend to be outgoing (Courtney Behm) while Romantics with an Observer wing tend to be withdrawn or quiet.

The agenda of Romantics is to avoid being seen as dull, routine, or conventional. They often long for something they don't have or had once but lost, which accounts for their melancholy moods and their tendency to envy others. Rock Ross' poem *Yonderling* expresses being tired of the longing, yearning, drama, and the thrust to be unique that can govern their lives, his ennui of ennui.

Grieving

Judy Meyer, a Romantic writing about her Asserter partner Martin's death in Chapter 8, says, "I grieved by crying a lot for six months. When we grieve, we are also grieving about our own demise." Romantics are attracted to suffering, the dark side, and the drama of life and death situations. As a young woman, Janet Hartzell read books about dying. Grieving can plunge Romantics beyond melancholy into depression. Being productive, paying attention to details, or organizing by means of their Perfectionist arrow can help pull them out of it. Giving attention to someone else—volunteer work, perhaps—by means of their Helper arrow can help take their mind off of their own troubles.

Shadow

Romantics' shadows sometimes take the form of the gifts they don't admit to or their own ordinariness (we're all ordinary on some levels, even though we don't like it). If Romantics don't feel special enough, they will envy others or become special in their own minds by way of their exquisite internal torment.

Shadow elements show up in the arrows. Among other things, the Perfectionist arrow represents following rules; Romantics are likely to be mavericks and break rules. The Helper arrow represents harmonizing with others; Romantics tend to be more interested in searching within themselves than devoting themselves to others.

> *Die? I should say not, dear fellow. No Barrymore would allow*
> *such a conventional thing to happen to him.*
> – John Barrymore's last words

The nine types of people

Learning the nine types' points of view helps individuals find balance, acceptance, and wholeness. The Enneagram is valuable both in facing an immediate crisis and in long-range growth.

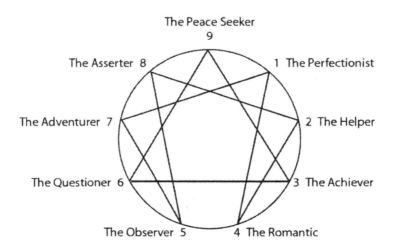

Contents

1. My Grief Process – Jayne Johnson
    (Her daughter and granddaughter are killed in an accident.)

2. If You Cry, I Will Never Tell You How I Feel – Charlotte Melleno
    (Man fearful of being encroached on and suspicious of people's
    love for him softens when diagnosed with lung cancer.)

3. Three Short Observer Stories – Jaki Girdner and Joan Degiorgio.

4. Letter to His Sister About His Meeting with Pema Chödrön –
    Dave Scherman
    (Dying man is accepting, kind after decades of illness.)

5. Death – David Brooks
    (Takes an interesting look at death around the farm.)

6. A Near-Death Experience – Tom L. Clark
    (Learns there is nothing to fear about death.)

7. My Father Had No More Fear – Elizabeth Wagele
    (Fred is prepared for his final illness.)

8. Symbolic Death and Rebirth: What Dreams Can Do – Elizabeth
    Wagele
    (A four-year-old's dream prepares her for her life.)

9. Assisted Death, Movie Review – Elizabeth Wagele
    (The only man he has loved asks him to help him die.)

10. My Obsession on Death and Dying – Michele Harrison
    (Her parents and doctor did a poor job of handling her fear of
    death. Later she might have killed herself but for love of
    family.)

11. About Observers

Chapter 5 – Observers

Reprinted from *The Happy Introvert,* Ulysses Press 2006. The I and E
stand for Introvert (the Observer) and Extravert.

What sets the principle characters of the stories in this chapter apart from the
other chapters is the amount of thought they have given to their philosophies
of life, including the meaning of death.

Writing styles

Observers tend to write clearly and to the point without wasting words. Note:
James Campbell has a minimalistic writing style typical of many Observers. He
is so private he wrote about the types of his mother, his sister, his lover, and
his father but not his own. See *Dr. Rasmussen's Need to Control Her Life*,
Chapter 1; *My Bipolar Sister*, Chapter 4; and *Significant Other: Real* and *My
Father: Can't We Have Some Peace?* in Chapter 9.

I (Elizabeth) am an Observer and I also wrote *Valerie's Worm* in Chapter 1;
Marge's Voice for the Last Time and *I Can't Tell My Mother How Sick I Am* in
Chapter 2; *I Couldn't Tell My Neighbors How You Died* in Chapter 4; *Alice,
Oldest Survivor* in Chapter 7; *Death by Assassination* in Chapter 8; and *My
Buddy Karl Kresge: Peace at Last* in Chapter 9.

Observer Jaki Girdner wrote *Uncle Wayne* in Chapter 7 and *Death of a Drug
Dealer* in Chapter 8.

1 My Grief Process

By Jayne Johnson, Observer

In this story, Jayne Johnson looks for patterns in her experiences that will bring order to the chaos and guide her through healing her grief. She's open to change and a new connection to life.

-1-

Grief. What does it even mean—all these thoughts and feelings? What is the *grief process*— my grief process? I hear something about a two-year time frame—sober—that it takes just to get past the numbness. There is so little information to help me out of the ambivalence I feel. And little of the information tells me the *what to do*, the *how to* of grieving. My own process is mostly one of hit or miss.

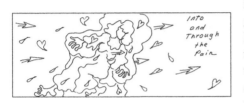

There are those clear moments when I am in the flow and intuitively recognize I am healing. During these precious times, I feel the movement of the current, the passage to some new level of acceptance. But I always seem to return to the hit or miss pattern. It might sound morbid to others, but I have been intrigued with death since my teens. I've had the good fortune to have many teachers who had living and dying as their main focus and I've known for a long time that life is a preparation for death. Still, I get confused and long for someone in my wandering to show me a clear path. In trying to make sense of my child's death, I am never really sure if what I am doing is helping or hurting me.

I write to make sense of the one year since the untimely death of my daughter, Christi, and my eleven-year-old granddaughter, Camran, in a single car accident June 24, 1996. I measure everything by this day. I sense at times I am healing. At other times I know I was better than I am. My recovery program has been my saving grace in this Great Teaching. I know the importance of reaching out to others despite longing to shut myself away.

When I first heard that they were dead, I didn't know I was in a state of shock, so I tried doing *business as usual.* I thought I had to get on with life, whatever that meant, and went back to work after a week. But my body knew differently. I didn't recognize the physical and emotional exhaustion I was in. Shock tricked and protected me for several months following the accident before I realized I wasn't keeping up. Eventually a colleague noticed. I took a long leave of absence. I needed the healing miracle of time and space, which I got through the support of lots of people.

I continued seeing my therapist and attending my twelve-step program daily. With more time available, I was able to join a dream group with a Jungian trained analyst, which I had wanted to do previous to the accident.

-2-

I knew at the time, from experience and from watching others, that I was ready to go into and through the pain—this was the only way to the other side. I had no idea how to do it on my own, however. I learned I must look inside myself and become willing to fully experience what I discover there. Since I started this process some months ago, I am beginning to open and sit with the pain. I am learning to breathe and relax when my body strains to push pain down or out and away. I soften my belly, chest, throat, and all the places where I want to grab my grief and tears and stuff them back in order to avoid. Although the pain feels too strong for me at times, I am always aware that these feelings are, strangely enough, a form of love. An exquisite form of love.

I am accepting that my loved ones are no longer here. Each new surrender brings me closer to the reality of letting go of the hopes and dreams of a tomorrow that will never come. I am letting go of all those saved items, fantasies and plans of what we will do or say in the endless tomorrows. I accept that what I did not do or say will never be done or said. Not now. Not ever. It is over. It is all done.

Hardest of all is giving up my guilt and self-pity. Letting go of the *should have beens, ought to have beens, could have beens.* Holding on to these means living in the illusion that I have some kind of control over their deaths. I am learning to follow something my daddy used to teach me when fishing together and I got my line tangled in the willow trees. You have to know when to "cut bait." I am learning to "cut bait" from my self-centered guilt and self-pity and experience life as the free fall it is. I am finding the willingness to touch that place of vulnerability so deep inside me that I didn't even know it existed. It is a smoky, hazy, vague place. Even now, as I attempt to describe it, I feel it evaporate.

Writing brings order out of chaos. It puts a border, a boundary around my thoughts and emotions, containing them in a way that allows me to make sense of them. So does talking at twelve-step meetings; their rooms are my refuge. And I read.

I read Christi's journals, poems, letters and stories. I read her term papers, even her diaries and recipes. I see her in my mind's eye, working over them as I have seen her do so many times. I cry a lot. The long hours of overwhelming, exhaustive crying are subsiding. But, still, I cry. Her father, my husband, asks if it is necessary for me to go through her papers, to "go through all that?" I reassure him that, yes, it is necessary. I ask him not to worry about me. But, of course, he does as I do about him. He wants to fix me. But I am broken. Mending takes time.

I drink in memories of her. I visit her old hang outs sometimes and sit in my car or on a bench and watch the kids come and go just as she once did. Beside my bed is a jewelry box that once belonged to her grandmother. Inside is a lock of baby hair I cut so many years ago. Sometimes I open the box and touch it. Usually I leave it closed.

-3-

Mercifully, I set grief down at times. I have pictures at my altar in my home and a candle burns. There is an *Over the Rainbow* clown music box that was Christi's as a child, which she, in turn, gave Camran when she was born. I leave my grief there at the altar sometimes and can be comfortable for days on end with only a quiet, gentle hum of reminder, barely audible in my heart-mind. But grief eventually calls again; she comes in many forms: as a slow fog rolling in off the ocean of South Florida, the place of their birth, or as mist on the early morning pastures of South Georgia, the ancestral home. Sometimes grief settles in my bones for days at a time, bringing a chill that only solitude and silence can warm again. Grieving is a private business.

There are times when grief comes in bright colorful bursts of images. The two of them appear suddenly laughing and teasing. I am soothed by this gift of spirit from out of nowhere or out of everywhere. I feel a tactile sense of their presence snuggled next to me sometimes in bed. I have experienced the light, wispy feel of Christi's hair brushing my outstretched arm as if she is placing her head on it, as I lie falling asleep. I have felt them leaning over me as if trying to see the page I am reading. And, when I have been too long forgetting, too long avoiding, it comes like an old friend tapping me on the shoulder, jolting me awake and reminding me I can never forget.

A hot knot of grief grabs my throat when my husband cries out for his child or my other daughter for her sister. Then I sense the layers and layers of my own powerlessness, an even deeper level of surrender, and an utter letting go. I feel the sharp pang of grief when Grandpa forgets Camran is dead and asks me, "is she a big girl now, does she still make A's?" After a moment I remind him she is dead. He is silent. Then replies he had forgotten, she is up there with Christi. They are buried in the family cemetery near his home. I imagine their sweet bodies lying there in the red Georgia clay beneath the stone slabs with sand dollars on top reminding them they are Florida girls with sand in their shoes, something I often reminded them of in life.

More than anything, my process allows me to recognize and accept not only what I have lost but what I have now that I did not have before their deaths. Until I could see the gifts they gave me through dying, I could not move out of the confusion, numbness, hopelessness, and rage at the sheer pointlessness of it all. Of course, I still relapse into confusion and anger, but more and more, I see gifts everywhere.

Their deaths have taught me the profundity of vulnerability. I cannot question this evidence of my own powerlessness in the face of Death. It is clear testimony that they are not my children but, rather, the children of Life and therefore of Death. Their passage is not so much about the death of their lives as about the Life of their deaths. It has taught me that death is not only the completion of life, but, and more important, the purpose of life. When I face each day in the spirit of the Lakota Sioux, I know that today is, indeed, a good day to die. And so it is also a very good day to live.

-4-

Many days now I feel content to live in this moment. To live each day well, willing to stand poised on the threshold of life and death is the miracle of recovery. For me this means to let go of each day, each hour, even each minute sometimes, trusting I am safe to pass through whatever I may find.

Their deaths became a doorway into a psychic relationship that, although invisible, is more real in many ways than the one I knew when they were alive.

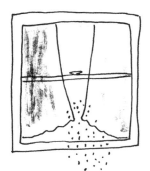

Without *our great warring egos*, our personalities, there is a dance of spirit not bound by worldly laws. They have become guides for my soul and have opened me to a deeper interior of self. My understanding and values have changed, as has my view of life and death. They have brought an opening, a calming, and a connection to life unlike anything I have ever known. I feel compassion and love and I treasure others in a wholly different way. Life is much lighter. And I regard my own life and death with a different acceptance.

Their deaths have brought congruence to the opposition of life and death, a mystery my mind was unable to integrate before. And, they have left me with a certain notion that one must not leave deeds undone, words unsaid, life unsettled, for the day comes in the snap of a finger.

I miss them very much. – Jayne Johnson '97

2 "If you cry, I will never tell you how I feel."

By Charlotte Melleno, Romantic (uses both wings), Social subtype

In contrast to Jayne Johnson's relatively objective, though moving, telling of her grief process, this story, though about a withholding Observer, is suffused with the feelings and the style of the Romantic who writes about him.

Three years ago, when I got a rare lung disease, we bought a glass-faced niche large enough to hold two urns in the San Francisco columbarium, a copper-domed masterpiece of Neo-Classical architecture. We wrangled over whose ashes would go on the top and whose would go on the bottom—a classic power struggle in the history of our thirty-seven year old relationship, including a thirteen-year marriage in the middle. Finally, another niche became available in a sunlit room where our urns could sit side by side, so, to Frank's displeasure, we traded up. He let me know if only I knew my place and would stay on the bottom, everything would be fine. I never thought he'd die first. A portion of the life insurance policy he left our son paid for the balance of the niche and I'm sure he would have been relieved that he, at least, didn't have to spend money on something he found so unreasonable.

One year ago, Saturday, while a January storm thundered outside my window, I reclined in bed, reading a *New Yorker* about Haiti's earthquake and a young woman who became an uncommon leader. After a lifetime of loss and failure, she had found the courage to fight and bring relief to her community. She foraged bags of rice and beans, drums of clean water, medical supplies, and bedding and trucked them back to the rock-strewn ravine where a few hundred residents of her town lived under tin roofs, cooking and sleeping among the devastation and the dead. Suddenly, I felt so grateful for my life and prayed, *Thank you God for keeping me safe, for keeping the storm outside, and easing the pain when I lie down, for helping me to see that I am surrounded by love and friendship.*

Slowing my breathing, I relaxed and, still holding the magazine in my hand, I fell asleep to the sound of the rain and a feeling of peace in my breast. The phone woke me an hour later.

"Hi, little lady," Frank said.

"Frank, how are you?" I asked, glad to hear from him.

"Not so good."

I caught my breath. Frank doesn't say things like this.

"Tell me."

"You know the doctor took a CT scan on Tuesday? He called yesterday to tell me it's not degenerative arthritis, as he thought. It's in my pelvis and my ribs. He's saying things like cancer and lymphoma, maybe a bad infection. I can't remember everything he said. I wrote it down somewhere. I have to have a pelvic biopsy next Tuesday."

Time stretched and tumbled. I felt a dark sadness in my throat and behind my eyes. I told him so, but mostly, we talked facts and logistics, which we do well together. During our marriage, Frank told me that my strong feelings overwhelmed him so he couldn't find his own. While a quiet standoff prolonged the marriage, our connection shriveled because I kept myself apart from him. He is the strong, silent type whose mantra goes, "I can handle it." Over the years, I had learned to hold my feelings close and keep them to myself or suffer. And ultimately I found closeness elsewhere.

Frank has suffered from chronic pain since last summer. I've had mixed feelings. As an empath, it hurt to see him dragging his leg as we walked down 9th Avenue. On the other hand, I felt that now he'd know what I suffered. Frank is a stoic. Weeks ago he told me he didn't want me to offer advice but would ask if he needed to know something. It was hard to keep my hard-won wisdom about pain to myself, since I had learned several tools to eliminate unnecessary suffering during my own health challenges. I had joined a twelve-step program, Chronic Pain Anonymous, a couple of years prior, which had helped me to manage loss, helplessness, and grief. These emotions are difficult for most people to handle, but are especially daunting for people like Frank and myself, who prize self-sufficiency and have difficulty depending on others.

I picked Frank up from his apartment to take him to a pelvic biopsy at the Kaiser hospital on my way to my own therapy appointment. I called a block from his house to give him a heads up. He said it might take a while to get downstairs. When he walked through the front door, leaning on his cane (which strengthened his identification with the irascible Dr. House, his TV hero), my throat closed. I watched him approach the car door, his grimace expressing the awful effort of each step. He looked like both a baby and a very old man, his face almost skeletal, his skull completely bald. This man once reveled in his muscles, his forearms strong and furred with blond hair, the blue veins roping them like a package. More than once he'd said, I am short but I carry myself like a big man. Frank was the most alive and vital man I'd ever known. Now he sat in the passenger seat and lifted his right leg into the car with both hands. Then he leaned out and pulled the door closed.

A week later, carrying a shopping bag with the ingredients for dinner in one hand and holding the banister in the other, I climbed the two steep flights to Frank's apartment with difficulty. When he answered the door, Frank's hug was more affectionate than usual—a two-armed embrace rather than the one-armed casual lean-in. He hobbled through his narrow hall, its walls covered with religious art and artifacts—a crown of thorns, paintings of Mary holding the infant Jesus and the Sacred Heart of Christ. After he reached his kitchen chair, I began taking dinner out of the bag—comfort food from New York, where I grew up—fixin's for a Reuben sandwich and knishes imported from

Coney Island and looked around for cooking utensils. He began to stand, to try and help, but I recognized the grimace around his mouth and forehead. He was in bad pain. My usual dose of morphine was doing its job of blunting my own and I could manage without him.

"Sit, just sit. It's okay. You don't have to do anything," I said, looking into his eyes.

I felt as though he was looking at a stranger. He sank back in his chair. "I was thinking today," he began slowly, "I bite my tongue for every evil thought I ever had about your illness."

I felt stunned and allowed myself a moment to take it in. "I have lived to hear those words," I laughed. He did, too.

Bending hurts my trunk and makes the nerves in my ribs and abs fire like an AK47 ripping through the center of my body. I remembered how, two months ago at Christmas, he had rolled his eyes when I asked him to fetch a platter for me from a low shelf. I had flared, "I pray to God you never have to know the strength it takes to live with a chronic illness." Now, I understood that my prayer was half a curse, which both failed and succeeded. I don't remember what he said next, but it was strange enough that I asked him to stop and repeat it.

"Oh, didn't I tell you? These drugs make me forget. I have lung cancer," he said, with a casualness that telegraphed exactly the kind of response he wanted. My eyes filled as a thousand cars collided in a tiny part of my brain, but his message was as clear as if he'd spoken, *"Don't cry. If you cry, I will never tell you how I feel."*

A few days later, his doctor diagnosed his cancer at stage 4 and told him it had metastasized to the bone and was inoperable. He gave him three to six months to live. An Air-force brat, and later, Captain in Viet Nam, Frank's first tendency in any crisis was to make lists centered on details and delegation. He focused on issues like whether he'd stay in his apartment and, if so, how, during daily radiation treatments, he'd manage the stairs. An experienced manager, he immediately created several support networks to deal with issues of daily living, i.e., grocery shopping, cooking and housekeeping. Beside myself, two people were his closest support system; our son, Daniel, and Frank's lover, Don.

When Frank was first diagnosed, I asked if Don could help him. He said, "Don has to take care of his mother, and besides, we don't love each other." I said, "That's baloney. He loves you and I think your willingness to spend ten years of Saturday nights with anyone is, in some way, a love connection for you." He never really admitted that, but the week before his death he told me how grateful he felt to Don for all his support and how surprised he was at Don's generosity. Frank was so fearful of being encroached on by anyone and was so suspicious of people's love for him, he barely gave it credence. He found rejection and struggle a headier and more exciting, albeit painful, experience.

He talked with us about his funeral arrangements and intended to look into Hospice and make a will. All of this was normal Frank, tried and true.

What surprised me was the person who emerged after he was given the news—an open and unguarded man—one I had rarely seen since we first met him thirty-six years prior in an encounter group at San Francisco State. His father, a high-ranking officer, who didn't meet Frank until his second birthday, had denigrated his early, loving relationship to his mother, and called him a sissy when Frank showed more interest in books and music than sports. Since his father put down self-expression and his mother took any expression of negative feelings personally, he had developed a poker face by the time he was six. Then, the fledgling human potential movement opened Frank briefly to a beautiful vulnerability that I fell in love with. Now, these two Franks braided together in an unusual manner. Once unwilling to express his needs for fear of indicating weakness, he now drew up a list of simple house rules for visitors, beginning with a brief explanation of his illness. He asked for help in an assertive and direct manner:

Please put food back in the refrigerator exactly where you found it.
Please hang up any clothes, books, or items you may have moved during your visit.
Please take down the trash when you leave.

At the time, I'd been ill for almost four years and many household chores had become difficult, but I never thought to hand out a list to my friends asking them to be mindful in order to ease my physical suffering. He was teaching me something about being entitled to ask for help.

More surprising was how the news shook the starch out of him and loosened his tongue. He began to talk with other people in an easy, eager, and comfortable manner. Our mutual friends had never seen him so easy-going nor heard him disclose his feelings in such a vulnerable manner, accompanied by dark humor.

He had never cared much about money nor saved for retirement and only began to make more than a living wage in the last ten years of his life. His main ride at sixty-six was still a motorcycle. He didn't own property and had feared that once he grew old he'd have to depend on the kindness of friends or move into a senior residence like the one he had managed as a facilities director in his early forties. It would take more than his social security to feed his love of travel, learning, and adventure. He had retired as a young man—having adventures, visiting exotic countries—and only buckled down when our son was born shortly before his fortieth birthday. "There's a certain relief in going out before I have to worry about how I'll support my old age."

I realized I had passed his test when I didn't cry after he told me his diagnosis. Over the next month, he called me more often than he had in the previous six. Sometimes, just to give me the news of the day; the family member he had told, how different it felt to connect with other people, the internal freedom he had never known. The watchfulness deep in the back of his skull was gone.

"I spoke to Mary Lou yesterday," he said, referring to his closest Aunt, who had, herself, been living and dying with lung cancer over the past year. "After she got sick, I began to call less and less. I didn't know what to say. Poor Mary Lou." They had been so close when he was small. She was only twelve years older, his father's little sister. "Now, we're like Chatty Kathy," a talking doll from the 1950s, "We don't want to stop."

I heard the pleasure in his voice and realized he was also talking about us. "No one else knows what to do with me," he said. "They're all giving me advice. I'm just delighted with you." Shortly after, I received a text, "...a bushel and a peck and a hug around the neck." These acts of tender openness meant the world to me. It was as if his dying had opened a vault, a safety deposit box.

Thirty-six years ago, Frank somersaulted from a seated position into the middle of the circle after a month of silence in our encounter group. He had previously avoided contact with any of us, He took a small bow and extended his arms to take us all in and said, "The ice has thawed." By that time, I was convinced I'd never get to know him, although, just like everyone else in the group, I was drawn to him. He was like Brando—magnetic in his nonchalance. His pose was one of passionate disinterest. A one-to-one subtype, while sitting in the outermost part of the room, he'd pull the attention of others towards him as if his silence was a rope.

Years later, he told me that, from his earliest memories, when his father was displeased with him, he would withdraw and freeze him out. They would sit in their living rooms on numerous Air Force bases, the tension thick as quicksand, while his father played a game of power designed to humiliate him. His father continually demonstrated his strength and invulnerability in contrast to Frank's feelings and dependency. He learned to hide his emotions as soon as he was capable. During our marriage, I discovered that Frank had learned from a master. When he wanted to win or control, he became a refrigerator, capable of sitting out any argument or debate in unfeeling silence. When he wanted to hurt me, he became emotionally cruel, signaling displeasure and occasionally the kind of contempt his father had demonstrated towards him. As my own therapy helped me to grow and stop taking his behavior so personally, I became intimately aware of how it felt to be Frank when he was a child. Psychotherapy threatened him. The idea that he would have to reveal parts of himself he'd kept secret since childhood made him feel too exposed—open to the kind of invasive abuse his father had casually dealt out as if he were interacting with an object rather than a person.

A year before, he'd shared a novel with me, *Something to Tell You*, about a psychoanalyst who had experienced a similar childhood to his and felt like an outsider. "I wish I'd read this sooner," he said with some regret. "It's the first book I've ever read about therapy that made me wish I'd done it." I was sad, too, because I knew what Frank had lost by keeping himself at such a distance from others, including me.

Less than a week before his death, we shared dinner in his apartment. I had brought a video, *Sweet and Lowdown*, and we stretched out on his bed, facing the large screen TV, which loomed over us on the opposite wall. We smoked a joint, laughed and ate, took our pain pills, and occasionally stopped the movie to talk about our lives. We agreed that, although our marriage and divorce had been hard, we had no regrets because, somehow, our relationship seemed meant to be. Our son, Daniel, had been the joy of Frank's life from the moment of his birth, which he had experienced as a golden glow. I have never known a father, or any parent for that matter, to love a child as much as Frank loved Daniel—his face open and beaming, laughing and attuned, his posture relaxed and easy, where, with most people, he carried a kind of alert tension. That night, I asked how he'd been able to love our Daniel so openly when he was so guarded with others. He responded without hesitation, "Daniel was a chance for a completely new beginning—a blank slate, someone without judgment or preconditions. Loving him was the easiest thing I've ever done."

When we parted that night, I had no idea it would be our last time together, although I looked back just before he closed the door, to hold him in my eyes and my memory. The following Friday, he completed two weeks of radiation to reduce the pain. We had a tentative date to get together and had spoken in the afternoon, but we were both too exhausted and promised to reschedule soon. That night, he spiked a fever and became delirious. At Kaiser hospital, he told Don that his cousin, Brenda, who died twenty-five years ago, was in the next room and that *they* were coming to take him. Those were his last words. He died the following evening, after receiving Extreme Unction (last rites) and surrounded by many people who loved him, five weeks after his initial phone call on that stormy afternoon. He never had enough time to meditate on his dying—to light the candles and incense, or throw the *I-Ching*, as he had wanted to do—but he was changed and finally at peace.

3 Three Short Observer Stories

These stories demonstrate Observers' ability to focus and to be unobtrusive.

My father was an Observer. In the last moments of his life, when he was experiencing radical changes in his body, I believe I saw not fear but an intense focus on what was happening to him, an Observer to the end. – *Joan Degiorgio*

Maurice, a bookstore owner, likely an Observer, went away and hid when he died so he wouldn't bother anyone. – *Jaki Girdner, Observer*

My mother, also an Observer, gave death a lot of thought and decided to die when the rest of her family had gone to Hawaii. – *Jaki Girdner, Observer*

I have never been hurt by anything I didn't say. – Calvin Coolidge

I never found the companion that was so companionable as solitude.
I am for the most part more lonely when I go abroad among men than when I stay in my chambers. – Henry David Thoreau, Walden

4 Letter to His Sister About His Meeting with Pema Chödrön

By Dave Scherman, Observer

Dave had Hepatitis C from his early twenties. After decades it morphed into liver cancer and about a year later he died. About six weeks before he died his sister made arrangements for him to go with her to a weekend workshop with spiritual teacher Pema Chödrön. Dave's friend, Tom L. Clark obtained this letter Dave wrote to another sister.

Yep—it happened. After Saturday morning's talk, an assistant led Jen and I to a curtain while Pema did what she needed to do to transfer her energy over to another subject, and then led us in. Pema took a seat, and rather than go through a formal bow and sit face to face on cushions, which I sort of expected, Pema stood up and looked directly into my eyes with more empathy and compassion than I've ever felt from one person. She has beautiful, crystal blue eyes. She said, "I hear you are very sick." I nodded and told her that I was dealing with cirrhosis and recently diagnosed cancer. She listened with loving concern as I told her I was not so worried with getting to the end, but with the uncertainty about what happens in the final moments and where we go afterwards. I've never believed in any of the various myths and traditions that are put in front of us: the Christian Heaven/Hell, the Buddhist bardo, or any of that stuff. She blew me away by saying almost with a roll of her eyes that the bottom line is nobody really knows what happens. Thank goodness she spared me from more junky dogma! She said every religion or group has a mythology that they use for comfort, if necessary, but the reality is that we don't know. It was a strange feeling of relief not to have to worry about behaving correctly in an afterlife to reassure my next birth would be in human form.

I then asked her if she knew of any practices I could do, both during the interim and at the final moment, to try to calm the fear and anxiety that I am sure will come (and, it goes without saying, to us all). She said there are two: *tonglen*, which, I told her, I frequently do for people at the cancer clinic (tonglen is the practice of breathing in the pain and suffering of the world and exhaling love and compassion, intended to relieve stress and anxiety) and *pause*, which involves turning your head, breathing in and out and then pausing, feeling the space, then coming back and repeating to the other side. She explained that this dispels anxiety, and when done at the moment of death can allow a person to go without struggle as the space widens out.

She asked Jen to write and keep her up to date on my progress. She smiled and wished me well. We thanked each other and I left.

Meeting someone face to face who is so full of compassion was the most incredible experience of my life. I will never forget it; it plays back like a movie all the time.

That's it! Now I have to go cry for the umpteenth time!
Much love. Dave.

In a gentle way, you can shake the world.
– Gandhi

5 Death

By David Brooks, Observer, Romantic wing

David makes poetry out of what many of us want to hide from.

I hesitate writing about Death; one, superstitiously, wants to do nothing to invite it or hasten it. Any thinking you do on it becomes, willy-nilly, part of your own Death's story.

Growing up on a Texas farm afforded this Observer type ample opportunity to glimpse Death in his many raiments, dispatched as he was equally by man's doing as by Nature's wordless own. A black calf, ornery and wild-eyed, might disappear from her muddy enclosure at her mother's side, to end up as white, waxy-paper frozen bricks and shards in our freezer, thence to our dinner plates; a cruel rooster, his head perforated with a single bullet, might do a macabre chicken-yard dance for a full half an hour, surrounded by the fidgeting hens he once dominated; a poky little puppy might be found drowned in a spring puddle; new piglets, as cleanly pink and diminutively adorable as a child's school eraser, might be found flattened by their grunting,  insouciant sow; a black rattlesnake, coiled under a plank of plywood, bothering only the mice who craved the maize leaked from holey burlap, would be shot and raked out, its scaly length to be doubled over a strand of rusted barbed-wire; an ancient lone mule might simply timber over into a grey, fly-riddled mound of dusty leather, hoof and exposed yellow molars; a treasured dog might be shot for worrying the neighbor's sheep and mauling our own Leghorns; an unfortunately black chick might be pecked to death by its own yellow siblings; a beloved family cat, now emaciated, might, unseen, toddle arthritically down to the garden and expire amid fragrant dewy stalks of sage.

Death was very much something that happened.

Its banal routine would encourage a child to doubt his visions of a bearded Jehovah, where all animals are seen by Him and relayed in turn to their own custom-made Heavens; and instead come to view Death as something more akin to the Hindu concept of Kali: a slavering, cruel mother who mindlessly spewed from her infinitely fecund womb all of life's wriggling creatures... only to eat them gleefully and voraciously with her own sharp teeth.

When my beloved family members died, it did require a shift, in my childish brain, to imagine that their destinies were substantially different from those of the pageant of dying flora and fauna of our barnyards. No, they were special, demi-angels almost, only partially monkeys as it turned out, and would be sent from their lacquered boxes and green swards to a fun never-land, somewhere northward into clouds, where angels flitted with golden wings and plucked ethereal strains from harps, and bathed eternally in the unceasing Love of the Father, fastidiously agleam in his pearled throne.

"Death is not an outrage," said Dr. Kübler-Ross. Teenagers imagine that death is surely the worst thing that can happen to us; we in our less-blinkered forties and beyond know differently. In fact, poised at midlife, we begin to realize that death is probably a welcome relief from many different things... not only from cancers and aches and nightmares and disappointments, insulin shots and ungrateful children and tooth decay, but also from the burden of Desire... knowing that we must eat or we shall die... knowing that our hearts and lungs must never cease their rhythms, and we are paroled from the social wars of ambition, morality, reputation... released from feeding, plucking, shaving, wiping and cleaning ourselves, and exonerated from finding bills in the mail.

On the other hand, Indian swamis warn us that death does not unburden us of our cumulative and private Karmas... So, there you go.

6 A Near Death Experience

By Tom L. Clark, Observer, Romantic wing

Tom Clark ponders this amazing experience from his youth and incorporates it into his philosophy of life.

The conquest of the fear of death is the recovery of life's joy. – Joseph Campbell

During the 1950s, when I was a teenager, I hitchhiked across the country in both directions, an odyssey that produced a full set of adventures, reunions, hard times, joyous good times and, on one occasion, an experience that was, for me, mysterious and apparently inexplicable. I was hitchhiking on a stretch of empty highway in New Mexico, close to midnight. There were no towns nearby and the moonless sky was dark in a way that is unique to the desert or the open sea. I held out my thumb gamely, still hoping for a ride at that late hour, as I was wending my way back to the East Coast from California.

Those were kinder, gentler times, and so it did not seem at all surprising to me that riding in the car that picked me up there was a family: a mother, father and two teen-aged daughters. They were returning from a vacation and headed for home in Paris, Texas. They had decided to drive through the night to avoid the summer heat and hoped that I might share some of the driving.

At about 2:00 a.m. one of the girls was taking a shift at the wheel—she was my age, nineteen. Her family was asleep in the back seat. We sat in relative silence, exchanging small pleasantries from time to time. She was holding the car, a four-door Plymouth sedan, at a steady 75 mph.

There was a sudden, loud bang when the right front tire blew out. I saw the girl clutch tightly at the steering wheel. In an instant the car was out of control, and it swerved rapidly to the right and left of the highway. Traveling at a high rate of speed, the car turned over—it rolled at least three or four times.

And as the car was rolling violently onto the desert sand, my sense of time suddenly and dramatically altered. Slower than slow motion, in a way I could not understand, time seemed virtually to stop. There was no sense of motion at all. In a calm and reflective way I wondered if I might die. This thought came to me without a trace of fear. Either possibility—living or dying—seemed equally acceptable to me at that moment.

I had heard stories about people seeing their whole lives flash before them when they are close to death. And when this happened to me, it seemed like a perfectly natural event. I wouldn't describe it as a flash, however, because of my radically altered sense of time. It seemed as though I was presented with a vision of my life, all nineteen years of it, and the vision contained everything; nothing was missing. It was a wonderful gift for me to appreciate and learn from.

When the car stopped rolling over (it was by now some distance from the highway), it landed upright. The windshield in front of me had been entirely smashed out, and I sat there looking at the dark night sky. It seemed to me there was a long period of complete and almost magical silence. I was struck by the brilliance of the stars.

Cries of pain and anguish then began. Two of the family had been thrown from the car—this was in the days before seat belts. The father's back was broken and his wife also sustained serious injuries. The others had, at the very least, broken bones and multiple lacerations. There was a lot of blood.

I alone was uninjured. Despite having been seated in the so-called "death seat," I did not have so much as a scratch or a bruise.

There was much to be done. I flagged down a truck, which promised to have an ambulance sent from the next town. Other cars stopped, and so I soon had some help in administering first aid to the injured family. Soon enough two ambulances came, and the four people from Paris, Texas, were taken to a small hospital in a small New Mexico town. A policeman gave me a ride back into town and, since I had no place to stay and hardly any money, I was allowed to spend the rest of the night in the town jail. Before leaving the next morning, I went to the hospital to visit the family. Soon thereafter, I began my hitchhiking journey again.

I believe I came close to death that night. My altered sense of time, calm reflection about dying, and vision of my life combined to change my own consciousness about life and death. On a deep, cellular level I learned that there is nothing to fear about death. And I was left with the enduring belief that there is something beyond the narrow band of consciousness, which so often passes for reality. I can't say that I know what that something is. I just know it's there.

Now, at this later stage of my life, I am leaning more into that experience I had so many years ago, understanding it more, embracing the opportunity I was given when time stopped, when I came so close to "that undiscovered country from whose borne no traveler returns." When I was younger, I used to try to make sense out of my near-death experience. At least I know now there is no sense to be made of it. It is not about rational understanding. It is not about God or the soul or the hereafter or spirituality. The experience I had, ultimately, is not even about death. It is only about the door that opened for me into that spacious presence that surrounds us, always. That's all.

7 My Father Had No More to Fear

By Elizabeth Wagele, Observer, Romantic wing

Fred had an active mind, which made him a good scientist. He also noticed things that might go wrong and tended to fret a lot until something happened that made his fretting unnecessary.

Around 1890, two Jewish families ran away from death from pogroms and arrived in Council Bluffs, Iowa. One family came from Odessa, Russia, the other from Romania. David and Lily were children at the time. They grew up, met, and married each other. Neither learned to speak English well because they each had spoken Yiddish at home and had only two or three years of education. When their first child, Sol Frederick, my father, was six months old, they moved to Salt Lake City, Utah. David Ravitz bought a bar and invested in copper and other kinds of mines. Their orthodox Jewish rabbi taught young Sol Hebrew, but not what the words meant, so Sol refused to continue with Hebrew school. As he grew up, he excelled in math and science, played tennis, became an Eagle Scout, and joined social clubs. His family called him Sol, however he introduced himself as Fred. He also developed the sense of humor and inner resources that saw him through his life.

When he was seventy-two he became ill with pancreatic and liver cancer. He didn't want us to agonize over his illness and cracked jokes to help us feel comfortable (friends often compared his sense of humor to comedian Groucho Marx). When I took him to see his doctor for what we expected would be (and was) the diagnosis of lymphoma, he was caught holding the door open for three women coming out of the parking garage. One of them casually thanked him. My father told her she could tip him when she returned after her appointment.

When the cancer created a blockage, his doctor wanted to perform surgery to extend his life for perhaps six months. He felt he'd be doing it more for the doctor's sake (as a guinea pig) than for his and asked him to

The blossoms never looked more blossomy!

make his life as short as possible instead. The decision was easy. A social subtype Observer with a strong Questioner wing, Fred had run many end-of-life possibilities through his head and was prepared.

Fred disliked strong emotions: he chose light music to listen to and read a lot but avoided novels. Even Oriental carpets depressed him. Objective and logical, he looked for what is real. *What's going on medically? What is the most likely outcome?*

Janice and Fred

At a dance at the University of Utah, he met Janice Fuller, who had been raised in Cripple Creek, Colorado, and they fell in love. A year later, he went to Cal Tech to get a PhD in physics and chemistry while she stayed in Salt Lake City. His parents offered him a trip around the world if he would not marry her since she wasn't Jewish. When he rejected their offer and Janice eloped to Pasadena—in 1930—my grandmother sat in a low chair and mourned in the Jewish tradition. Happily, his parents later had a change of heart and accepted her as their daughter.

Mom and Dad had a difficult first year of marriage, so my mother told me. Writing love letters while apart for a year or two, they had idealized each other. Living together, reality set in.

A few years later, back in Salt Lake City, my parents had a son who died at birth, then my sister was born. I came along four years later. In 1950 we moved to Berkeley when my father became a metallurgy professor at the University of California.

Family dynamics

My expected birth represented the last chance for my father to have a son to share his love of science with. My sister was unhappy about having a sibling. My mother was delicate emotionally. When I was two, the family moved to a two-bedroom apartment because their big house was too much for her. My father may have felt pressure to do things he didn't want to do: his wife wanted to go dancing and camping, while he had his mind on intellectual pursuits and his work. He had stomachaches and headaches, was prone to depression, and sensitive to noise for most of my childhood.

Fred's interest in me increased when I became a teenager. His health and bad moods also improved. We would occasionally sit up late into the night talking. I loved hearing about his thoughts and his philosophy of life and having someone to share my ideas and feelings with.

Dying

My father was a worrier until he found out he was dying. When the end was near, there was nothing fretting could achieve. The frowns on his face relaxed. He looked at me in a new, open way. What could go wrong was no longer an issue. His new attitude reminded me of what British writer Dennis Potter said in his interview with Melvyn Bragg one week before Potter died: white flowers looked whiter and blossoms never looked more blossomy.

During his last weeks we discussed, among other things, the Mozart, Beethoven, and Brahms recordings I brought him. He could now enjoy music that was beautiful in its seriousness and sadness instead of silly, not-quite-classical music. His back ached from the cancer, so I cut foam-rubber pillows to fit under his shoulder blades and relieve pressure. I was glad I could *do* something for him.

Dad accepted his death graciously. At the end he lay sleeping for a few days as the doctors increased morphine "for pain." Two days before he died, he woke up long enough to tell us goodbye one by one. He said he'd been dreaming about an interesting place, like Pakistan. I was both surprised and not surprised by his parting words to me: "We were lucky—we got to know each other very well. Not many people get to do that." I wondered if he was thinking about those late night talks we had about the meaning of life.

Do not give your love—it may get lost.
Radiate it like the sun. – Sunyata

8 Symbolic Death and Rebirth: What Dreams Can Do

By Elizabeth Wagele, Observer, Romantic wing

Observers like to concentrate on one thing in depth. This Observer has spent a lifetime pondering one short dream.

Peace comes from within. Do not seek it without. – Buddha

When I was four years old, my unconscious invented a dream I responded to with horror. Gradually I have realized how it helped me find my self and my way.

Before the dream, I was having trouble getting beyond the toddler stage. For one thing, I felt too attached to my mother. Though I could speak normally, I was always reverting to baby talk around her. It also bothered me that I kept asking her permission to go to the bathroom when I didn't need to ask. As an Observer type, I kept these concerns about growing up to myself. To express them would only have made me feel worse.

I tried to deny it as long as possible, but I was also troubled by the recent realization my sister, who was four years older than I, didn't like me. Looking back, perhaps her anger with my parents for burdening her with a sibling partially explains her tantrums and dark moods.

It seems to me my parents treated us differently. They were ineffective at calming her or preventing her from bullying me, possibly from guilt over having disturbed her happier life as an only child. Yet they were both tough on me. Even though I was quiet and wanted to please, my father was unnecessarily strict with me. My mother disciplined me for small infractions by rejecting me for days at a time. I'd have to ask her forgiveness before she'd speak to me again. Decades later she told me she didn't know why she would become so angry with me.

Dreams often seem like stories coming to us from a far-off place, but I knew I had generated this one myself, during the Second World War.

A hybrid of American Indians and Japanese soldiers rampage through my toy drum, now as large as the three-story apartment house we live in. They crawl like ants in and out of round holes in the drum. As my family and I eat dinner, they throw torches through our dining room windows. The torches catch our lacy curtains on fire. The fire spreads to the tablecloth, then to my mother, father, and sister and burns them to death. I escape by running through the kitchen, down the hall, and to my bedroom and safety.

When I woke I felt guilty, as if I had killed my parents and sister myself. Shock that I had harbored enemies in my toy drum haunted me for years. I told no one about it until I was well into adulthood. At age four, I couldn't reconcile this dream with my image of myself as a good girl. At the same time, the fantasy of life without my family pleased me, adding to my guilt.

Feeling I had something to do with killing my family shocked me into changing my attitude about myself. After I *killed my family* I could no longer think of myself as too babyish—that innocent part of myself had died with the dream. By morning, my reborn self was already seeking to detach from my family and put more trust in my own private world. I started to depend more on my imagination and look for my own meaning and direction.

In the dream, my psyche used shadow images to do the work of killing my family. (I knew the Japanese were our country's enemies from my mother reading newspaper accounts of the war to me as she held me on her lap.) It took me decades to accept the killers were also playing positive roles as protective animus symbols—male guides whose tasks were to liberate me. The drum that housed the murderers was also a shaman's drum, guiding me toward my inborn gift for music. My unconscious had plans for me. The container of the warriors could have been any kind of box-like object, a bee's nest for example, but it was a drum for playing music. The drum with small holes also resembled the unconscious: dark inside with few windows. The torches' flames represented my rage and my creative energy. My bedroom represented the sacred sleeping place incubating the vision my psyche had for me: to become more independent and to march to my own drummer.

I had loved music before the dream, but after the dream I wanted to carry it around inside me, so at the age of four I figured out how to pick out tunes and chords on the piano. I figured out nursery rhyme songs, then themes from my parents' classical records, starting with *Scheherazade*. Soon I would come home from movies and play the theme music I had heard. Drawing became an important way of entertaining myself, too.

I was around forty when I started thinking seriously about what this dream meant. I've talked about it in dream groups and studied Jung's and others' interpretations of dreams. Now I refer to the huge toy drum as Mother Music—my other mother, whose warriors stood up for me and helped guide me on my path. I think back to my parents' collection of 78-rpm records I loved when I was a child—black discs the same shape and color as the top of my toy drum. Black circles or spheres have populated dozens of my dreams since then, along with white squares or cubes, generally representing the round feminine and square masculine. In one dream, I dive to the bottom of the ocean and bring up a black ball in one hand and a white cube in the other. They're treasures, like gold. Like the drum dream, they're gifts from the deep.

The story of my dream at four-years-old expresses the Observer type by showing the importance of introversion in my life, keeping things to myself, disliking intrusion. I felt pushed by my family. My mother may have wanted me to stay her baby; I felt squashed by my father's authoritarian demands. Both parents were weak when it came to protecting me from my sister. So I made my own music and became curious about things that didn't depend on interacting with other people so much.

Eventually my mother's and father's stress levels went down and they put their hearts into raising and educating me. In the end they were loving parents and excellent grandparents to my children.

9 Assisted Death

Movie review by Elizabeth Wagele, Observer, Romantic wing

The Observer in this movie shows the complexity of the introvert's psyche given his need to be alone and his discomfort with, yet need for, relationships. He becomes energized when his emotions come to life.

In the opening scene, master violin-maker, Stephan removes the top of the violin he's working on and we see what looks like an empty, coffin-like box. I assume he is the person referred to in the title, *Un Coeur en Hiver (A Heart In Winter)*. Right away I'm curious. I'm hooked by Ravel's chamber music and the artful cinematography. The story is presented in rondo form, as is the music, a technique that moves the story along. I wasn't bored for a second. Even during the opening credits, the music is passionate, delicate, tumultuous, and mysterious—a taste of some of the musical and nonmusical themes to follow. Openings and closings—of doors, hearts, minds, lives, and relationships—are the motifs in this film. When Stephan is working close to his apprentice, the

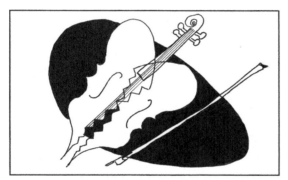

depth of field is shallow and the room appears crowded. When Stephan, an Observer, is working alone, the same room appears spacious. His friend, Maxim, an Achiever, calls Stephan's living space Spartan, trying to put him down. This Observer is relaxed and comfortable when left to himself.

The three main characters have studied violin with Louis Lachaume, a likable elderly man who lives retired in the country with his female friend. Lachaume keeps the fact that he's dying a secret, while Stephan, the closed and unreadable main character, played by Daniel Auteuil, seems to keep his own aliveness a secret. The Ravel music expresses what is in Stephan's heart, however. We know he's sensitive to the sound potentials in the violins he repairs.

Stephan, an Observer, comes to life when he's with Lachaume, the man who was the only person he ever loved. Stephan's eyebrows become relaxed—he even raises them expressively a couple of times—his face is looser, and he smiles more broadly (though it's never a full smile). Finally, Lachaume can no longer talk. He's old, in pain, and wants to die. His female friend says, "He's been asking me for three days, but I can't do it." When

Lachaume sees Stephan, he smiles faintly at him, looks at the syringe, and nods. To help the person with whom he feels the most alive to die is difficult, but Stephan takes the syringe and caringly administers the lethal dose that ends his friend's suffering. The others go outside to seek peace by walking in the woods. They know their beloved Lachaume's life is over when they see Stephan open the shutters to his room to give a sign and to let the air in. Look to Observers for nonverbal messages and kindnesses. They don't always have the words...

After this, Stephan grows more confident (goes toward his Asserter arrow). He takes charge by opening his own shop, taking some of the customers with him. Light shines onto his new, attractive, and roomy work area through skylights. After an 8½ month gestation period, Stephan meets Camille in a restaurant. He tells her he had thought the only person he had loved was Lachaume, but now he is able to admit that he also loved her and it wasn't just a game (his Adventurer side). We watch Stephan look out the window as Camille leaves to get into Maxim's car. The window reflects onto the car window, window piled upon window like the stretto of a fugue as they drive away. Camille looks back at Stephan.

As the music from the opening scene returns, one recalls Stephan dissembling the violin, exposing the interior to light, and applying fresh glue. By now the precious violin is mended and Stephan is stronger, too...

Always know how much we are loved and carry that love in our heart.
– David Bennett

10 My Obsession on Death and Dying

By Michele Harrison, Observer

Observers are prone to fear and are often curious about where we came from and where we're going. Michele's parents handled her fear of death poorly.

I was obsessed with death and dying from an early age. I frequently watched the news about Vietnam and Biafra children and adults dying. I covered my ears up with cushions so I couldn't hear what was being said. I was scared. I kept telling my Mum I thought I was going to die, I told her day after day I was sure I was.

She was so concerned about me, as I was about seven years old, that she spoke to our general practitioner. He thought I was attention-seeking and told her to say something that made matters worse. One day my Mum told me, "go away and die then."

I then believed my Mum and Dad wanted me to die and were going to kill me. Night after night I had the same dream that they came during the night and suffocated me with a red velvet heart-shaped cushion, I can't remember when or why the dream stopped, but it did.

However, my fear of death didn't go away until I had a near death experience at the age of forty after an operation that went wrong. I hemorrhaged and lost a lot of blood. I slipped into near unconsciousness and thought if this is death it's not that bad.

But I still have the occasional fear from not knowing how and when I will die. My Mum took three days to die and was distressed throughout, my brother died instantly. The not experiencing anything anymore: sunrise, sunset, food, sights, sounds. Not being able to have a conversation with the people I love, to tell them things or to touch them.

At the period I told you about, I believed that once you died you just ceased to be in body, soul, and spirit. Since then I have had some experiences that are convincing me that is not the case. I will only become totally convinced, however, when I do die, which I hope is not for a long time as I'm only fifty-five. There are some things worse than death to me.

Having said that there are times since I developed M.E. (myalgic encephalomyelitis, essentially the same as chronic fatigue syndrome), that on my darkest days I feel I would sooner be dead than carry on unable-to-live life. I know that if I didn't have four grown-up children and four grandchildren I would have taken my own life.

But I wouldn't leave them with that legacy or grief.

11 About Observers

Before you speak, ask yourself, is it kind, is it necessary, is it true, and does it improve the silence? – Shirdi Sai Baba

The fifth type, the Observer, belongs to the Head or Fear Center of the Enneagram, along with the Questioner and the Adventurer. Most Observers are thinking types. They are motivated to learn, regard knowledge as power (Bill Gates), are often calm and quiet, and sometimes shy. Being politically correct isn't important to many of them. Career areas include the sciences, working with computers, writing, categorizing things (i.e. library work), and working with machines. Observers with a Romantic wing are more likely to have occupations in the arts, writing, or psychology. Observers with Questioner wings are more likely to be attracted to the sciences.

Observers can use their Asserter arrow as a model for building confidence to put their ideas and projects out into the world. Their Adventurer arrow contributes to their sense of humor, their interest in a large variety of subjects, and a tendency in some to talk too much (to lecture instead of having conversations).

Since Observers guard themselves against intrusion (Fred Ravitz and Frank), they respect others' privacy, too. At their best they're logical and objective (Fred), sensitive and nonjudgmental (Dave Scherman), interesting and original (David Brooks), kind and gentle (Dave and Stephan), good listeners (Tom Clark), and open to new ways of thinking about things (David Brooks, who is also a talented musician and artist). At their worst they are withholding or overly critical.

Observers are often idiosyncratic, easily feel like outsiders, and can feel frustrated when the social graces elude them.

Observers want to do what they like doing—to work on projects and to learn—without being bothered. Being curious, they often search for the truth, thus the many Observer scientists (Albert Einstein and others). David Brooks examines cruelty and fantasy in death honestly. Tom L. Clark helps his clients search for what's bothering them in his psychotherapy practice.

Grieving

Processing feelings and memories is crucial for accepting one's new reality after a significant loss. A state of shock protected Jayne Johnson for a while following the deaths in Jayne's family but wore off in a few months. As she says, mending takes time and grieving is a private business. Having led a thoughtful life helped her cope with her daughter's and granddaughter's deaths. Jayne knew the only way to the other side of her grief was to go into and through the pain.

Expressing what they need when grieving might be more difficult for Observers with Questioner wings—or Observers who are unfamiliar with the feeling side of life. In *A Heart in Winter*, expressing his love for his violin teacher by his actions strengthens Stephan emotionally. Grieving helps thaw his heart.

The Shadow

Integrating shadow material into our lives can be painful and difficult, but rewarding, work. Jayne Johnson integrated the deaths of her daughter and granddaughter in the first story of this chapter, bringing congruence to the opposition of life and death.

Shadow elements show up in arrows. Among other things, a quiet and shy Observer's shadow side might be represented by his gregarious Adventurer arrow. A mild-mannered Observer's shadow side might be represented by his bold and angry Asserter arrow.

Nine types of people

Learning the nine types' points of view helps individuals find balance, acceptance, and wholeness. The Enneagram is valuable both in facing an immediate crisis and in long-range growth.

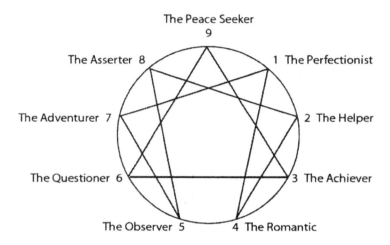

Contents

1. Sorrow and Fear of Living in an Unpredictable World – Dave Hall
    (His friend's cancer produces in David fearful anger and mental reactivity.)

2. 1967: Not the Summer of Love – Shelley Berman
    (Her Adventurer father took off with a girlfriend when Shelley was six, had a bad drug trip, and jumped out of a hotel window, taking a part of her soul.)

3. Accepting Death Without Fear – Georgia Bailey
    (After a brush with her own mortality and others' illnesses, she finds ways to connect more with her physical being.)

4. My Father's Death – Mario Sikora
    (His Questioner father uses vodka to help him cope with the terrors of war, poverty, and refugee camps.)

5. Thinking of Death – Marilyn Margulius
    1. What My Near-death Experience Taught Me
    (Feels no fear when a thief holds a knife to her throat.)
    2. Death with Love as Precious and Spiritual
    (Contrasts her mother's death, where they kept her alive as long as possible, with the peaceful, spiritual death of her mother in law.)

6. "I Was Taught We Don't Have a Body" – Samantha Mercer
    (Her father was murdered, when she was four years old. Afterwards, her mother acted as though nothing had happened.)

7. "Death Will be Graduation Day" – Tom Purcell
    (Religious Questioner father manages to get through life so he can make it to Heaven.)

8. About Questioners

Chapter Six - Questioners

Be patient toward all that is unsolved in your heart, & try to love the questions themselves. – Rainer Rilke

What sets the principle characters of the stories in this chapter apart from the other chapters more than anything is the way fear has a hold on their lives and at the same time seems to sharpen their mental focus.

Writing Styles

Questioners write in a broad range of styles, from angry to humorous to intellectual to poetic, all in the service of unearthing what, to them, is the truth. Note: Questioner Connie Frecker also wrote *He Keeps His Audience Wanting More* in Chapter 3.

1 Sorrow and Fear of Living in an Unpredictable World

By David Hall, Questioner, Observer wing, Social subtype

In this story, David tries to balance his grief with his defense of anger over having a friend dying of brain cancer. His partner Katy Taylor reacts to the same friend's illness in the first story in the chapter on Perfectionists.

I've been watching how the reactive parts of my personality keep rising up and blocking a pure experience of grief and love for my friend who is dying of a brain tumor. Almost every time I think of him, I sit with some form of reactivity until it dissipates—then I return to the real grief, loss, and love I feel.

For starters, I'm really angry about cancer these days. It seems to be everywhere. I don't know if cancer is on the rise, but I'm ready to believe it is. I don't know if most cancer is caused by human toxic activity, like polluting air and food and ground water, but I'm ready to ascribe it to this. I certainly don't know if my friend's case of cancer is in any way anybody's fault, but this generalized feeling of fearful anger, as if there are careless and irresponsible Other People out there persecuting all of us with their toxic activities, wells up every time. Then I have to sit with that reactive energy, allowing that it's there but not getting caught up in the judgment or the stories, until it fades away and I can feel what's under it: sorrow, love for my friend, and fear for myself and everyone else who lives in such an unpredictable and unsafe world.

This is an edge I have to keep working. I actually value the critical intelligence that helps me to understand some of the human factors that are likely responsible for a lot of cancer. At the same time, I see how I avoid the direct experience of pain in my heart by diverting my attention to this understanding and by getting caught up in a net of judgment and story telling.

After telling his story, David answered some questions the author asked:

- I believe part of our growth path is to be able to look at the truth, which includes dying and death. That we are all going to die is an inextricable part of the experience of being human.
- If I am in pain when I'm dying, ideally I'll die consciously. I hope my suffering will not cloud my mind too much and I'll know when it is time to release myself and do it with grace and grit (to steal a nice phrase from Ken Wilber).
- I don't think people are necessarily depressed when they talk about death. Talking about anything can be bound up with depression. And talking about death can come from an infinite variety of places within us.
- People should have more freedom to choose the option of suicide than they generally do in the United States. I would like to know it was an option if I was in unbearable pain.

2 1967: Not the Summer of Love

By Shelley Berman, counter-phobic Questioner

This is a story of what happens when people are neither honest nor sensitive with children about the deaths of their loved ones. Shelley's trauma of losing her father was compounded by sibling abuse and having a mother who had difficulty coping with six children.

My life changed two weeks after my seventh birthday with the unexpected death of my father. Before his death, I was a typical six-year-old tom boy-girl: happy, inquisitive, thoughtful, intuitive, and playful. After his death, my life was altered when violence and neglect took over.

My father was the sun: he was the center of our universe. There was many a night he piled four or five kids into his two-seater and took us to see the sunset. There was many a night my father, a young doctor, charmed the panties off of many a nurse. I knew of his infidelity. I started seeing the inappropriate flirtations with nurses at the hospital when I was a wee tot of four. I hated it. I hated hearing my mother crying in the bathroom because she knew too. And what could I do about it? I was only four or five or six. I tried to help my mother, to cry with her in the bathroom. I tried and it didn't matter because my mother didn't suit my father, and perhaps even marriage didn't suit my father—and these two people left their indelible emotional scars on my siblings and me. I knew—casket side—there was no way I'd be a parent or a spouse. This was my pledge to myself two weeks into my seventh year: I would never have children, I would never get married, and I would never do drugs. I've kept that pledge, with one interesting exception.

My father seemed to me to be a happy man. But how could he have been? He was unhappily married. He had to marry my mother because he impregnated her. I joke that he missed that day in medical school when sex education was taught. But it was not a joke, it was a huge mistake, and one huge mistake begot the next and the next and the next. He kept having more children with a woman he didn't love and how could he have been happy? My father was a man who had his way ups and his way downs, which he helped by taking uppers from the hospital. These days, people lament that he was manic-depressive but it doesn't really matter now. What matters is that he left us, took off with one of those nurse/girlfriends, had a bad drug trip, jumped out of a hotel window, and ended up dead. With him, he took a part of my soul.

It's not a good idea to give a dead person that much power, but when you are young and life changes for the worse, it's hard to find ways to rub a soul salve on oneself.

Mystery, shadows, and half-truths should have no place in death. Let me shout to the world and beyond that heartfelt honesty is the only way to begin to fill the chasm unlocked by trauma. It was not until very recently, not until I turned fifty years old, that I found out more of the story behind my father's death. Why did it take so long? What was the point of keeping this part of the truth from me?

This is what I now know about my father's death.

On his way to Carmel, in the "Summer of Love" in 1967, my father and his Nurse Du Jour spent the night at Esalen on the California Coast. It's supposed to be a beautiful place, nestled amongst the redwoods and overlooking the Pacific Ocean. My father, a man who was used to control, upset the apple cart by arguing against experimentation with LSD. Whether through outrage or a misguided sense of play, I will never know, but someone slipped LSD into my father's coffee the next morning.

That is how the last trip in my father's life began. A day that ended in a paranoid mixed-up naked cop-chasing hotel to the window terra firma gone and dead.

Ever have an A-HA moment? I've had two in my life. The first when a good friend asked me twenty odd years ago if I thought my parents would have gotten married had he not gotten her pregnant. The skies opened and the little birds starting chirping and the sun finally broke through and cleared up all the questions in my life. It all made sense: the pain and the unhappiness of that marriage.

When I heard about the slip of the LSD, I had my second. My father's death was truly a tragic accident. My father didn't willingly take the hallucinogenic that ultimately killed him. He was scared. He was so scared and he was used to being in control. He didn't understand what was happening to him. And how could he?

I once had the same sort of thing happen to me, with a much different result. I was house sitting, rummaging through the fridge and finally I uncovered a ziploc bag of brownies in the freezer. They were small and freezer burned, not so great, but chocolate is chocolate and I ate several. It didn't take long before strange things started to happen. I was tripping. I could read everybody's mind. I was in a play and everyone was an actor in my play. I had a pain in my heart and finally I called the ambulance because I thought I was having a heart attack. The EMT (emergency medical team) asked me what I took. I was indignant. I took nothing. I have never taken anything. My body was experiencing something that I had never experienced before. I remember telling that bastard that he could shut the hell up and help me because something was indeed happening to me. To me, it was an emergency. He accused me of taking him and his ambulance away from a real emergency. He told me I was going to have to pay thousands of dollars for calling the ambulance when I didn't really need it. By the time I arrived at the hospital, I was in tears, terrified, and having a full-blown panic attack. I was being checked for everything. Hooked to a monitor, waiting in a little room off to the side, my mind began to wander through the evening. When it meandered back to the brownies, tucked away in a back of a freezer, cut into tiny squares, I knew exactly what had happened. At that moment, I was relieved. There was nothing physically wrong with me. Then, I was appalled. I, unwillingly and unknowingly, ingested a substance that I had promised myself and my dead father I would never use.

Now I see, given a different set of circumstances, this could have ended way worse than a fight with the ambulance attendant. I had an argument; he ran naked from a cop. I was driven to the hospital. He was driven to the morgue.

I hear Joni Mitchell singing, "forty-three falls and forty-three summers gone now. One chin turns to three through the town…" Middle age. I look at myself in the mirror and see the age markings, but inside, I'm just as devastated as when I was seven. The tomboy turned lesbian and the violence turned to anger and rage. I've spent half my life in therapy trying to undo the damage, and if not undo, then at least understand. My nuclear family is not close and my mother is emotionally stunted. My younger brother has replaced my older sister as her spousal stand in and my mother chooses whom she will love amongst her children and whom she will ignore. I grew up knowing this inequality and, if there is one thing to be proud of in my life, it is not passing on the dysfunction to another generation by having children of my own.

I was visiting relatives in San Diego when my father died. I was inexplicably escorted on a jetliner back to my family home where people milled around not seeing me. My well-honed ultra sensitivity and intuition told me there was only pain in that house. Not to mention the extra clue that I was seeing people I only saw at weddings and Bat Mitzvahs. I knew something was terribly wrong. I asked and nobody would tell me. I remember getting angry. Why go to the trouble to bring me home and then not tell me why? It was a feeling I'll never forget. Kind of like being tossed into the Bering Sea with a wetsuit on and knowing that even with that suit, the icy sea will drain the warmth from your soul and your organs will shut down one by one and you will drown. I felt that way. Knowing there was something dreadful, not knowing what it was and drowning in a sea of relatives.

The perfect mother would have wrapped me in her arms, told me she loved me, then told me the tragic news and let me have a safe place for tears. I didn't live in that world. When I finally was able to wrench out the truth of my father's death, I didn't cry. I decided not to shed a tear, let bygones be bygones and move on into the next chapter of my life. The next chapter was from an entirely different book: abuse prevailed where love had once been. There were five other children in my family and each handled the death of my father differently. My older brother dealt with his anger by choosing me as his punching bag. I dealt with my newfound violence by beating my younger siblings. My mother didn't stop the violence, whether through indifference, numbness, or depression, and I don't remember laughter after my father died, unless it was mean spirited.

In the Jewish tradition, we go back to the gravesite one year later and unveil the tombstone and place markers on the grave in the form of small rocks. When my father's grave marker was unveiled, I cried. Seeing that cold stone marking the place of my father's body sent me reeling. It was the ultimate pain in the ultimate year of pain. Since that day, forty-three years ago, I've only been back to that gravesite a handful of times: once to bury my grandmother, once for my grandfather, once for my aunt, and once for a cousin.

This past year, I went back to the cemetery just for a visit. With a pocketful of stones, I went around that cemetery and placed one on each of the grave markers of family members. I tried to say a few words to each and appreciate what each did to make my life fuller. When I got to my father, I cried. I don't know what would have happened had he lived. He was ready for divorce; my family would have been torn apart in a different fashion. He would have taken the money and a couple of his favorite children with him, but not me.

Even so, had my father lived, I imagine he would have pushed me to be the best self I could be and appreciated my intuition and loyal nature. I imagine he would have made sure that I knew I was smart and worth the effort. I imagine that instead of looking in the mirror and seeing the broken heart of a seven year old, I could see an adorable sparkling baby blue-eyed dyke fifty year old.

3 Accepting Death Without Fear

By Georgia Bailey, Questioner with an Observer wing, Social subtype

Questioners tend to live in their heads. Georgia's route to reducing her fear of death was to connect with her body and the world of feelings.

I'm a sixty-six year-old Questioner living in Bakersfield, California.

I felt called to become a massage therapist after retiring at fifty-one from working for years in corporate America. The year before my retirement I got my first massage, but I resisted having my body worked on. In fact, it was years before I could truly receive a massage myself, even though I knew I wanted to massage other people after only ten minutes. Massage is rhythmic like dancing and is done to music; they both require disconnecting one's thinking.

When I turned sixty I went through a major life change from losing people who were important to me. My dear friend died of bone cancer; I still feel great sorrow when I think of her six years later. My mother has late stage Alzheimer's. My sister is ill, 600 miles away, with late stage Type II diabetes. I became so afraid of death; I would lie in my bed, alone in my house, and literally shake with fear.

This fearfulness continued until I took up my second career as a massage therapist. Through this training I became aware that there are other ways of knowing than just your mind. For example, when I visit my mother and I know when she knows me and when she doesn't, it's an energetic thing—not what she says. At this same time I began doing couples dancing several times a week. These two activities overlapped in many ways. As a follower, I had to learn to stop thinking. My center was moving from my head to my belly. I began to understand others in a whole new way.

When I became interested in the Enneagram I was stunned to find I could so easily see people's type. What a revelation that I could become conscious of personality energy! The training was a peak two weeks in my life. When I lean toward my Peace Seeker arrow, I feel connected to others and to the earth and I have no fear of dying. I used to think of dying as being cut off from life, being left out and, I guess, knowing it. But now recognizing the connectedness of all things has reduced my fear in general. It couldn't have happened by reading or talking—only through feeling.

My own reaction to high death risk was when I had a mastectomy for breast cancer in 2004. The greatest risk came with the staph infection resulting from insertion of the expander. I was hospitalized twice and had IV's for weeks at home. My attitude was one of a dumb animal—I did what I was told and didn't think about the future. Facing the death of my two remaining family members makes me cry and feel sad to be alone. Even caring for them is better than not having them.

I no longer fear death (unless I'm fooling myself!). I am not religious at all and believe I will return to whatever I was or wasn't before I came into consciousness. I am incredibly lucky to have enough in retirement to get by and not need to be married. I have a large circle of friends and acquaintances around me. The work I try to do on myself involves accepting others as they are, compassion, and kindness toward everyone. When I succeed at these things I genuinely feel better; I don't do them in order to get me anything later—I don't believe that will happen.

> *One can experience an unconditional affirmation of life only when one has accepted death, not as contrary to life but as an aspect of life.* – Joseph Campbell

4 My Father's Death

By Mario Sikora, Asserter

Mario's father knew the terrors of World War II, similar to Elli Boray in Chapter 2. While Elli at first found refuge in sleep and eventually recovered, Mario's father became a perpetual outsider.

Note: My father was a Questioner who died from liver disease after a life of serious drinking, probably caused by horrible experiences as a child during World War II. His last month was a descent into pure fear--hallucinations of demons and reliving real and imagined terrors--the worst of the Questioner's world. – Mario Sikora

My father's final month was the same as the previous sixty-two years: full of fear that sometimes bordered on terror. But it was also worse than the previous sixty-two years, because he knew what was coming.

It was the alcohol, of course. The alcohol that was the Refuge for decades, starting every morning with vodka in his coffee and taking him through the day until he finally faded into fitful sleep each night. It catches up.

He had a Reason for seeking such Refuge, and one difficult to argue against and one that he generally kept to himself. But it was a Reason you need to know if you want to understand my father's life and death. Born in his mother's country, near the border, a few years before Hitler invaded his father's country. His father went back to fight a futile defense, took a bullet and ended up in the RAF in England. My father stayed with his mother, and the rest of his short childhood was a series of refugee camps and not knowing, ever. Not knowing how you would eat tomorrow, not knowing if it would be a bomb or a bullet that came out of the blue; he'd seen the wreckage that each one left behind and always wondered when it would be his turn and if it would hurt and if he would even know what happened or if it would all just suddenly go black.

The not knowing fed the fear, and the fear became the focus of his life. It accompanied him from Germany to England to Argentina to the States. Always an outsider, never really understanding the rules; torn between pride in his heritage and shame.

He did what one was supposed to do: got a job, found a girl, started a family. He was an only child, and his parents fit in even less well than he did. It fell on him to solve their problems, and all that he did was never enough (his parents had their Reasons as well). He tried to keep everyone happy, but that's difficult when you never know what's the right thing and you know you don't know. It becomes harder still when people realize that you don't know but expect you to know anyway.

To understand my father you have to understand his parents, as much as anyone can under such circumstances. His father, whom he called "Papo," was hard and straight. Small, but tough. The kind of guy who could take a bullet, but none too happy about that or anything else. His mother, whom he called "Mamo," was another story. Tough and mean, but with a bucket full of fear to go with it. His father saw his mother in him, without the tough and mean, and was none too happy about that. Disappointed, really, and my father knew it.

To understand my father's death you have to understand his son, at least a little. His son was hard as well; bigger and stronger and certain. My father admired that some days. "You'll live your own life," he'd say. "That's good." Other days, especially when the vodka took over, it pissed him off. "What do you know?" he'd say. "You'll see; they'll drag you down too."

"We'll see," the son would say. We'll see.

The last ten years my father and his mother lived together; his father long dead. She clung to him, afraid when he left her sight, and with good Reason. "You're all that's left," she said one night. "Everyone else is gone. Everything is gone." Being the only thing left was hard  for him. It was too much pressure, so he took Refuge.

When his last month began his mother was already tucked away securely in a place for people who were near the end and might have known it, as much as anyone in that state can know anything. She started to go first, but he went faster. You can't start your day every day with vodka in your coffee—for decades—and not pay a price. The price was his liver, as it goes in these stories; and in the end he was swollen and yellow-brown and mostly out of his mind. His son took care of him, with some help of course; but it pretty much fell on his son to listen to the hallucinations and feed him and clean him and wait as the story played out.

The son still remembers, clearly, when they sent his father home from the hospital. "Nothing to do really," the doctor said. "Here's what the next few months will look like..."

My father's street was under construction; torn up, undrivable. Which meant walking the last 100 feet. The unnatural yellow-brown giving people pause. Construction workers, neighbors, in the midst of living life, all fell silent and watched. My father's hospital gown and slippers—all that would fit over the swollen body—told the story. He walked with help, shuffled really, slightly aware of the audience but his mind on bigger things. That last walk his own road to Gol'gotha, his past was the cross he bore. One can debate how much one deserves the cross, any of us, but that debate doesn't matter. We all get one, custom fit.

The doctor was wrong; it wasn't a few months. It was a few weeks. It seemed longer; it was a bad time either way. The fear got worse, and sometimes crossed the border into terror. Visions of demons and monsters, no longer able to be contained, Refuge no longer an option. Near the end there was a final moment of clarity, sort of. My father's eyes focused on his son, and first in Polish and then in German and then in Spanish and then, finding the language his son understood, he said in English "You are a cruel son of a bitch, Papo." The son no longer the son, perhaps, but who's to know what people are thinking in that state and why they say what they say.

From there, it went fast. Back to the hospital. A morphine drip. No more words; the eyes stayed shut; the breathing slow. Peace at last, perhaps, but who's to know. He slipped away in the middle of the night. "Slipped away" are the right words in this case. After the war and the bullets and the bombs, after crossing the ocean to a new land and then another, after the drama and the sheepish calls in the middle of the night asking for help at the police station or the accident scene, after the angry tirades about everyone who had done him wrong and plotted against him and made it impossible for him to be happy, the breathing simply stopped and he was gone.

5 Thinking of Death

By Marilyn Margulius, counter-phobic Questioner

Marilyn is a decorator and artist. She uses eye contact to hold her listener's attention, describes herself as non-conforming and as vacillating from one extreme to another, and says fear plays an important role in her life.

1. What My Near-death Experience Taught Me

One day, when I was a young woman, I was coming up the stairs from the subway in New York City at 34th and 5th Ave to visit my father-in-law at his office. It was not a bad neighborhood. I thought it was strange that a man in a Harris Tweed jacket would turn around and look at me. I was not at all street smart then or I would not have kept walking upstairs so close to the wall. As I reached a landing, the man came at me suddenly and held me pinned against the wall with his knee. He had one hand on the side of me ready to push me down the stairs while he held a knife at my throat. It all happened very fast. The most amazing thing about the whole thing was that I learned I had no fear of dying. I asked him to please take anything he wanted but to not harm me, as there were people who needed me. Then, I took my purse and threw it up the stairs away from me. He stunned me and split my lip with his knee, then ran to get the bag.

Many people went by as if nothing were happening, just keeping going until he left the scene. Then people came to help me. For the first time in my life, I understood why so many Germans went along with Hitler. People have to protect themselves. It was a tough way to learn that and to learn about the necessity of being streetwise. I never walk near walls and always make sure I know who is around me.

2. Death with Love as Precious and Spiritual

I do not like contemplating the adventure of death.

I spent a lot of time with my mother while she deteriorated from congestive heart failure. It was awful to see her decline. We all suffered when they kept her alive as long as possible with pain and other medications. Something is wrong about that. I feel badly that I was not there to be with her the night she passed away all by herself.

Many years ago, my mother in law, who was alone most of her life, passed away in the hospital. Every one of us whom she loved was by her bedside, holding her hand, and proceeding with her from being conscious and grateful that we were all there, through the many slow stages of leaving her energy behind. It was a spiritual experience and one I think of often and as being precious. How lucky she was to be surrounded by love. How peaceful she seemed. I have had a similar feeling of awe, mystery and amazement about the unknown while being a coach at a birth, standing in Chartres Cathedral, or in front of a Rembrandt painting for the first time. And at those very special and very rare times when I am in the process of painting and magic happens with no explanation possible.

I am grateful for the opportunity to think about it.

6 I Was Taught We Don't Have a Body

Interview by Elizabeth Wagele of Samantha Mercer, Questioner

This is one of three stories in this book where how children were told of a parent's death was mishandled. These children were also deprived of sensitive care around their mourning. Samantha's shift from a limiting belief system (all spirit) to a connecting one facilitates her healing. (The other stories are There is to be no Grieving *in Chapter 2 and* Not the Summer of Love *in this chapter.)*

Samantha's personal history has given her an unusual attitude toward pain, suffering, and sympathy. Her dad was murdered when she was four years old. Sam remembers hearing her mother, who put a positive spin on everything, talking on the phone that night to the Christian Science practitioner, saying, "I'm completely healed of grief." The next day she removed all the photos of him from their house and never mentioned him again. Sam's father was gone and her mother was not available to comfort her.

A year earlier, there had been a robbery in their home and she and her sister and mother had been tied up and left on the bed while the dad was put in the closet. The robbery was apparently connected to the fact that the father owned a lumber company and wouldn't go along with the union. The day of the murder was payday. One man came to his business and pulled a gun, allegedly to rob him. Another man shot him.

Since Sam was not allowed to grieve in her family, she shifted her need for parents onto religion and became obsessed that God, whom she feared, would take care of her. Eventually she found a cousin she could talk to about her father. Growing up, she didn't have courage to do things on her own, didn't trust life, and had no dreams of her own. She gave birth to four children believing she would be flawed if she felt pain. As a psychiatric social worker she was competent, but was afraid to do anything new or go off on her own. She put all her creativity into cooking and working with the disadvantaged.

"I watch my ability to have access to my own wisdom," she told me. "Sometimes I'm so clear and sometimes I'm so unconnected. I've had years and years of insomnia due to the trauma of losing my father and not being able to mourn his death. When I'm tired, it's hard to trust, allow, and let go of pain. If there's anything bad happening in your life, you're taught in Christian

Science not to tell anyone, because either you have to deal with their fears or they'll see you as a person in pain. You have to defend yourself against other people's thoughts. Christian Scientists believe people are only spirits and can't experience pain. Since pain is an illusion, sympathy is forbidden.

I don't like to be the recipient of sympathy. Until I smiled, my Mom just wouldn't talk to me. In God's eyes, we don't have a body. I didn't know there would be pain in childbirth and thought I was being punished. These ideas are in your cells."

Now at seventy-eight, Samantha is anti-authoritarian; she runs through stop signs and steals magazines. She likes to surprise her partner, Mary, with her cooking. "I don't think about death because I don't know what the circumstances will be, but perhaps the anxiety I sometimes experience is about death. I just have to trust I'll be able to deal with it. It's important to me to be here now, especially since I've become a Buddhist."

If we take a small step in understanding the stressors in life, with understanding we can find the triggers and forgive, or let go. – David Bennett

7 Death Will Be Graduation Day

By Tom Purcell, Peace Seeker

Questioners tend to be skeptical and mistrustful, as is Tom's father, to feel they are protecting themselves. He trusts his church and the afterlife, but he's pretty grumpy about life on earth.

My father died at age ninety-three, a month before his ninety-fourth birthday. He was a social subtype Questioner through and through. He often complained about "the powers that be," yet enjoyed socializing with them; he was instrumental in the campaigns to re-elect our local Member of Parliament, yet refused to run for office himself; he was friendly with everyone he met, especially the underdogs of society. Yet he often said he was unable to trust anyone.

My loving father maintained his intellectual faculties until the last few months. During his last ten years, following a few minor surgeries, he experienced brief periods of memory impairment, but bounced back quickly. The official cause of death was old age.

He was a devout Roman Catholic with an unshakeable belief that he was going to heaven. His concept of heaven wasn't elaborate, but he did expect to see predeceased friends and family members there when he arrived. He never disclosed to me what they were, but in his later years he expressed regret about mistakes he had made in his life.

Overall, he was accepting of his fate. He didn't believe the world was such a great place with all the moral corruption, poverty, wars, and suffering. Life on earth was a test of faith, and death was graduation day.

In light of the current health consciousness and the focus on physical well-being, I found it interesting that my father ate red meat daily, drank alcohol, smoked, never exercised, carried at least seventy extra pounds, was always worried about something, had high blood pressure and cholesterol, and was never particularly happy or relaxed. However, he was proud of the fact that he never ever missed Sunday Mass. Perhaps he was onto something.

A major theme of his stories was a mistrust of authority figures and an inability to express emotion. He felt powerless to change any aspect of the world. As a skeptic, he believed politicians were skillful liars and the news media were the mouthpieces of rich and powerful interests, but he was loyal to his wife, his family, his employers, his religious faith and his political views.

He was afraid of losing his job, although he held the same position for over twenty-three years, and he often expressed suspicion of other managers at his workplace. His co-workers wouldn't listen to him when he said their employer was headed for bankruptcy, but his fear of being out of work inspired him to seek out another job. Three months later he found out his former employer had indeed gone out of business. My father had landed a much better position,

even though he was already in his mid-fifties. He attributed his success to prayer and God's work—never giving himself credit for his own virtues. I wished he'd take pride in his reputation for scrupulous honesty and loyalty to his employer.

I questioned his blind faith in a belief system that had evolved through many centuries. In its highest expression, through the example of the loving kindness of Christ, it commands its followers to "love thy neighbor as thyself." My father, however, divided the world into members of his club and nonmembers. It bothered me deeply as a young man when he spoke negatively about people who did not agree with his beliefs. I became even more frustrated when he refused to discuss religiously based beliefs at all. Now, however, I can understand my youthful desire to seek the essential truth in all religions as rather threatening to my dogmatic father.

When I was a teenager, I would try to engage him in theological debates about other religious traditions, but he would dismiss anything that didn't conform to his own narrow and rigid interpretation of official Catholic dogma. Later in his life, he softened somewhat and relaxed his rigid views when he acknowledged, "good people of all faiths go to heaven."

Out beyond ideas of wrongdoing and right doing, there is a field.
I will meet you there. – Rumi

8 About Questioners

Questioners like honesty and dislike flattery. They want to know where they stand so they can figure out how to protect themselves from harm. Sometimes they behave timidly (the phobic or fearful ones), sometimes assertively (the counter-phobic ones), and sometimes they vacillate from one style to the other. Marilyn Margulius is an example of a counter-phobic Questioner: she is not afraid when she is attacked with a knife. Georgia Bailey shaking from fear in her bed is an example of a phobic or fearful Questioner.

The Questioner's fear can distract him from grief, joy, or a heart connection. Dave Hall describes his reactivity taking his attention from loving his dying friend. He sees how he avoids the direct experience of pain "by getting caught up in a net of judgment and story telling." Fear can also result in over-controlling, blaming, and rage.

The Questioners' Achiever arrow inspires them to work hard or find a goal to pursue and to go after it. Questioners, including Georgia Bailey, often seek the calmness of their Peace Seeker arrow.

The Observer wing influences the Questioner to be focused and to stay on track. The Adventurer wing can influence the Questioner to be more highly strung.

Questioners are often attracted to a cause or institutions that can provide authority: the police force, science, and the law. Counter-phobic Questioners may become daredevils to try to prove they are not afraid. Phobic Questioners tend to be overly cautious.

A typical defense mechanism for the Questioner is restlessness of the mind—worrying, fretting, or being reactive. Humor is often used as a defense.

Professional comedians are frequently Questioners because they can be witty and quick and good at reading what others find funny. Humor can deflect feelings or express feelings ironically (Shelley Berman writes with humor). Needing to numb out, Mario Sikora's father used alcohol to forget or avoid his problems.

Grieving

Feeling safe is of utmost importance for Questioners when under the stress of a recent or impending death. One defense they often use against grieving is to project their power onto someone else, avoiding responsibility for their own feelings. Questioners are often afraid of their own rage.

To avoid feeling overwhelmed, Questioners can plan ahead by thinking of how they can feel taken care of and empower themselves. They can make an appointment with a grief counselor, sign up for a grief group, and make arrangements to be with soothing friends on a regular basis.

In spite of your fear, do what you have to do. – Chin-Ning Chu

Shadow

For Questioners who trust authority (for example a church, their government, the military), their shadow is the part of themselves that secretly wants to rebel. Anti-authoritarian Questioners are outwardly rebellious, so their shadow side is secretly obedient.

Questioners, like Tom Purcell's father, who are suspicious and project their own shortcomings onto others, who subscribe to unrealistic conspiracy theories, or who are overly pessimistic, often live among people who don't share their reality.

Shadow elements show up in the arrows. Questioners tend to be relatively doubting and pessimistic. Among other things, their Achiever arrow represents confidence and optimism and their Peace Seeker arrow represents relaxation and optimism.

When you are free from desire and fear
you will live a life that is so different from all you know,
so much more interesting and intense,
that, truly, by losing all, you gain all.

– With respects to Sri Nisargadatta Maharaj
I Am That, Dialog 97
Sunyata

The nine types of people

Learning the nine types' points of view helps individuals find balance, acceptance, and wholeness. The Enneagram is valuable both in facing an immediate crisis and in long-range growth.

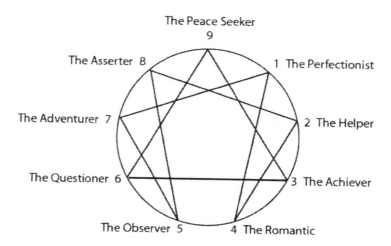

Contents

1. For the Birds – Kathy Heuser
   (She traces a healing experience to understanding fears from her childhood.)

2. Avon Calling – Kathy Heuser
   (Her first experience of knowing someone her age who died.)

3. I Opened to the Essential Beauty and Awfulness of Loving Someone Deeply – Catherine Williams
   (After fighting with father for twenty years, they become friends. Controlling gives way to love.)

4. My Happy Reactions to Death – John Stabb
   (His unusual responses cause raised eyebrows.)

5. Uncle Wayne – Jaki Girdner
   (Went to great lengths to enjoy the stars.)

6. Evidence: Clarity – Poem by Dah
   (Love of garden and quiet...)

7. She Laughed in the Concentration Camp – Elizabeth Wagele
   (Oldest survivor also unusually optimistic.)

8. Party Girl Too Young to Die – Pat Helin
   (Young woman has an early death.)

9. Dying Having a Good Time - Valentine Illidge
   (A child's father's friend dies.)

10. A Reason for Urgency – Harriet Berman Glaser
    (Deaths in her family change the way she expresses her feelings to people.)

11. Victor the Adventurer – Vicki Zenoff
    (An 18 year old pushed the limits.)

12. About Adventurers

Chapter Seven – Adventurers

Death is only a few bad moments at the end of life. It's not worth wasting any anxiety over. – Montaigne

What sets the principle characters of the stories in this chapter apart from the other chapters more than anything is their feeling of lightness and their enjoyment in entertaining us.

Writing styles

Adventurers often write to entertain in a breezy and easy-going style with humorous touches. Note: Adventurer Pat Helin also wrote *Mimi, Dying with Class* in Chapter 3 and *Two Hospice Stories* in Chapter 8.

1 For the Birds

By Kathy Heuser, Adventurer, Asserter wing

In this story, we accompany a little girl to her grandmother's house where her grandfather has recently died. Adventurers love to be fascinated and her experiences there are indeed fascinating.

1 My first experience with death

Cosby Green Fowler, my mother's father, died when I was in the fourth grade. My only recollection of him was during a trip to visit my grandparents when I was approximately five years old. I have an image of him sitting on the porch of his rundown clapboard house in Malden, Missouri, rocking in a chair and whittling on a stick. Oddly, I don't remember hearing him say a single word. He did give me his small pocketknife, however, before we left to head back to my home in California. I had it for many years, and I feel a tinge of sadness when I think that somewhere along the way I carelessly lost it.

Grandma Fowler was the opposite of Grandpa in temperament. She was loud, laughed and raged a lot, and delighted in chasing her grandkids around with a switch or a broom when we didn't behave as she expected. She taught  me how to quilt. She also taught me to stand by her side quietly as she knocked on doors from house to house preaching the gospel and encouraging the neighbors to attend the local Pentecostal church to save their souls.

Brother Johnny, the town's preacher, who had recently taken a new wife, had shiny black hair and vivid blue eyes; in all of my ten years, I swear I had never seen such a handsome man. I was in love with him, and my memories of attending the town's Four Square Pentecostal Church revolved more around wishing he were my boyfriend than receiving the Holy Spirit. I was optimistic in spite of the fact that not only was he married and fifteen or twenty years older than I, but I had not yet even approached puberty! He crosses my mind every few years and I wonder if he is now at Jesus' feet in heaven, as he used to describe to us during those endless Saturday night revivals. Grandma teased me for years afterward about that first little-girl crush.

Shortly after our arrival to be with the family for Grandpa's funeral, Grandma informed me that when Grandpa died, he had made quite the exit from both his home and his body. The story was nothing short of amazing to this small girl sitting at Grandma's feet. Grandma said she knew the very moment Grandpa's spirit left his body because as she was sitting in the parlor she saw a large ball of white light come out of the bedroom, through the parlor, and out the front door screen. She went into the bedroom, and found his lifeless shell.

My parents felt conflicted about whether or not I should attend Grandpa Fowler's funeral. I desperately wanted to go, especially curious to see if the ball of white light would show up to peek in on his own visitation at the mortuary. The truth is I do not remember if my parents allowed me to attend. I do remember sitting on the edge of Grandpa's bed after the funeral as I tried to will his spirit back. I so wanted to witness that mysterious orb.

Grandma and Grandpa had seven live children at the time (one died as an infant before the birth of my mother); three of them were boys. My uncles Haywood, C.G., and Jimmy had military experience and were rowdy drinkers and womanizers. Jimmy the youngest, was probably not more than twenty at the time Grandpa died. I recall being somewhat uncomfortable with the energy of these men—and aware I should never drop my guard around them. My mom noticed this and once told me to not be so standoffish around them.

Grandpa's was not the only death I experienced during that trip. Hearing popping sounds in Grandma's backyard on a day shortly after Grandpa's funeral, I wandered outside to find out what the noise was all about. All three of my uncles were taking turns firing a BB gun, systematically wiping out all the sparrows that sat on the overhead phone lines. They'd hit one, hoot and laugh while watching it fall to the ground, wait while the other sparrows frantically fluttered around, then fire again when the remaining birds settled back down on a place to land. My screaming and crying in horrified protest did nothing to stop the slaughter. In fact, Mom came out of the house and told me that if I were bothered by all that, to come inside and not watch. I remember nothing about the remainder of that trip; however, that event solidified both my opinion of my Fowler uncles and my lifelong love and empathy for birds. It also stands as the single-most painful death memory I hold, even more so than that of my father, one of the most beloved and important people in my life.

2. Grief as liberator

Recently, while straightening up at my office after seeing the last client of the day, I glanced up to study a print hanging on my wall. The image depicts a number of colorful silhouetted birds sitting on a wire. Many glances throughout each workday at this whimsical print usually yield an equal number of smiles, many of which I hold inside as a delicious secret that I keep for myself. To me, birds represent freedom, joy, and lightness. I simply cannot see a bird and not smile. I've kept companion birds off and on throughout my life, and I am certain that I am a better human because they have allowed me to provide care to them.

On this particular day, my gaze at the wall print did not produce any smile. I had just finished a session where a client and I were working on some severe symptoms related to multiple childhood traumas. During the session, her flashbacks were worse than usual. Being present to someone's suffering demands that the heart is open to touch the pain they experience. This was one of those sessions where my heart was aching; my client experienced her trauma and resulting grief at a similar subtle but deep level to my own.

We decided to work with a therapeutic technology called *Eye Movement Desensitization and Reprocessing* (EMDR), a powerful modality of healing that has been demonstrated to aid the mind in integrating traumatic material. As often happens with EMDR, this client's suffering was metabolized during the session. She was left with a sense of raised-eyebrow wonder at the quiet equanimity with which she experienced recalling the horror of her childhood memories.

As always, I felt grateful for this technology and the courage of my client to place such trust in the process. After saying goodbye, I also noticed that I was experiencing some residual effect—a sort of "vicarious traumatization"—from being witness to my client's horrific memories. Stealing my breath, grief took hold and seemed to saturate me, evidenced by the unexpected tears staining my face and shirt. This vulnerable opening, combined with the glimpse of my favorite print at exactly the perfectly precise moment, brought into sharp and painful focus my own trauma and grief around those birds and how they died.

A thought occurred to me then: *heal this.*

Locking my door and closing the blinds, I pulled the EMDR light board toward where I would sit on the sofa. Moving my eyes from side to side and following the lights on the board, I focused on the memory-image of those sparrows being killed and the sound of the BB gun. Tears turned into raging waters. My pulse pounded like a Native war drum. *I am there.* I stayed with it and after a time, the horror rolled into sadness, and sadness softened to stillness. At that point, I closed my eyes and asked what those birds wanted me to know. As I waited in still-minded quiet, they began to speak.

Where I found myself next was astounding, and whether the experience was metaphorical or literal makes no difference to me. In answer to my question, I heard that the sparrows were an embodiment of guides, specially sent to foster my developmental unfolding. Because of a powerful and joyous earlier childhood experience and memory I had involving birds, the messenger-guides felt that the timing and impact of this particular event would establish itself into my consciousness. They knew that I would eventually examine and ultimately understand its meaning for my betterment. Yes, the event certainly got the attention of every cell in my being.

The message seemed to smack me in my chest physically but gently and my suffering vaporized in an instant. My grandfather's death, that trip to Malden, my uncles' participation in an event that my system took in as a trauma and endured for years within; all part of a perfection of sorts that yielded a capacity inside that can be unafraid of suffering. Good grief, the message was right in front of me for all these years, and it took a raw, open heart and an inexpensively framed print on the wall to heal the wound.

Good. Grief.

2 Avon Calling

By Kathy Heuser, Adventurer, Asserter wing

Most Adventurers love parties. Kathy remembers a party long ago and relates what she heard had happened to one of her daring childhood friends.

Ricky S. and his twin sister Cathy were classmates of mine during the time I attended Betsy Ross Elementary School, from kindergarten until midway through fifth grade. I had an on-again, off-again crush on Ricky during my elementary school career. Girls chased Ricky around the playground during recess in search of a kiss. In fourth grade he tried to romance me during recess. I barely remember his appearance except for his dark hair and plaid shirts; however, he must have been impressive, given my abiding good taste in men. He was popular and always picked first for dodge ball teams. He was daring, funny, and best friends with Marty, the pornographic poet.

Cathy was also popular, but mostly with the girls. Her mother was a pillar of high fashion and held in awe by all the girls in fifth grade. She was, after all, the neighborhood Avon representative and Cathy drew attention at school whenever she appeared with new colors of fingernail polish or an unusual fragrance, usually applied too heavy-handedly. She was always polite but aloof toward the less popular girls such as me.

Somehow I had the good fortune to be invited to the Dougherty's home for Cathy's eleventh birthday party. In retrospect, I believe that Cathy's mother probably persuaded her to invite all the girls in the class. I'm thankful I did not have that insight at the time. The party took place in the small and tidily maintained living room of the family's Lakewood tract home, and was led by Cathy's beautifully made up, heavenly smelling, and socially astute mother.

As we played one party game after another, I was astonished to realize that I was winning most of them. Cathy was clearly not pleased and became more and more competitive, as the grand prize was the privilege of selecting a coveted Avon item from a large basket of temptingly arranged cosmetics. The final blow to her esteem was when I won the game of picking up the most cotton balls from an aluminum pie pan with a spatula while blindfolded. To Cathy's humiliation, her mother made her personally present the cosmetic basket to me, so I could make my selection. I had my eye on a tube of white lipstick, the latest rage at that time. I knew attempting to purchase it would be forbidden by my mother. Winning it was my only chance. Poor Cathy could not bear the thought of me winning a prize of such enormous significance, so she maliciously swung that damned basket back and forth, not stopping to allow me thorough inspection of the goods inside. In my excitement and anxiety, I chose something in a lipstick-shaped box. As it ended up, it was a stick of yellowish-toned blemish cover. My self-esteem deflated in direct proportion to Cathy's hateful glee. She gloated throughout the rest of the party, and I returned home to look for pimples that needed covering.

When I was eighteen, I ran into an old elementary school classmate whom I had not seen since that fifth grade year. She told me Ricky was dead. When he was sixteen years old, his Volkswagen bug had been struck by a train in a town not far from where we attended school. My friend had not heard whether it had been an accident or a suicide. We decided he must have been playing chicken with the train, consistent with our memory of him being so daring when younger.

This was my first experience of knowing someone my age who died. I felt sad and troubled. How to make sense of a death of someone so young and vibrant? I also thought about Cathy. How she must have ached for her womb-mate in that physical proximity kind-of-way that twins share. I do not know what became of her after Ricky's death.

As upset as I felt hearing the news that Ricky had died and all my thoughts about the impact of his death on Cathy, it was his mother for whom I felt the worst. Nearly forty years later, I still wonder how she survived such a tremendous loss. Perhaps she is gone now, too. If so, I enjoy the fantasy that she has had the opportunity to see Ricky again. The possibility of outliving my children touches the saddest place in me. I imagine that I am not alone with such a fear.

3 I Opened to the Essential Beauty and Awfulness of Loving Someone Deeply

By Catherine Williams, Adventurer, Questioner wing, Social subtype

In this story the feelings of a man and his daughter for each other go up and down until they reach a happy conclusion.

Death is the dark backing a mirror needs if we are to see anything. – Saul Bellow

The most significant death in my life so far is my dad (a social subtype Perfectionist) who died of cancer in June of 2005 at seventy-nine.

I adored him as a child. He recited poetry and sang to me daily, "Thank heavens for little girls." He drank too much. When tipsy, he went into a jovial, outgoing Adventurer mode. Otherwise he seemed contracted, worried, and very controlling. In my late teens this Adventurer found the controlling intolerable. As a result, we fought for the next twenty plus years.

Finally, after much therapy and 12-step work, I made amends to him. For years it hadn't occurred to me that I might have hurt him, too. We were both ready for healing and our hearts somehow opened again to each other, so for the next eight years or so we were able to feel and express our love for each other. Since I had hardly been able to take in love from anyone until that point, being able to feel how much he loved me was a profound experience. Feeling his love allowed me to feel more real, a little like the *Velveteen Rabbit*.

At the end, he quit eating and was ready to go. The family was together in the house he and Mom had designed on the Mississippi Gulf Coast (two months before Katrina wiped the house away). I experienced my father in his dying as boiled down to his essence, a pure expression of love. If there is such a thing as a good death that's what he had. We got to tell him how much we loved him and to say goodbye. Nobody seemed too fixated in those essential moments.

Just before he died, he spoke a lot, though it was unintelligible. That he would occasionally reach both of his arms out—to what or whom I will never know—moved me to my roots. I wondered if he was seeing his parents or friends who had gone before him. I had never heard him speak of a belief in an afterlife, though my mom spoke to him as he was dying with her belief that he would be going to paradise.

I went to bed and my brother woke me to say he'd passed. I'm glad I got to see his body from which his being had departed. My brothers and I became momentarily and comically obsessed with trying to close his mouth by tying a scarf around his head. We were unsuccessful and let go of it, laughing ruefully.

I experienced grief in a deeper and more physical way than I ever had before; my entire chest area ached for months, as though it were a large metallic disc. As I'd feel the love I'd feel grateful for the healing, which seemed to go hand in hand with the sadness at his loss. I opened up to the essential beauty and awfulness of loving someone deeply.

I've never been able to avoid emotional pain. I know my mother misses him terribly. I asked her (an Achiever) how she deals with the loss and if she cries. She said she keeps busy and does not cry. I can't pretend to know what her experience is, but I can see how her Achiever strategy helps her cope.

Talking about death may signify a realistic understanding of life, or it may indicate depression. When I was depressed for several years, I did think more about death. I contemplated suicide daily. Something in me knew that suicide wouldn't solve my problems, and I persevered, despite seeing no light at the end of a tunnel. My Adventurer strategies of keeping busy and having a good time didn't hold up well in the face of crushing depression. Eventually, after trying everything holistic, I succumbed to taking anti-depressants, and lo, the depression lifted.

4 My Happy Reactions to Death

By John Stabb, Adventurer

Adventurers are known for being upbeat and happy. But being happy about deaths is likely to shock someone.

> *Life in its becoming is always shedding death,*
> *and on the point of death. –* Joseph Campbell

As a kid, ages 11 to 15 or so, I remember reacting to death by feeling light-hearted, happy.

The first was the death of Bill, resident manager at Camp Wauwepex, which I had attended as a camper. I knew him fairly well, not closely, but I knew him. I was attending a work weekend with the Order of the Arrow, and word got out that Bill had died. I was happy! Happy for him. I can't say why. That was my reaction.

I had a similar reaction when my grandfather died. We were in New York; he was in Chicago, so I didn't have a close relationship with him. My mom got the word and shared it with me. When my dad got home, I was pleased to be the first to share the news. "Grandpa Lilleberg died," I told him, with a big smile on my face. As I recall, my dad almost smacked me for seeming to be happy when I told him. He made it clear that my emotions were inappropriate for the occasion.

Then there was Vietnam. I lost two close friends in that war; one, Ralph, a childhood companion, the other, Charlie, a fraternity brother from college. I heard that the Army GLO (gunfire liaison officer) who worked with us in Phu Quoc had been killed. I heard that some not so close friends from my ROTC unit had been killed, all some time after the fact. I don't recall having a strong response to any of that. Death is a part of life. No big deal.

Many years later, I had the chance to go with Ralph's parents to the Memorial Day ceremony at Arlington Cemetery. Dan Quayle was the speaker. Afterwards we went to visit Ralph's grave, a group grave, actually, of Ralph and his two crewmen because the human remains were so intertwined. No DNA labs back in the day. Visiting with Bill and Thelma, I felt a profound sadness for THEIR loss.

I think my religious faith plays a part in all of this. I don't see death as an ending but as a beginning. I have a strong traditional Christian faith and believe, as the creed says, in "the resurrection of the dead."

I did have a simulated death experience once when I was in the Navy. It took place as part of battle training at Guantanamo. I was Chief Engineer, in charge of the propulsion plant from "main control" in the forward engine room. As part of the training, main control was wiped out due to an explosion or something. Everyone else was supposed to recognize that and the after engine room was supposed to take over duties as "main control." So, all of a sudden, the trainers said we were dead. We were not to answer the phone or respond to the "squawk box," just play possum for a while. I LOVED it! The Captain called down, "Main Control—Bridge. What's going on down there?" We ignored him. It felt SO good to ignore the Captain, if only for a short time. I enjoyed being "dead."

And then, after the Navy, I went to seminary and became a Lutheran Pastor. Lots of death, dying, funerals. The first dead body I ever saw was when I was doing my hospital training in San Diego. I was the on duty chaplain and the ER doc requested my presence. A patient had died, and she wanted me to be with her when she informed the family. They wanted to see the body, but he was all tubed up and wrapped up with the implements of the heroic ER life-saving efforts that had failed. Not a pretty sight. So I sat and prayed with the family, periodically checking to see if the body was ready to be seen. It took a while. How did I feel? Saddened but professional. I was doing my job.

And then when I was a parish pastor, I comforted many families during times of death and dying. I did lots of funerals. It was important to me to just BE with them, not address any theological issues, like "What kind of God would permit this to happen to MY wife?" Sudden deaths. Suicides. What does one say? I learned in seminary that Presence is more important than Answers. People ask profound unanswerable questions, but what they most need is their Pastor's non-anxious presence, to help them through their grief. I was good at that.

So as an Adventurer I don't think that I have turned away and ignored the implications of dying and death. I can't ever recall being grief-stricken at hearing news of the death of a friend or loved one. As a Pastor I resisted the urge to spout platitudes like, "Well she's in a better place." I've been able to just be with folks and listen to them.

5 Uncle Wayne

By Jaki Girdner, Observer

Adventurers want to experience life to the fullest, like Uncle Wayne.

If our lives are a tapestry then lets fill them with Positive Colorful experiences.
– Dave Bennett

Uncle Wayne was such a jovial Adventurer, his doctor missed how much pain he was in. As a result, his cancer wasn't diagnosed in time. He had big doors added to his bedroom in order to have his hospital bed rolled outside every night so he could look at the stars.

Drawing by Harry Gans

6 Evidence: Clarity

By Dah, Adventurer

Of all the types, Adventurers appear to like themselves the most.

Evidence: clarity's crimson
-colored light. Death says:

Do not turn away from
the black roses that fill my hands.

Solitude: A quiet so painfully
aching with joy—even

unspoken words become
disruptive, chattering about,
 running underneath my tongue.

My cherished wealth:
Each blade of grass, each flower,
each tree branch, the birdbath

--all of this from my garden,
I am overly in love with.

Death says: *I have given you*
a syllabus of hours, each
one is your life decaying.

In the end,
earth will open her body,
and make love to my remains.

7 She Laughed in the Concentration Camp

By Elizabeth Wagele, Observer, Romantic wing

Adventurers try to make the best of the worst circumstances. It's hard to imagine staying good-natured in a concentration camp, but that's how positive Alice was.

> *Life is not about waiting for the storms to pass,*
> *it's about learning to dance in the rain.*

The movie, *Alice Dancing Under the Gallows*, documents the life of Alice Herz-Sommers, 107, the oldest survivor of the Nazi Holocaust. A well-known concert pianist living in Prague, she was deported to a Nazi concentration camp in 1942 at age thirty-nine. *Theresienstadt* or *Terezin* was a propaganda camp and transfer station to other camps. It was the only camp where children were allowed to stay with their parents. Every day she saw fellow prisoners get sent from there to *Auschwitz* and other death camps. It was seemingly only a matter of time before she and her son would be sent there, too. But the war ended and they survived. Through it all, she retained her good nature. Still happy and optimistic, she now lives in London and continues to play the piano.

One of Terezin's purposes was to show the world how well the prisoners were allegedly being treated. Starving prisoners were encouraged to paint, perform, and play music. This was a moral support to the other prisoners, however, not entertainment. Alice gave more than one hundred concerts, performing all of Chopin's etudes by memory and pieces by Schumann, Beethoven, and Bach.

To Alice, music is a sort of religion. "Music is God. You feel it especially in difficult times," she said. "Sometimes I'm thankful to have been there because I'm richer than other people." Her optimism gave her and her son strength. He sang in the children's opera there. Her friend, also a survivor, said her own father told her, "Put as much as you can into your head so no one can take it away from you."

"That's what music is," she said. "You can put music into your head and go into another world that is better."

8 Party Girl Too Young to Die

By Pat Helin, Adventurer

Everyone wanted to be around this young woman because she made them feel good.

Enthusiasm is contagious. Be a carrier. – Susan Rabin

One of our patients where I'm a hospice nurse was a highly energetic young Adventurer woman who was raised by a single mom. Suffering from a rare lung disorder, she wanted to live so badly. She had been a party girl at Chico State University in California and had just finished nursing school at thirty-four years old. She liked to go to movies and was proactive during her illness, continually looking for new clinical trials on the computer. "I know why I'm dying," she told me. "Because I used up my life too fast."

After college she worked at the grocery store for many years, went to Hawaii, then nursing school. I connected with a lot of her friends at her memorial. Mothers with their kids said they always waited to shop until she was working on her shift.

She had a beautiful boyfriend in Hawaii who rigged up an inner tube with an oxygen tube on it so they could go in the water. They didn't marry until she was on her deathbed because she had a lot of debt, but the marriage wasn't official. He placed leis all over her bed and a Hawaiian quilt over her.

9 Dying Having a Good Time

By Valentine Illidge, Helper

Mr. Sharp seemed to be a charming person, in keeping with many of this type.

Being a soul in wonder allows you to live as yourself... how better can we learn to understand the depth of our world & our place in it. – David Bennett

My father had known a friendly and popular man by the name of Mr. Sharp for years. Daddy was a bicycle racer and Mr. Sharp was a retired professional cricket player with a general sense of wellbeing and a roaring laugh you couldn't ignore. I never heard them yell or argue and he was always friendly to us kids. One day when Daddy was fifty-three and I was almost twelve, Mr. Sharp parked his tiny new fire-engine-red station wagon in front of our house. I later overheard Daddy saying to Mammy that Mr. Sharp had bought that station wagon to take with him to St. Martin Island where he was about to begin a brand new life. We all headed there together as my family was on our way to moving to the United States of America from Aruba. The shiny red station wagon was being hoisted into the belly of the ship as we walked the plank to get on. On board, Daddy and Mr. Sharp spent hours together laughing, telling stories, and playing table games.

We approached the island of St.

Vincent, where we were going to dock for a few hours. As we waited for a small boat to come to take us to shore, Mr. Sharp yelled out with his hands overhead, "This island is so beautiful, I could live here!" The island was endowed with the green beauty of vegetation. He was one of the first to leave for its port. Our family took a small tour of the island, met with friendly people, saw an old church with a cemetery in its yard, went through a hospital, and rushed back to the ship to be on time for departure. Mr. Sharp wasn't accounted for, so we waited and waited. When he still didn't return to the boat everyone became distressed. Then a small boat rowed out and a man said someone had died of a heart attack while playing cricket at the sports park that afternoon. Everyone's face froze at the shocking news! He was a dear friend of my father's and my father cried. We lived on to remember him as a happy and lively man. The next stop of the ship was St. Martin's. Mr. Sharp had been so close yet so far. It was as if it were his destiny to die doing something he loved doing.

10 A Reason for Urgency

By Harriet Berman Glaser, Adventurer

Harriet was also deeply affected by the death of Shelley's father, from the story in Chapter 6, Not the Summer of Love. *He was her older brother.*

My most compelling fear is the death of my loved ones, not my own.

When my brother died at thirty-five, (I was twenty-eight) I was shocked, sad, mad, hurt, and devastated for his children, my parents, my sister, my other brother, and myself. I'm embarrassed to say I felt bad that people would feel sorry for me, that I wasn't as perfect as they (I) thought, that there was another flaw in my family—a major one. Happy wasn't so happy (my nickname is Happy).

This death changed me. I knew I had to express my feelings for people now, not wait until it was too late. My mom died of Alzheimer's at seventy-four, more acceptable to me, more natural, but scary because she really lost it and I was afraid I would lose it too. Then my dad died at eighty-seven, happily of natural causes. What a difference a long, good life, makes for those left behind. Next my sister died tragically in a car crash with lethal doses of lithium in her system. Another senseless death in our family.

So how do I feel about death? It's not about mine, although I'd like to get my act together and leave my messes in order so my kids don't have to go through piles of nothingness. It's about living my life fully and creating memories for my children and grandchildren, so that they can pass on the legacy of a strong sense and knowledge of Jewishness and the joy of holidays and a love of music and art and poetry and family closeness throughout the generations of our family.

11 Victor the Adventurer

By Vicki Zenoff, Helper

In this story, a Pied Piper on acid goes climbing around in Yosemite with disastrous results.

My nephew Victor collected snakes and loved the Grateful Dead. I was his favorite aunt because I didn't care that he was a free spirit and didn't have boundaries. He was almost unstoppable, but he died when he was eighteen.

He was the one in the family that sold dope and was always in trouble. His parents were very straight and he was always pushing the limits with discipline. Not feeling understood must have felt painful. He was a bad student and couldn't concentrate. He couldn't make it in a regular school so his parents put him in an experiential school. He was good with his hands, physical, artistic, popular, and extraverted. He made so many friends, I think of him as the Pied Piper.

After attending an all night party at Yosemite and doing acid, he ran down a steep hill with many switchbacks. On the way down he went over the edge to his death. I don't think he had a death wish. I think he was immortal in his own mind.

Let a man in a garret burn with enough intensity, and he will set fire to the world. – Antoine de Saint-Exupery

12 About Adventurers

Adventurers are fun loving and optimistic people, enjoy what life has to offer, and don't like feeling obligated. They crave excitement; Victor went too close to the edge and fell off. Dah expects the earth to envelop him lovingly when it's time for him to go. Alice Herz-Sommers was able to laugh in a concentration camp with death all around her.

The agenda of Adventurers is to remain youthful and make sure they'll always have something to do by planning options. Developing the ability to tell stories helps them feel comfortable in different social circles. Many feel responsible for keeping others' spirits up—Happy Glaser felt she'd let people down if she weren't happy. John Stabb got in trouble for being too happy when his grandfather died.

Adventurers become more systematic when they follow their Perfectionist arrow and are more able to concentrate on one thing at a time when they follow their Observer arrow.

When they talk too much, it's usually out of anxiety; as one Adventurer said, "I don't have the courage to shut up;" their Questioner wing may be influencing them. Their Asserter wing influences them to be more competitive and strong-willed.

Grief

When Adventurers feel bad, according to Enneagram teacher Tom Condon, they create a fantasy of the future and make elaborate plans to keep pain at bay. To let grief in, Condon says they need to nibble away at the emotions. After Catherine Williams' father died, she appreciated the healing that came with the "beauty and awfulness of loving someone deeply." Kathy Heuser stayed with her sad feelings long enough to heal an old wound and diminish her fear of suffering.

Adventurers feel more fully connected when they share the whole range of feelings with other people—not just happy ones. Until that happens, they may subtly feel that something is missing.

Openness doesn't come from resisting our fears but from getting to know them well. – Pema Chödrön

Shadow

The shadow for Adventurers is the part of life that is boring, stagnant, or dark. They avoid "nothing happening" in favor of lightness, excitement, and always meeting new friends.

Shadow elements show up in the arrows. Among other things, the Observer arrow represents quiet and the isolated part of the Adventurer that is often deeply buried. The Perfectionist arrow represents being serious and following the rules.

Nine types of people

Learning the nine types' points of view helps individuals find balance, acceptance, and wholeness. The Enneagram is valuable both in facing an

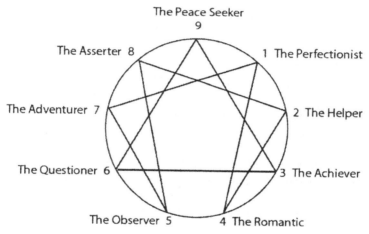

immediate crisis and in long-range growth.

Contents

1. "If you don't give me the time I'm requesting, I'll push you out forever." – Helen Clarkson
(Woman in 40s may be dying of cancer, is annoyed by people giving advice.)

2. Two Guns – Mario Sikora
(Someone points a gun at him. He also has a medical crisis.)

3. Lester – Jan Conlon
(Grief counselor helps man with ALS.)

4. Two Hospice Stories – Pat Helin
(The first Asserter is angry, the second is afraid.)

5. Martin – Judy Meyer
(Hepatitis C leads to liver cancer.)

6. Death by Assassination – Elizabeth Wagele
(Dr. Martin Luther King.)

7. Bolu Bauri is Dead – Tom Rosin
(Laborer from Rajasthan tries to make it to the doctor.)

8. Killer: Jim Schnobrich – Elizabeth Wagele
(Grizzly war story.)

9. Death of a Drug Dealer – Jaki Girdner
(Mourners take on the grieved one's personality.)

10. About Asserters

Chapter Eight - Asserters

I just feel that my competitive drive is far greater than anyone else that I've met, and I think that I thrive on that. – Michael Jordan

What sets the principle characters of the stories in this chapter apart from the other chapters more than anything is their powerful personalities and how readily they express anger.

Writing styles

Asserters tend to write in a direct or bold style. Asserters submitted fewer stories to this chapter than were submitted by people of other types to their type chapters. Note: Mario Sikora also wrote *My Father's Death* in Chapter 6.

1 "If you don't give me the time I'm requesting, I'll push you out forever."

By Helen Clarkson, Asserter, Adventurer wing, One-to-one subtype

In this story, a decisive and bold British cancer patient keeps her boundaries. She is one of several in this book with a fatal illness who feel blessed by the gifts gained from the knowledge they're going to die.

When I was first diagnosed with bowel cancer at forty-one years old, I came home, rang my dear friend, and we cried. She then asked if I was going to ring my (then) boyfriend at work. I said "No, I want to get my own head round it before I speak to him. I'll tell him when he gets home." I also rang my brother and cousin (my only remaining family left—I have lost most of my other family to cancer). Once my boyfriend knew, I rang my large group of close friends and delegated some of those to tell my other close friends. I gave them all the facts and then said I needed some time to myself to research and make my decision about what to do. "I know you're worried about me, however I have to do this and if you don't give me the time I am requesting I will push you out forever."

I became very business-like. I locked myself away and put my phones on silent and wouldn't answer my door buzzer. My boyfriend and I researched for hours on end. I asked my surgeon and oncologist direct and candid questions and told them I expected the same back, with

statistics to support what they were saying. I then reached what I believed (and still do) was a well-informed decision. Based on all sorts of research, speaking to my friends who are consultants, doctors, and nurses and pulling on watching eight family members go through conventional treatment, I decided to decline what the professionals had suggested, which was intense radiotherapy and chemotherapy.

I shocked and outraged my surgeon, oncologist and friends and was furious when they questioned my decision. They (friends) barely knew what I had experienced with cancer.

However, I did question my decision, changed my mind, and on my forty-second birthday I signed papers to have the conventional treatment. I then became extremely ill and I couldn't eat for three days. As I got out the shower on day four, I saw how thin and ill I looked and decided that chemotherapy would kill me. Deep down in my stomach I knew it wasn't right for me and I went back to my initial decision. I informed the professionals and my friends. Until they had experienced what I had and lost seven family members, my decision was NOT up for discussion.

One friend offered a contact that had been through a "similar" experience to mine and asked if I wanted to email her. No I didn't. I'd heard all the stories I wanted to hear; it was now up to me. This friend then proceeded to email me the person's story. I was so incensed!! It wasn't even akin to my family history. I wanted to ring her and scream down the phone at her, "What right do you have when I had already said no?!" However, I realised it was all about her angst and I had to think about what her positive intention was, which was to keep me alive. I ranted at my boyfriend that other people's worry and fear doesn't help me. I don't want to see or speak to anyone. If anyone is worried about me they need to be told I am not choosing to die. I am choosing how I live the rest of my life and that is MY decision no one else's.

Luckily for me my surgeon removed my tumor without any of their treatment, which meant two major operations and they wanted to leave six months in between time. I asked how quickly the second one could be done. They said, "Six weeks, though that is never going to happen." Wrong thing to say to me, especially when it meant it would get rid of the ileostomy bag. So I used all the energy I had and I pushed and pushed until I got what I wanted—what I *knew* was right for me. Much to the shock of the nurses and staff on the ward! Both times I came home sooner than my wonderful surgeon wanted me to. I remember him saying, "You're putting me in an awkward situation asking to leave." I replied "I'm putting myself in a worse situation if I stay! I need two things to get well, wholesome food and sleep, and I'm getting neither here. I have to go home to get well!"

While I was in hospital, the only people I wanted to visit were my boyfriend and my two close friends, who were only allowed in because they were cooking for me. I stated, "I don't need to be speaking to visitors and making them feel better by saying I'm okay. I don't want to be drained by a conversation I can't be bothered to have. I want to be sleeping and healing and left alone."

One day my partner persuaded me to let another friend visit. However, the night before had been terribly painful for me and there had been complications, so I just needed to sleep. I sent her a text saying I was too ill to see her. She then refused to answer my subsequent texts (asking her for help) and emails. Her boyfriend said she'd been put out because I wouldn't see her. I sent her an email telling her I didn't need friends like her and this was about me not her! I said, "Why should I put myself out to see you when I'm ill, just to make you feel better?!" She was wiped out.

Even for months after I came out of hospital I refused to let anyone visit. I wanted and needed my time and space to get my head around what was happening and what was going to happen.

Every time I saw my nephews and niece, after they left I would sit and sob and ask myself, "By not having chemo am I denying them their only Auntie?" I was grateful for that because it made me question my decision over and over. Though I always came back to the same decision my gut had initially told me!

I fell (understandably) into depression. I did recognise it, though didn't want to accept it.

I've always accepted that death is a natural part of life, and as much as I don't want to die, I accept that it's a big possibility for me now, especially as the cancer has come back. This would have happened regardless of conventional treatment or not.

Even now, I have a feeling that everything is going to be all right, though I'm aware that I could die soon.

I stay positive and optimistic most of the time, though obviously I have my moments where I sob and feel terribly sad for myself.

I love myself for the fact that I got drunk not so long ago (I rarely drink) and I was still a funny drunk and I still found everything absolutely hilarious.

On the rare occasions that a thought crosses my mind like, "I'll never see my nephews and niece grow up" or "I'll never have a moment like this again" I laugh. I think, how will I know when I'm dead anyway? So what's the point of wasting valuable time worrying about something I won't, in my opinion, be aware of anyway?!

My biggest fear is the thought of becoming dependent on other people. It's just so not what I want for me or any of my family and friends.

I often think, "If when you die, it's at a point in your life where you are surrounded by beautiful, loving, special and amazing people, then it really is your time to go." I've had lots of fun, learnt lots, and shared really fab times with special and amazing people. How lucky am I! Some people don't get that at all, even though they may get longer on this earth than me. My biggest challenge is accepting I have no control over any of this. I'm constantly "working on myself" to heal and correct my emotional, spiritual and physical self, and I totally believe I am in control of it. However, even though I've apparently only got about a year left to live, I look and feel well, so I'm positive and optimistic. I truly hope I'm like this if I get really ill.

As mad as it sounds, I feel totally blessed to know that I may be going to die. It has given me a chance to do and say even more things that I may not have done. That said, I didn't rush to make amends with the people I had fallen out with as I still believe I pushed them out of my life for a reason. However, I was persuaded (by others) to give them the chance if they wanted to make amends. I contacted mutual friends and asked them to inform the other party and said, "It's up to them if they want to make contact, I'm really not bothered either way," and I meant that. All three of them did want contact (of course they did; I'm a great friend) and although I have been in touch with them, I have kept them at a distance.

I wrote a wish list, which started with lots more travelling to far out exotic places. Then crossed all of that out and wrote I still want to holiday though I'm not bothered about doing all that travelling; what's more important is spending time with the people that are important to me, telling them how much I love them, reminiscing on all of our good and fun times, and concentrating on having more.

I love holidays and I love holidaying alone. However, since I got my terminal verdict, when I holiday alone, I get homesick. I have never ever been homesick and to quote one of my friends "I'm usually sick to come home!" So getting used to that feeling was and still is very strange for me.

For the first time in my life I have felt down about my body. I have a roll of fat on my stomach (from the operations) that I have never had and it really knocks my self-esteem. Interestingly I have terrible scarring on my stomach yet I can accept that that is part of the operations, though not the roll of fat!

I remember being in a changing room trying to get clothes to fit and flatter me and breaking down sobbing on the floor. I looked at myself in the mirror and said to myself, you cannot leave until you have taken at least three positives from this experience. I went home without any clothes. However, I kept my sanity and pulled myself together! I've constantly got to be taking the positives out of every unpleasant experience if not (in my world) what's the point in being here anyway?! I have to be enjoying, resting, sleeping, healing, meditating or having fun.

My friends always ask when my next set of results are and I'm reluctant to say, simply because (there is a part of me that feels bad saying this) what happens is on the morning of getting them I get lots of texts wishing me luck. Now I know that would please most people, however for me (and this is why I feel bad) they just irritate me. I know all my friends are thinking of me, I don't need loads of texts from them telling me so, especially on that particular day (though I do like and want it normally!). What I need on that actual day is a clear head and my phone to be silent.

I notice I detach myself from myself in order to cope with my stress and to make well-informed decisions. While organising Mum's funeral with her I remember watching myself all the way through it, and thinking I feel like I'm watching a film. Yet when I organized my own funeral I associated with it all and myself, probably because I want everything right and how I want it!

I've never been big on compromising my needs, however now I refuse to waste any of my valuable time. I won't even spend five minutes more than I want to do something or being with someone I don't want to communicate with any more.

Sex is at the forefront of my mind often. However, whenever a family member has been dying and now I (maybe) am, it's constant. I obviously use it as a distraction, though because my senses are more heightened; any sexual experience becomes at least doubly sensitive, which makes me want sex even more! Years ago I'd allow sex to be my total focus when I was physically away from the upset and trauma going on, however now I'm more evolved I have it under control. Though my friends may argue with that!! Ok, I have it *more* under control.

2 Two Guns

By Mario Sikora, Asserter, Peace Seeker wing

Among other things he can't control, Mario struggles with the possibility his sons will not be old enough to remember him if he dies now.

It sticks in your mind, I can tell you, the first time someone points a gun at you in anger.

More than twenty years ago but it feels like last night; the feel of the carpet under my bare feet, and smell of the bourbon on his breath. John, my housemate's brother who was sleeping on the sofa until he got back on his feet, had been on the short-end of a bar fight and came back for his brother's gun with the intention of settling the score. Roused from bed by his girlfriend's screams, I went downstairs to see what was going on. When I got between him and the door he pointed the Browning Hi-Power 9 mm, a gun I well knew to be loaded, directly at my nose.

As I said, it sticks in your mind.

I wish I could say I had a more profound thought at that moment. Oddly enough, I'm writing this at an outdoor cafe off Boulevard des Philosophes in Geneva, home of Rousseau and Calvin, a long way from that Southwest Philly row home. Perhaps an insight on civility and society in honor of Rousseau, or more apropos, something on the perseverance of the saints or the ramifications of God's hand in human affairs in honor of Calvin. ("Hath not the potter power over the clay..." as St. Paul wrote to the Romans.)

But all I could think at the time was: I refuse to die at the hands of this idiot.

I was younger then, of course. Fast and good with my hands. John was drunk so his reactions would be a little slow, maybe giving me a slight edge. But he was a bad drunk and I didn't know how much time I had and I wasn't waiting around to see which way things would go. I had coiled my legs just a little to get some spring and I was trying to shift my angle ever so slightly to see whether John had released the safety when he lowered the gun and eventually calmed down.

Anti-climactic, perhaps, but not when it's you. I went to bed a little dizzy and wondering if I would have felt the impact of the bullet or if the lights just would have gone out.

The second gun pointed at me was metaphorical.

"It could be no big deal, or it could be something like non-Hodgkin's lymphoma," my cardiologist said. "But let's not get ahead of ourselves. On Monday I'll call a pulmonologist I know— he's very good—and we'll get you in to see him as soon as we can."

It was late on a Friday afternoon. Five minutes after I hung up I called him back.

"Doc, I'm not a sit-and-wait kind of guy. I won't make it through the weekend just waiting. I need to do something today. Right now. This hour."

I had gotten to know him over the preceding weeks, as one test after another had shown nothing to be wrong with my heart. But my symptoms were "troubling" to him and he kept looking. A CAT scan the previous day had proved *irregular*. Probably an Asserter himself, my cardiologist said, "Okay, go to the hospital, I'll admit you. We'll get some tests done over the weekend."

I hadn't gotten used to the fact that there was someone in the world who I was calling "my cardiologist;" by Saturday afternoon I had an oncologist and a pulmonologist as well.

Five days in the hospital and seven more waiting for the results of the biopsy of the nodes scraped from my chest through an incision at the base of my neck. This provided a lot of time to think. Twelve days is a long time when you're waiting for that kind of news.

My thoughts didn't turn to the afterlife; I'd long ago stopped speculating on such things. The threat of hell and enticement of heaven had lost their efficacy when I was twenty. There is a certain appeal to Eastern notions of the dance of Shiva or recycling through continuing stages or of somehow becoming one with some universal consciousness, but we're adults, right? So let's be serious.

I can't count the times I've read Camus' "Myth of Sisyphus." Camus takes 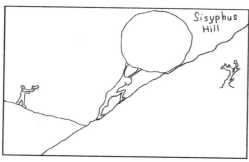 what others see as the bleakest of fates—Sisyphus condemned to endlessly push a rock up a hill only to let it roll back down and do it again—and turns it into something noble. Like each of us must do, Camus' Sisyphus has come to terms with his fate, and thus "one must imagine Sisyphus happy."

My view of the life after death had settled into what I like to think of as a mildly Shinto-istic existentialism: that we leave a mark on those things and people we interact with; they carry our memory, they are reshaped by our having come into contact. While our lights may go out when that last electrical spark emits from the brain, others carry us with them and the way we shaped them lingers on, and thus do we. Like Shinto's "kami," or spirits, the memory of us lurks in those we have touched, longing to be seen.

I met a man once who was wearing the shoes of his son who had died five years prior. I always thought of those shoes as the most sacred of shrines, an intimacy beyond the comprehension of most of us. Speculations on the afterlife feel hollow in the face of such acts.

On the occasion or two that thoughts about what happens next did cross my mind over the course of those twelve days, they passed quickly. *Pascal's Wager* had always seemed a coward's ploy to me and I wasn't going to blink now.

So here were the choices--it could be no big deal, or I could be in for a long sickness and unpleasant treatment or I could be dying. The pain in my chest and shortness of breath that sent me to the doctor in the first place were real. They weren't stress—sure I have stress, I'm self-employed, our fourth son had been born a few months earlier, but I'm not that way. So maybe it was no big deal, but it was something.

For the most part, I put it out of my mind. It seems like they shouldn't, but the events of the day go on--and it is surprisingly easy to fill up the time and be distracted.

But I'll let you in on something; I'll tell you what woke me up at night, what filled me with terror and heartache and despair, what made me get in the car by myself and drive fast and scream until nothing more would come out and I thought my throat would bleed: the knowledge that my sons would forget me.

I often travel on business. Once, toward the end of a three-week trip, Alexei, son number three, said, "Mommy, I'm starting to forget what Daddy looks like a little." Alexei is five now but he was only three during those twelve days. After three weeks the memory gets a little fuzzy; what happens in three years, or ten?

Sure, I could make one of those "dying-dad" videos, but I always imagine they end up in a closet somewhere, unwatched, or watched as something obligatory and oddly historical. My wife would tell them fond stories for a while, but life would go on and the stories would become less and less frequent and eventually stop. What terrified me was that I had not had enough time with them to leave my mark on these four little boys who I cherished, that I wouldn't be there to guide them and shape them, to pick them up and dust them off when they fell, to hold them when they needed it or push them when they didn't think they could go on.

One afternoon Warren Zevon's *Keep Me in Your Heart* shuffled onto my iPod in the car. At the line, "If I leave you it doesn't mean I love you any less," the dam broke. They wouldn't understand and I feared they would hate me for not being there.

I feared my kami would wander alone, unbeckoned and unnoticed.

When the diagnosis arrived, it too was anti-climactic: enlarged lymph nodes, non-cancerous, consistent with sarcoidosis. I had a condition with no known cause and no known cure. "It can be fatal in African-Americans," my pulmonologist said, "but typically it just shows up in some people and in a year or two it goes away. You'll be fine. Stay away from saw dust and talcum powder."

I have a scar at the base of my throat (which I jokingly tell people was from a knife fight if they ask). I saw the hospital bill that my insurance company paid. A quarter of a million dollars.

"Stay away from talcum powder."

Six months later, the symptoms were gone.

I wish I could say something was different, that having stared into the abyss and survived I had some profound insight or made a significant change in the way I live my life. But life goes on pretty much as it did before.

My one aim, my one straight and true goal, is to last long enough to matter to my sons. I don't feel an urgency to mold them like clay (St Paul's potter I am not), but I'm acutely aware that every inadvertent moment leaves a mark, and gives the kami breath.

So every once in a while in the midst of the chaos when everyone is yelling and we're in a hurry to get them out the door to school and son number one can't find his shoes and son number four is flailing on the floor because he wants the car that son number three is playing with and son number two realizes he forgot to do his homework and says you know I don't like jelly on my sandwiches, I take a moment to remember Sisyphus. I feel my muscles brought alive by the weight of the rock and my heels digging in to the dirt so as not to lose traction. I take a slow breath and I press my cheek against the cool, rough surface, losing awareness of where the rock stops and I start. In such moments all sounds are muffled, and everything happens—briefly—in slow motion. I look down the hill and see a long way to the bottom; I look ahead and see a long way to the top.

Feeling momentarily in on the joke, I raise my face to the gods and I smile.

3 Lester

By Jan Conlon, Perfectionist, Peace Seeker wing

Asserters are known as being powerful and able to show their anger with no difficulty. Lester shows no restraint and remains difficult and fierce to the end.

> *I have always had a dread of becoming a passenger in life.*
> – Margarethe II, Queen of Denmark.

Lester was sixty-four years old when he was diagnosed with amyotrophic lateral sclerosis (ALS), Lou Gehrig's disease. For months he had been having difficulty with hand coordination and weakness. Even simple tasks, such as holding a spoon and feeding himself, were challenging as he lost control of the use of his muscles.

When I met him, he had just learned of his diagnosis. Lester told me he would like me to visit him at least once a week during the progression of his disease. He didn't know how long he would be willing to live with the inevitable successive losses. He wanted someone there consistently to support him in his choices. When I made the decision to tell him I would continue to see him until the end of his life, I felt as though I had walked into a room that held only me and him and I could hear the door closing quietly behind us.

As an Asserter, Lester had difficulty giving up his power and sense of control. Each week, when I came to see him, he shared his latest physical losses. He'd point to his right foot and explain that he couldn't move it anymore. Or he'd lift up his gown and show me his new diaper. But right after his sharing he would look at me with his fierce eyes and remind me of the important positions he had held in his younger days. He demanded confirmation that I understood and saw him as a powerful man. During the ensuing months, I witnessed explosive diatribes that seemed to come out of nowhere, leveled towards the hospital staff, his wife, and friends. We found it impossible to prepare for his moods.

Eventually, his friends and most of his family stopped coming to see him.

Some of the most poignant and heartbreaking moments came when I would walk into his room and see that his body had collapsed into itself. His head would be tucked into his chest, and his arms wrapped around himself. With eyes full of pain, he would look up at me in deep fear. I experienced his need to not be seen as a weakling. He seemed to feel he had become someone to  be tossed aside, who didn't matter. On those days, he would talk about wanting to die. He believed that he wasn't of any use anymore.

But the next time I arrived he might be all fired up again, exuding his power. As he lost his ability to speak and started using alternative methods of communication, he would use me to present his demands to the hospital staff. These were often out of line, overly controlling, and sometimes incomprehensible. I could see the almost feverish light in his eyes as he fed off of his ability to control us. What he ended up getting didn't seem to matter; it was his ability to still be in control that lit the fire within.

Two years went by. Lester was moved into three care facilities; in each case the staff claimed he was too difficult and wouldn't work with him anymore. I could understand their position; after even one afternoon with him I would sometimes leave feeling exhausted from our interactions.

As the end drew near, there was nothing much left that Lester could do voluntarily. Tubes fed him and breathed for him. He had no more movement available to most of his body. Even blinking his eyes to communicate became too tiring for him. There were days when I came and simply stroked his hands, his feet, or his face and we just looked at each other. I still felt an indomitable strength in him, and, when many others with ALS would have given up, he fiercely let us know that he was not ready to die. He delighted in not giving in to what *they* wanted him to do, which was to let go and die.

One morning Lester's wife called and told me that he was finally ready to end his life. I immediately went to his hospital bed. The doctor was called and Lester was given morphine and taken off of life support. I still remember the fierce light in his eyes as he looked at us while he died. I sang a song that came to me, about a man who claimed his ultimate power by letting go. His eyes never left mine as the light finally faded from them.

4 Two Hospice Stories

By Pat Helin, Adventurer

In this story, an Adventurer hospice worker figures out different ways to work with two Asserter clients.

1. Gaining Trust

When I was a hospice chaplain at Kaiser Hospital, one gentleman was alert, bed ridden, and angry. He spewed vulgarities and would only allow a nurse in his house, no other member of our team. So I was frustrated as the spiritual care worker. This blazing Asserter had been the boss his whole life. One day the nurse said, "We've got to get you in there somehow because his wife is going nuts. Don't go in his room, just talk to his wife." Knowing he didn't want to see anyone, I just wanted to take a peek at him and say hello. Looking in from his doorway, wondering what would happen, I saw a bold man sitting up in bed with pillows behind him. I am an Adventurer so I could be light in my response.

I scanned his wall and saw a graduation diploma from Chicago Loyola and said, "John, you're a Jesuit guy." He said, "Of course." And I said, "I'm a Jesuit girl." And he started melting. Then for five or six months he increasingly unwound and the tapestries of his life unfolded, including a huge conflict with his  brother, the need to defend himself from his father, three wives, and the need to trust me. When he allowed me to sit on the end of his bed the nurses couldn't believe it. I tried to not be weak in his presence.

2. Baby Guide

Another Asserter, Tom, had lung cancer. He was bold enough to smoke with his oxygen tank in his small condo. On my first visit, I told him I'd wait outside until he finished his cigarette. The nurse said he needed a priest because he seemed afraid of dying. The priest was a Peace Seeker. Tom had wanted to be a priest, too, but he liked girls too much to give them up. He ended up being a volunteer fireman and driving a fire truck.

He and his wife lost their first baby due to a hole in her heart. They took baby Anna home to enjoy her as long as they could and she died within two weeks. Breaking apart inside, he went to the pastor's parish two days after she died to get his grief off his head. But the priest said, "Come back in two days. I'm on my way out." Tom needed to talk about her and cry right then. He banged the steering wheel. Then he saw the priest get in his car with a pair of skis on top to go skiing and that was the day he left the church forever. When I proposed he see a kind priest that I knew, Tom looked at me full of rage. He said, "Hell no, I'd never tell a priest what I just told you."

I visited him once a week after that. His language was wonderfully earthy and real. He was alone a lot of the time. His second wife, who was younger than he, had to work because they were very poor. I had him restructure an image of god using his daughter Anna as his guide. Racing to the hospital to try to save her life when he saw her turning blue, he had driven to Seattle instead of a closer hospital. So he felt guilty. Giving her a turn to guide him gave him a lot of peace. He'd say, "I was talking to Anna today."

Bend with the movement and the flow life is taking.
Transform into someone greater. – David Bennett

5 Martin

By Judy Meyer, Romantic

Martin's Hepatitis C turns into liver cancer. His attitude transforms from denial to acceptance.

There was never any fear for me, no fear of failure.
If I miss a shot, so what? – Michael Jordan

My partner, Martin Linhart, was the Asserter. He was hearty and prone to denial. Since I grew up in family where alcoholism was denied, I was particularly angered at this ability of his. He was diagnosed with Hepatitis C—asymptomatic—in about 1999. He could have contracted it from a blood transfusion in the mid-seventies or earlier on in one drug incident.

Martin had the best-case scenario for eliminating the hepatitis, but he was the sort who wanted to deal with things on his own. There are two types of Hepatitis C and his was the one that was curable by taking interferon. But upon looking at its side effects, he decided not to do it, which was a mistake. He had been told that some people live without any problems with the disease. He had also been told that it wasn't communicated sexually. But in the liver tumor handbook, it says otherwise. It was only about five years ago that he really considered interferon because I had insisted on safe sex after the diagnosis. He would say, "You're not going to get it." (It had been twenty years and I hadn't contracted it.) And I would say, "Who *are* you—God? It's MY body."

He was diagnosed with a tumor and cirrhosis within a year of a previous blood test where the tumor marker was borderline. Since he was not a candidate for a transplant, he went online to research and found alternatives, including chemo-embolization, and his blood results improved. But he suddenly turned yellow, ended up in the hospital, and was advised of hospice care. We had a gathering for him and many people came. He felt greatly loved and sat in the sun and improved.

I thought if anyone could beat this it was Martin. He stalwartly ingested his alternatives, but he gradually diminished in weight. One day, he sat his eldest daughter down at the kitchen table and said, "Well, I guess this is it." And he peacefully went into another place. I think that the LSD that he took in the sixties and seventies helped him to make this leap. People would visit in the beautiful, sunlit room/kitchen that he built and feel its tranquility with him in it.

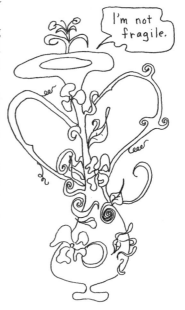

He had no pain. Once, when he was trying to go off the small amount of morphine he had been on so he could drive, he told me in fear, "I don't want to die." There again, was the denial. I told him he just had to accept his body and the time it wanted to take. It took twenty-five days after his acceptance for his body to go along with the program.

I never talked with him about where he would go afterwards. But I know that he was quite capable of making leaps into other realms. He liked the *Seth* books with Jane Roberts. He believed in other universes, parallel realities. He died like a prince, transformed, in 2010. The edge that he always carried (Brooklyn: Italian-Jewish neighborhood) left him.

Towards the end of your life I think it's a good idea to practice letting go of agendas and accepting what is. I don't know if I will be able to accept death so graciously. Martin resisted the fragility of his body at first, and caused us a lot of distress about his falling. I cried with him and said he had to let me take over. He seemed to listen. Still, every day was a lesson in not engaging the ego, that is, going along with his needs with as much tranquility as possible while not making him feel totally inadequate.

I have come to accept *what is* more every day. I used to think I was a Perfectionist until I found how much I was stuck in the morass of tragedy and unfulfilled dreams and realized I'm a Romantic. I don't have too many agendas about how things should be now. I hope every day is a spiritual experience. Life seems to flow much easier, and I don't go into that place of dissatisfaction with my surroundings. I do think about the fragility of life and that is depressing. I do think that my and others' potential demise is depressing— even though some part of me feels that this earth plane is not the best experience one can have. I think we are reincarnated to improve ourselves with another go-round.

Here's a poem I wrote shortly after Martin's death:

Now that I am living on the edge of the world
And the future stretches its cat's paw to a more unknown
Now that you are like the birds that come to light on our deck
And then have flown
I know more nothing than before
I know the in-between
In-between what you say?
The condolences and the grasping at the edge

And each new day is a roller coaster, a balancing act
Between the doing, as if there were some meaning
The humor, as if there were some laughter
That could swallow up the distance of the other sphere you're in
And still, I am in-between it all
In-between and tenuous

Sometimes I wish to just loosen the grasp
And leave this life
That holds us all in such brevity
Too much, too much
The shock
And sometimes not enough
Shock

To propel us into the quickening
That this moment is all we have
And we best fill it with love.

6 Death by Assassination

By Elizabeth Wagele, Observer, Romantic wing

Dr. Martin Luther King, Jr. won the 1964 Nobel Peace Prize and was the most prominent African American leader in the civil rights movement of the 1950s and 1960s. People frequently project their repressed anger onto Asserters in a negative way. Dr. King's story, however, goes against this stereotype.

Heads of companies and world leaders are often Asserter types: Lyndon Johnson, Golda Meir, and Franklin Delano Roosevelt, for example. Dr. King stands out as the most notable civil rights leader the United States of America has ever known. Starting in 1965, this gifted, dignified, and brave man, who started out as a minister, began to express doubts about the United States' role in the Vietnam War. When he went to Memphis, Tennessee, to support a strike of black garbage men in the spring of 1968, he was shot and killed by James Earl Ray. Many doubted if Ray acted alone.

At the time of his murder, Dr. King had been increasingly expressing his opposition to the war and calling for a redistribution of resources to correct racial and economic injustice. On April 4, 1967—exactly one year before his death—Dr. King delivered a speech titled *Beyond Vietnam*, calling the U.S. government "the greatest purveyor of violence in the world today." He argued that, "A nation that continues year after year to spend more money on military defense than on programs of social uplift is approaching spiritual death."

Dr. King's life had been threatened many times and he was obsessed with the possibility that he would be killed. He had trouble sleeping, suffered from depression, and had nightmares when he did sleep. His assassination produced shock, anger, and mourning across America and throughout the world. African-Americans rioted in more than 100 cities and on many campuses.

Our scientific power has outrun our spiritual power.
We have guided missiles and misguided men. – Dr. Martin Luther King, Jr.

7 Bolu Bauri is Dead

By Thomas Rosin, Peace Keeper

Anthropologist Dr. Rosin describes a tough, dignified Asserter of lowly social stature in India.

He was eight days sick, complaining of severe, body-twisting pain in his abdomen. First he ignored it, came into the village center to talk to friends. He had been quarrelsome back in his hamlet, irascible with his wife and relatives. Often he slept nights in the village, as though it were the flaring arguments within his family that gave him pain.

Finally he came to the Priest Sukhdev and sat down before him in the courtyard of the temple. "Master, these pains have me doubled over."

Sukhdev listened, looking intently at this dear friend whose family had always stood supportive of his own. His brows furrowed, he became stern. "You must go. You must go to the doctor in Makrana." Moolsingh and another friend, Warriors by caste, came forward. They supported him from each side, and they began the third of a mile walk out of the village to the bus stop on the route to the neighboring town.

The track skirted around the reservoir, following its high embankment and then dipping down over the bed of the arroyo. Halfway as they came down from the embankment, Bolu Bauri faltered. The pain was great. They pushed on, each of the men supporting more and more of his weight.

They passed the shepherds Herla and Gopi, then the carpenter Kishna; ahead they could see Perohit leaving on his cart drawn by water buffalo. Women passed with hoes going out to their fields. As Bolu passed each person, so they say, "He drew his hands up to salute each and every one. He spoke his "Ram Ram Sa," an invocation to Lord Ram, the noblest of greetings spoken by peasant and shepherd in the Marwar desert of Northwestern India. Bolu Bauri was always ready to give honor to those he respected. And, as a lowly Bauri miner ought, he spoke praise, but only to those among his social superiors he felt were special and to those poorer and in greater trouble who worked hard physically to make their living.

When times became difficult between the landlords and their tenants, Boluji was remembered as the man who could stand alone. He was ready with his seven-foot staff of bamboo to fight. So fierce was he with the staff, twisting and turning it, swinging it right and left, that others could never get near him to strike. He alone, they would say, could hold off four or five men sent to give him a beating. He had earned his right to speak out. "Roshinji," he had said to me, "I am just not afraid. So I speak my mind." A man who speaks exactly what he sees and feels in his heart develops a presence and clarity of mind.

We had been joined together, Bolu and I, on a long trek to retrieve Sukhdevji's cow. She had wandered thirty miles out past Kuchamen City, where the roads turn to sandy tracks, to rejoin the herd of her owner of ten years before. A party had gone before us, but the herdsman had refused to release her.

Sukhdevji and I had set out on motorcycle. We were to meet Boluji at dawn the next day in a village several hours on foot from the hamlet of Bolu's in-laws with whom he was staying. Sukhdevji and I had arrived in the night after the moon had set, pushing a cycle no longer able to plow through the sand. We entered the large, unlit square of the village. A man emerged next to us in the dark; I could not see his face.

"Having trouble with that cycle?"

"Boluji, Boluji, it is your voice I hear. How did you get here?"

"Master, I walked here. Feared that if I waited 'til morning, that bus would never come in time." When he saw that we were settled, he went off seeking his own caste brethren for a night's meal and a place to sleep. He did not know

Sukhdev on left, Boluji on right.

any Bauri in this village, but had set off in the deepening dark of evening from his in-laws' hours before, without even taking an evening meal.

The next morning before sunrise we began walking the miles to the next village, where we would pick up a Warrior who was willing to be an ally in this affair, and go on to the outlying hamlet to inquire about and perhaps demand the cow.

It was winter in the desert. Bolu felt the cold more than I, for he had far fewer wraps. Halfway there, Boluji dragged brambles from the roadside fencing down to the track and lighted them with a match, adding new fuel of thorn, as the pile burned rapidly. He and Sukhdev took its warmth, while I took photographs of them before the fire. We never did get back the cow.

I remember him wearing a seaman's pea jacket, yet could he possibly have been so clothed? He was tough, rustic in the way he spoke his words, always a Bauri well-digger, miner, quarry worker of the laboring class, but he would quote those wonderful Marwari sayings for the occasion. And priest Sukhdev would elucidate, showing how rich in content Bolu's references actually were. With his rustic Bauri pronunciation, his was among the most difficult speech for me to understand, for none of the standard city Hindi language would intrude. He had no pretensions, other than to be a Bauri.

When a man of lowly social stature, but of great personal dignity and fortitude praises, strange how it calls forth the best from those around him. The warriors and priests he favored were finer men in his company.

Moolsingh was working hard to hold Boluji up as they reached our corral, not far away from the bus stand. We were not home that weekend. Had we been home, how we would have called out to him, "Ram Ram Sa, Oh Boluji." Not far from our gate he stopped, then doubled over with pain, and died there.

In India it is said that one can recognize the signs of impending death. Those closest to you will know. If you are ill upon a string cot, they will lift you down to lie upon the earth, cradling your head in their lap.

In the time that now passes—it may be hours, it may be days—those who have lived their lives near you will come. They will greet you upon entering, and perhaps upon leaving. They will sit beside you and talk, knowing that this is the last farewell. But on Bolu Boari's last farewell, he is the one who sets forth, who rises and greets each and everyone. He braves the painful course to the bus stop, knowing perhaps that his efforts to get medical care are too late.

In the Rajasthani countryside there is no farewell. There is rather the invocation that unites us. As we exchange our "Lord Ram" in greetings, we are invoking the powers that sustain us in this moment that our lives cross. How I wish I had been there, chanting back to his call, "Ram Ram Sa, Oh Boluji"— how I yearn to invoke again those moments of our encounter.

8 Killer: Jim Schnobrich

Interview by Elizabeth Wagele, Observer, Romantic wing

A man tells of his Korean War experience using shocking language. Enjoying shocking people is typical of some Asserters.

"I'll tell you what type I am," the retired pilot said. "Asshole." "And what type would your wife say you are?" I asked. "Fucking asshole." Oh dear, I thought to myself, should I bail out of this interview? But curious me. I stayed to see what was next.

We sat in the French Hotel café. Showing off to Jim's male friends who were there was probably the reason for his bravado.

The author taking notes on a napkin while two of Jim's friends listen. Jim is probably an Asserter with an Adventurer wing.

"My code name was 'Snow Fire 1,'" he said. He was stationed off of an aircraft carrier, controlling air strikes from the ground. The last forward controller before him had been killed. When he called in to check with the aircraft, the pilot said, "There's an enemy tank on the other side of the hill." Jim and seven other Americans were up a slope and just then they were overrun by sixteen of the enemy. The Americans killed eight of them and held their ground on the top of the hill. In the quiet of darkness they made a plan for the next morning.

I believe it's true that Jim was in the Korean War. From this point in the story, my ability to trust Jim's veracity dissolves, but you can judge for yourself. Jim said they planned that the next morning they would cut off the genitals of the enemy they had killed. Then they would charge down the hill, shooting and carrying their ammo and radios—with the genitals hanging out of their mouths.

He had one special friend in his outfit named Robert, who weighed about 195 pounds, was tall, handsome, and had been raised a Catholic and spoke German like Jim did. They had agreed if anyone got shot they wouldn't stop. There was gunfire. Robert got hit in the abdomen, and the rest kept going. When they were safe, Jim looked through his binoculars and could see Robert was still alive. "I took my rifle and shot Robert's head off."

"Did you do that so the enemy couldn't torture him?" I asked. He nodded yes. "Is your story true?" I asked. "I can only have true stories in my book."

"That's up to you to decide," he said.

I debated what to do. Asserters like power. Some Asserters use shock to get power. Some of the details seem far-fetched. But Jim really did tell us this story.

In an indifferent universe you have to wring every bit of juice out of the world and push until you can't push anymore. Then you crash and you regain your energy and push some more. – Mario Sikora

9 Death of a Drug Dealer

By Jaki Girdner, Observer

While the Asserter in the casket had no choice but to remain lying down, his buddies had taken on his persona and were feeling as tough as he had been. This was a bad time to mess with them by cutting into the funeral procession.

A friend of mine told me the story of an entrepreneurial Asserter drug dealer and biker he knew who died. At the funeral, everyone took on his personality somehow. They guy (the deathee?) had a heart attack, probably drug-related. His friends had an official funeral procession with cars and motorcycles. Some guy (the idiot?) cut into the procession in his car. A group of bikers surrounded that car and forced him off the road, asking, "What the f... do you think you were doing?" He and his friends replied in kind (mistake?). The bikers and the driver and the friends of the driver got into a big fistfight that the procession stopped to watch. When everyone finally reassembled, they all agreed that the dead guy would have loved the last fistfight; they had

provided a fitting, fighting send-off for their deceased friend.

Driving to the cemetery, a car got too close to my friend's car. Joe, a usually mild mannered fellow, leaped out and threatened the driver's life, later admitting he felt like the deceased more than his usual self.

10 About Asserters

The Asserter belongs to the three Gut or Anger Center types, along with the Peace Seeker and the Perfectionist. All three have issues with anger. Peace Seekers try to avoid anger and Perfectionists are resentful about the lack of perfection in themselves and the world, but try to keep it a secret. Asserters express anger directly, however. Their tough demeanor often goes hand in hand with a soft heart and an abundance of energy (fighter Mohamed Ali). They're frequently attracted to leadership roles, sports, law enforcement, or to the field of crime as perpetrators or enforcers. Most have strong personalities.

Asserters tend to be extraverted (especially those with an Adventurer wing).

They use their Observer arrow for research, as Helen Clarkson did when she learned she had cancer, to bolster their position of power, or to quench their curiosity. Their Helper arrow influences them to be protective and generous, though they avoid appearing vulnerable.

Sometimes Asserters like to shock people (Jim Schnobrich's war story and Helen Clarkson's bluntness). Control (Lester and John), self-confidence, and independence (Martin Linhart) also characterize the Asserter. Since they want to make an impact on the world, their nightmare would be to be forgotten by their children (Mario Sikora). (Achiever Manny Glaser, also a competitive type, has the same fear.)

Helen Clarkson's biggest fear is of becoming dependent on other people. She makes decisions based on what her gut tells her more than her head or heart.

Justice and truth are important Asserter themes. Martin Luther King strove for justice and equality for black people.

The agenda of Asserters revolves around power. Mainly, they don't want anyone to have power over them; they keep track of powerful people so they can be sure to avoid being dominated. Dying is difficult to accept, so if they're told they have a fatal illness (Martin Linhart) they might say, "I can beat this" whether it's realistic or not.

Grieving

If Asserters feel angry about their loss, they usually don't hold their feelings back. When they experience a loss, physical activity can help prevent and relieve stress. Since anger is a more comfortable state for them than sadness, they often don't experience their real feelings until they soften their armor. Talking with someone they trust is a good way to begin disarming themselves.

Shadow

Asserters value being tough and powerful. Their shadow, then, is their soft and vulnerable side. They often distain those who have a gentle persona because they see their own possible weaknesses reflected back to them. At the same time, they excel at helping people who really need it.

Shadow elements show up in the arrows. The Observer arrow represents shyness or the nerd in the Asserter. The Helper arrow represents vulnerability and caring about other people.

The nine types of people

Learning the nine types' points of view helps individuals find balance, acceptance, and wholeness. The Enneagram is valuable both in facing an immediate crisis and in long-range growth.

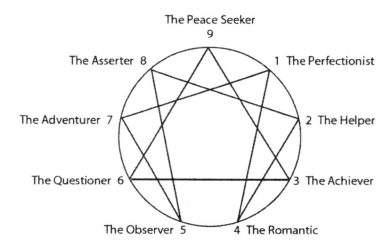

Contents

1. Breast Cancer – Mary Bast
   ("Grateful to the cancer because it brought me into greater presence.")

2. Death is Going Home – Tom Purcell
   (When close friends die his life changes.)

3. The Miracle of Life – Tom Rosin
   ("What-is is the real miracle.")

4. Real: Significant Other – Dr. Jim Campbell
   (A story of mysteries as a brain tumor develops.)

5. My Buddy Karl Kresge: Peace at Last – Elizabeth Wagele
   (The suicide of an old friend.)

6. Belaram Bulai Was Dying – Tom Rosin
   (An Indian seeks medical help from his American friend. Was it wanted?)

7. My Father: "Can't We Have Some Peace?" – James Campbell
   (A doctor writes about his passive father.)

8. Very Quiet Man – Jill Fanning
   (A Native American man dies at the traditional three a.m. time, even though he's in a coma.)

9. Love in Passing – Bertha Reilly
   (A poem about a hospice worker and her dying patient.)

10. Dying of Picks (Almost) – Joyce Dowling
    (An earache turns into TMJ, then a diagnosis of a serious brain ailment, then...)

11. About Peace Seekers

Chapter Nine - Peace Seekers

Our minds try to convince us we are separate... Our focus should be on our unity... We are but a fragment of the greater all. – David Bennett

What sets the principle characters of the stories in this chapter apart from the others is their humanistic outlook on life, their need to not participate in conflict, and their desire to keep their surroundings pleasant.

Writing Styles

Peace Seekers tend to tell stories when they talk and write. Their stories are often long in their desire to be all-inclusive and connect human to human.

1 Breast Cancer

By Mary Bast, Peace Seeker

The liberation Mary feels when she accepts the truth of her impermanence continues a theme of several of the stories in this book. When she gets cancer, she feels she also gets unexpected gifts.

I've been a life coach for more than twenty-five years. But there's no real preparation for being told you have breast cancer. I had a bilateral mastectomy in December 2010, and even though I have a low risk of recurrence, I'm going through all the stages of shock and renewal life-threatening illness can evoke.

I Choose Authenticity, February 2011

Authenticity is a daily practice. Choosing authenticity means: • cultivating the COURAGE to be imperfect, to set boundaries, and to allow ourselves to be vulnerable; • exercising the COMPASSION that comes from knowing we are all made of strength... and connected to each other through a loving and resilient human spirit; • nurturing the CONNECTION and sense of belonging that can only happen when we let go of what we are supposed to be and embrace who we are.

– Brené Brown, Ph.D.

Many people who've had cancer report significant changes in their lives and a gratitude that might seem strange to those who haven't been there. Having had cancer recently, I realize how difficult it is to put into words the gratitude I feel. Of course I'm grateful to be alive, grateful to all the helping professionals, friends, and acquaintances who are part of my healing, grateful to my body the cancer didn't spread through the lymph nodes, grateful I don't have to have chemo. But my gratitude spreads beyond those happy aspects— I'm grateful to the cancer because it brought me into greater presence than I'd ever experienced.

The question has become, "Now that I am present to my impermanence, how do I live every moment going forward?" The answer to this question has not been a conscious decision. It's bloomed in me as a consequence of opening myself, of having *yielded* to and *embraced* breast cancer. The biggest lesson has been how I'd contributed to the burden of caretaking I'd been feeling—in my life and in my work—by keeping the focus completely on other people and not asking for what I needed. I was giving, but not allowing myself to receive. Caretaking fed my ego and also exhausted me.

Having cancer required that I learn how to ask for help and to be clear to those around me what kind of help I needed—to be listened to, encouraged to talk about myself. Instead, my gift of focusing on the positive took charge, and left no room for feeling tired, disoriented, lonely, and that dreaded state— *needy*. Everyone was rejoicing in how brave and amazing I was, while some newly acknowledged part of me simply wanted to curl up and be held.

Exactly as Dr. Brené Brown's research on authenticity suggests, I'm more connected now because I learned a new kind of courage—to be imperfect (needy), to set boundaries (ask for what I want and don't want), to allow myself to be vulnerable (admitting these needs without shame), and along with this came true compassion (giving is no longer a one-way street). Thus,

I'm grateful to Dr. Brown for putting into words the lesson I most needed to learn.

So, now that my energy and mental balance have returned, instead of feeling back to my old self, I'm forward into a new self, one that has a *squishy* part I didn't have before. *Vulnerability* can be interpreted as defenseless, exposed, insecure. My new squishy part has none of those negative connotations. It has made me softer, more yielding, tender, sensitive, open, and accessible.

Cave Drawings, June 2011

Research suggests that trauma survivors can head off long-lasting symptoms by letting friends know what they're going through. – Susan Lien Whigham, *The Role of Metaphor in Recovery From Trauma*

I had not thought of my cancer diagnosis and surgery as *trauma* until I read the transcript of *How the Brain Helps Us to Survive Trauma* and understood that any life-threatening event can be traumatizing—war, a terrible car accident, a natural disaster, a heart attack, cancer.

And the measure of how well or quickly we recover, compared to those who might develop post-traumatic stress disorder, is whether or not we can discharge the energy created by the shock. Some of our response to stress is determined by our own emotional resiliency, but much of it depends on whether our caregivers, family, and friends contribute to our feeling helpless or support our gaining a sense of control. We can begin to take charge of our fate when we're able to talk about our feelings, absorb the reality of our circumstances, and move into action.

My strongest urge while convalescing from surgery was simply to be listened to. And yet, I didn't really have the words to express what I was experiencing. Some of my friends interpreted my early quasi-silence as a desire to have my spirit lifted, and entertained me with stories. I loved them for this, yet also needed help to find words for what I was experiencing.

So I was relieved to read how listening for metaphors can help recovery from trauma. I remembered an earlier blog entry where I tried to express my reaction to others' view of my "bravery":

It's like driving in a heavy rainstorm late at night. You'd rather be home by a cozy fire, but you're on full alert, every sense attuned to what's happening in your immediate environment. You don't have time to be afraid.

I didn't feel brave; I felt swept up in a tide of experience. During the two weeks of diagnosis, biopsy, and surgery I was in a kind of trance, floating, as if rocked on the waves of a deep ocean.

Notice the quality of water in these metaphors—rainstorm, tide, waves, ocean. And notice also how these water metaphors are hard to pin down (another metaphor); how fruitless it would be to try to capture water with a *pin* of any sort. And yet, these watery images have helped me embrace a shock too big to encompass with left-brain language.

Breast cancer brought death into my house. Paradoxically, the mastectomy brought a change to my body that meant I could stave off death, probably for many years, so I denied the surgery as trauma. It's taken almost six months for me to see the loss of my breasts as a *disfigurement*, to notice how I've dressed to hide it from the world, how quickly I cover myself after a shower—when I used to be so happily naked.

I was helped to finally let in the loss by following my metaphors, diving in to the ocean, being swept by the tide to a barren shore, finding a flat terrain with strange plants and unknown dangers, dark caves filled with ancient drawings, wondering *who are these others who have been here before me? How can I survive this?*

And I must find my way through this metaphorical territory, go into the dark caves, experience the fear, learn from the ancient drawings, find guidance from others who have been here for a while. They will encircle me as I weep for the loss of my breasts, they will chant with me as I celebrate life's changing seasons and embrace more enduring symbols of womanhood.

2 Death is Going Home

How the instant deaths of my friends changed my life

By Tom Purcell, Peace Seeker

In this story, we follow the adult life of a Peace Seeker to whom personal connections and resolving relationships are important.

A few days after my father passed away (see *Death Will Be Graduation Day*, Chapter Six) I had a vivid dream in which he appeared, not as an old man in pain, but a young, vibrant, confident man. The message was: "I'm fine, everything is okay, don't worry." Up to that point in my life, I had felt there had been unfinished business between us, we could not seem to agree on anything, and there was an emotional distance we could never bridge. I let him go and released many childhood feelings surrounding him.

At present in my mid-fifties, I don't think about my death and the afterlife as something to fear, but as a new adventure. I didn't think about my own death at all until I was twenty-two. Within one hour I was informed about the accidental death of my best friend and two others I had known very well. My best friend was like a brother to me. We met in high school and shared a house during our university years. One summer we toured California together and met some high school friends who took us on a sailboat ride in San Francisco Bay. We had similar Irish Catholic backgrounds and spent many a night laughing about our upbringing and making plans for our future as ex-Catholics, which would include every possible sin of self-indulgence.

The day he died marked the end of innocence for me and for the group who had come to our house every weekend for years to have a good time. Soon I moved to another city. After some lonely times, I eventually made new friends and embarked on a lifelong journey of self-discovery. Like some other baby boomers, I explored Eastern religions, lived in the Middle East for a couple of years, and immersed myself in the Islamic tradition, including the mystical Sufism. I practiced meditation, pursued transcendent experiences, and eventually came to the understanding that my essence will never die. My physical body will return to the earth, my ego identity will dissolve, but the divine presence of my living spirit is eternal. Death is going home.

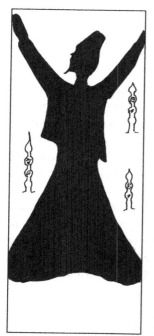

I've always felt lucky and assumed I would live into my nineties. When the joy of living goes, I prefer to die. I can't imagine that happening at this time, but being in pain may change that. An ideal way of dying, according to the ancient Egyptians, was if a man expired during sexual intercourse and his soul would travel into the womb of his lover. This would ensure his next incarnation would be through a woman he loved before he was born and eliminate the need for a father. That appeals to me.

As funerals are for the living, I don't care what the ritual is or what happens to my mortal coil, but I prefer to have my ashes spread in a forested area where they can fertilize new life forms. I also like the ancient Zoroastrian ritual of exposing the corpse in a tower so the birds can pick it clean.

I believe we are spirits having a human experience. Clinging to life when our spirits want to be free is similar to staying awake when we need to sleep. We come into this world kicking and screaming, fighting to breathe, and then, when all is said and done, desire a peaceful death.

Funeral rituals are at least partly designed to wake us up, to contemplate our own mortality, and to inspire us to feel gratitude for the miracle of human life. One channeled reading influenced my attitude toward life, i.e. immediately following the passing out of our bodies, we will be asked two questions—what have you learned and whom have you helped?

I've felt connected to an inner knowing through some out of body experiences that left me feeling very peaceful. Usually, my encounters with the great mystery have taken the form of angels in human form. When I have felt hopeless and confused and have asked for help, it has always come in the form of a stranger who just happened to strike up a conversation with me about the very issue I was perplexed about.

Create understanding and tolerance so we may work toward peace within and thereby outward. – David Bennett

3 The Miracle of Life

By Dr. Thomas Rosin, Peace Seeker

Dr. Rosin's view about the relationship of body to spirit is that what is material is the real miracle. Peace Seekers, as all the types, consist of people of many different ideologies.

The miracle of life, of everyday existence, of the now-of-experience is the emergence of spirit or soul out of matter. This sense is what I try to carry with me each day. What-is is, of course, the real miracle. The more we learn of the universe around and within us, the more intricate, detailed, and infinite in scope do we find it. Not only has life emerged, with its rich subjectivity for each such life so woven out of materiality, but also much of that life is conscious, and some of it even self-conscious and reflective.

Our knowing and experiencing life is a part of this unfolding, evolving, and miraculous creation. As consciousness and self-reflection emerge out of creation, each such monad allows the universe, as it were, to view itself within this cosmos. Yet, this consciousness, and even this self-reflective knowing, is woven out of the materiality of the universe. Mind and body, spirit and matter, are woven out of one another. Just as an electromagnetic field can be traced to a configuration of spinning planet with iron core, so too can spirit, subjectivity, consciousness be traced to the configurations of matter and energy that give it being.

I have before me in my study a sculpture by Don DeVeiros. I call it "The Quickening," the moment at which out of bone, sinew, horn, and wood, so carefully articulated and configured, emerges spirit. This sculpture is as though alive. Another who took it home from Don's Gallery was forced to return it, for his wife felt so powerfully the presence of a soul emerging, that she could not sit alone with it in the room.

"The Quickening" is that miraculous movement wherein life and spirit emerges out of matter. When matter is quickened, made alive by spirit. Such has almost happened, or is happening—if I linger but a moment more, that sculpture will quicken into life. I shall be confronted with a Deer Spirit. It shall move from the wall and engage me. Yet, such works of Creation, rather those of Don DeVeiros, do actually quicken into life, my life one among them. But we are a mysterious weaving of materiality: flesh, bone, nerve, and sinew set aflame into life and subjectivity. When that particular arrangement wears out, slows down, halts, I am dead. This particular arrangement of matter decays and falls apart, and this particular miracle of my own existence woven out of materiality disappears. I would wish it no other way, such are my convictions. Let us exult and give thanks for these miraculous moments when we and those we love have been quickened into life. May we exult in the living, honoring and revering and standing in awe before the miracle and the mystery That Is.

But the flame of life, as we have come to know it upon this planet goes on, that we do know, and can rejoice in that knowing. We in our own individuality are but a part of this great flow of life, temporarily here, but able to experience the infinitude of being present in each successive moment of our being. So may we rejoice and bare witness, this moment, to our universe.

4 Real: Significant Other

October 27, 1930 – February 13, 1981

By James Campbell, Observer

In this story, the arrow (see the diagram at the end of the chapter) becomes important. Real is influenced by the aspect of his Achiever arrow, the personality type that has a tendency to re-invent itself.

I met Real in June 1978 when he was working for the French Commercial Services in San Francisco. He was supposedly French and had been raised in Neuilly, one of the posh suburbs of Paris. He had a lovely apartment in Dolores Heights, loved to cook, and had a fine aesthetic sense. Most of all, he enjoyed his cabin in the woods about a mile from the Russian River. He had an outward easy going manner—typical of a Peace Seeker—and several friends, but seemed rather critical of most of them. At times he didn't want to speak with them. We always got along well. He seemed to fit into my agenda and even took up skiing, which he had never done before.

A year or more after I met him, his mother came for a visit. I speak some French, but not well. I had a difficult time understanding her French. When I asked her about Neuilly, Real immediately whisked me off into another room and warned me not to speak of it with her since she was going to have to sell the house there.

Around Thanksgiving of 1980, my mother visited; we had dinner with Real. She was fond of him; it was rare that she would say such kind things about any of my friends. A couple of days after I had taken her to the airport, a lovely French woman from Real's office phoned me to say that he was in San Francisco General Hospital with a stroke. When I visited him, the CAT scan of his head they showed me revealed a moderately large hemorrhage in the left hemisphere. He had partial paralysis of the right side of the body and fluent aphasia, i.e., words came out clearly but they didn't make

sense. He stayed in the hospital and later a rehab hospital through December 24, 1980, at which time he came home with me considerably improved. He walked well, prepared Christmas dinner using both hands (he was right handed) and made some limited conversation. It seemed as if the personality had vanished.

On December 26, as we were having breakfast together, he broke out into tears. The right side was paralyzed again. I called an ambulance to take him to University of California Hospital, walking distance from my house. He improved slightly, but it seemed like the beginning of the end. Conversations made less sense. He vomited at times. They did more scans of his head, which revealed a slowly growing mass deep within the left side of his brain. Most neurologists agreed that it was a malignant brain tumor, probably glioblastoma. A biopsy was needed to confirm the diagnosis, but I knew that a biopsy could cause further bleeding into his brain. The only treatment option was radiation of the brain, but I knew that this would only prolong life with several months of misery and wasn't likely to reverse his neurological deficit. Consequently, he didn't have to biopsy. He eventually stopped eating and vomited if he did eat. Early in February, he was transferred to a nursing home with feeding tube in place. I discussed the futility of the feeding tube with his primary care M.D. We agreed to discontinue it. He died on Friday, February 13.

On January 4, his mother came from Montreal, Quebec, to stay with him in the hospital all day every day until he died. We got along quite well and could eventually communicate in French. When Real became sick, a close friend

186

from Canada informed me that Real was from Quebec and not France. I needed to let Real know that I knew this, so I commented that I had a hard time understanding his mother's French and wondered where she was from. He said she was from the North (he was somewhat compromised mentally then). I replied, "You mean Canada?" He replied, "No, the north of France." I said no more on that subject. Also, around the time he became ill, I had to rummage through his documents because I was named his durable power of attorney. From this I learned that he was four years older than he had stated; it also confirmed his Canadian origin. I felt sad that he had to live with an altered persona. I couldn't understand his reasons for inventing a new life history.

Examination of the brain in an autopsy revealed glioblastoma, an incurable brain tumor. In retrospect, his family, friends, and I were glad about the decision to limit his care so early. I have had three more friends die of that disease since that time. Most lived about a year, but with many hospitalizations and much misery.

I was grievous about Real's medical condition from the day he became ill. As I saw the neurological deficits progress I would become tearful and had a hard time keeping the tears away when conversing with him. In late February 1981, his mother, a couple of close friends, and I took his ashes to his cabin at the Russian River and scattered them in the forest. My mother was very sympathetic about his death. I didn't take any time off work after he died. I was sad but could cope.

The mind of compassion is truly present when it is effective in removing another person's suffering. – Thich Nhat Hanh

5 My Buddy Karl Kresge: Peace at Last

By Elizabeth Wagele, Observer, Romantic wing.

Karl was comfortable to be with, a trait shared with many Peace Seekers. Perhaps Karl was too comfortable with his troubles than need be; seeking medical or psychological help as a teenager may have changed his life.

The phone call came during a neighborhood block party I had organized one summer. We'd gotten a permit from the city of Berkeley to shut off car traffic. We'd brought out picnic tables to the street from our back yards. I'd made potato salad and hors d'oeuvres, neighbors were roasting hot dogs and hamburgers, and children were running around shouting and playing badminton. I was standing on the sidewalk by our cement stairs, thinking about how many serving spoons to retrieve from my house...

Decades before, in the 1950s, Karl and I lived in the same neighborhood and went to the same church. My parents were good friends with his parents, Adah and Miles, and would get together on their own for Sunday afternoon drinks. I got to know Karl fairly well when he and his pal, Ron Riddle, who lived a few houses away from us, would stop by our house when walking my older sister home from high school. Before long we became best buddies, spending weekend afternoons washing his light green Plymouth and my family's beige Chevy together, going to jazz concerts, swimming in Lake Anza, or just hanging out. Had I been his age, I might have been concerned about his poor grades, but I was six years younger and I had other things besides Karl's education on my mind: my own schoolwork, practicing the piano, and other friends.

Karl was mild mannered and attractive, his big blue eyes outlined like a cat's by dark lashes. He loved to giggle, laugh, and make jokes in those days. Our relationship was pleasant and fun, not romantic. He seemed to have less life force than most kids I knew, had no consuming interests, and drank too much. When I'd get depressed in my adolescence, I'd future-trip and lament, what if my true love didn't come along? Would I have to end up with Karl? I hoped I'd marry someone more exciting, not someone who was almost sleepwalking through life, whom I'd have to worry about. But it seemed he'd always be there just in case.

Karl at my senior ball

When time for my high school senior ball rolled around I didn't want to go. My sweetheart, Gus, who later became my husband, was away on a trip at the time. He attended the University in Berkeley and might not have wanted to go to a high school dance anyway. But my friends pleaded with me to go. Karl felt he'd missed out on something by not attending his own senior ball so we went together and had a good time.

The other men in his family overshadowed Karl. His younger brother, Stephen, was an excellent student and won a big scholarship to college. His father, Miles, had been an important army officer who had been honored at the White House for his artillery innovations. Miles lost his first son, Mike, (by another marriage) when Karl was thirteen. Soon after Mike received his M.A from Stanford University and became engaged, a radio fell into his bathtub and electrocuted him. Mike had been the apple of his father's eye.

Karl was drafted into the army while I was still in high school. We wrote letters back and forth in which we would invent names. (One of his invented names was Janice Kif-Slissel-Shlessel.) His first schizo-phrenic episode occurred in the army. After he was discharged, he was in and out of mental hospitals. Gus and I cared about Karl, but since he usually fell asleep when he visited us, we started hoping he wouldn't show up at our house. Then he moved to San Francisco and we didn't see him any more.

Apparently, Karl's health and moods steadily worsened. His brother Stephen told us he couldn't make his life work. He couldn't keep jobs and had a poor social life. He had reached the point of being unable to control much of anything and was living in a halfway house.

Returning to the block party, someone in my house answered the phone, heard the message from my mother, and relayed it out to me on the street. My feelings were blocked off from my body for a few hours after I found out. I was stunned. There I was on a sunny day enjoying a party and my old buddy Karl, at age forty-three, had just jumped to his death from the Golden Gate Bridge. I felt devastated thinking about Karl's unhappiness and suicide for a few months, then less over the years. I mourn his death rather as one might mourn a child's. His life never quite got going.

Some people said Karl was courageous. Some feel suicide is cowardly. I'm not interested in applying an adjective to suicide. I just hope the next person who shows the same symptoms as Karl gets the help he needs when it's early enough to help.

Better than a thousand hollow words,
is one word that brings peace. – Buddha

6 Belaram Bulai Was Dying

By Dr. Thomas Rosin, Peace Seeker

Dr. Rosin is an anthropologist who has studied a small village in Northern India over many years. He offers his medicine to Belaram hoping to restore his peace, but unwittingly disturbs a greater peace that Belaram is seeking.

His daughter called us to his house. "I need you. His breath will not come." We followed her through the narrow lanes of the weaver neighborhood, through their gate and into his courtyard. His string bed took up central place, around which others squatted, their arms resting on the cot, their faces turned toward his ashen face. I knelt down beside them and pulled from my pocket the medicines I had for treating my own asthma, should I suffer an attack from the dust and the dander of India.

I held a small nebulizer in my hand, with doses of that ancient Chinese discovery of epinephrine, and gazed at this frail figure. Would he be able to handle this bolt, this shot of heart stimulant? He was leaning over, struggling with a breath. I touched his arm, showed him the nebulizer, brought it up to my mouth, and exaggerated my breathing. Exhaling slowly, forcefully, then as I drew in, I showed how I would trigger a blast. Inhaling deeply, I showed him how I would savor it deeply, linger, and then exhale again.

The unit was now in his hand. We exhaled together forcefully then I said. "Take a breath." And as he drew in, I gave his hand a squeeze, and a blast of epinephrine shot into his mouth, hopefully drawn by his weak breath down into his lungs. "Breathe in more." His breathing eased up. We tried another shot, and then put the spray away. It was working, he smiled. His daughter was pleased. The American medicine was good. Fearing he might overdo it if I left the nebulizer with him, I gave him a pill that in time would open up his bronchial tubes and ease his asthma. We checked him several times that day and the next, and matters were much improved. He said he liked my medicine, and we left the village for ten days.

Upon our return and a few days of settling in we came to see how he was doing. Now the scene had changed. His daughter did not seem anxious to see us, but was attentive, not wanting to act unappreciatively. "He is not well," she said. After we had gone, he got worse and worse. They took him by bullock cart to a doctor, but his relief was only temporary, and the trip so tired him out.

"Roshanji, he is on the ground," she said. The cot was gone from the center of the courtyard, which was clean and orderly. Belaram laid there on the ground, on the floor freshly plastered with a mixture of cow dung, straw, and mud, leaving a hard, clear surface, with the fresh aroma of ammonia. Some people left through the gate, others came in. They dropped down, squatting around him. We joined them; I pulled medicines from my pocket. "Here is a pill, like I have given you before."

"No," he said, nearly pushing my hand away. "No, that pill disturbs my mind, gives me no rest, agitates me." I pulled forth the nebulizer. "No." He was irritated by my presence. Someone took me aside, "Roshanji, he is now lying on the ground." Yes, I can see he is lying on the ground. Why don't we place him back on the cot, and let us tend to his asthma, I thought. Let us return him to his cot, make him comfortable, return him to the setting in which I saw him on my prior visit. As more people entered to drop down beside him and give him a warm and hearty, "Ram Ram Sa." ("Lord Ram, Lord Ram") I was being steered away from the gathering. His daughter thanked me, "Roshanji, he does not want your medicines; they make him feel agitated." I thanked her and left through their front gate.

Several days later, we heard the name Belaram called out four times from the lanes moving southward toward the village reservoir, where on the rim

Bulai Weavers buried their dead. They were carrying out his body on a plank, calling out his name to the region of death.

"He is lying on the ground," they had said to me, "Roshanji, he is no longer

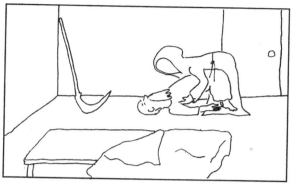

on the cot." They had spoken and I did not then understand. In Rajasthan, when one is dying, approaching death, one is lifted from the cot and placed upon the ground, for one's body should now be in touch with the earth, from which one has sprung, and from which all elements return. Once this movement is taken, then death is near and is expected. Belaram had chosen to be placed upon the earth.

He had chosen to recognize his impending death. It was too late. He was on the pathway to dying, and my offering him mind-disturbing medicines threatened the tranquility and withdrawal he had now chosen. People were coming to bid him farewell. In my innocence, wanting to heal him and quiet his labored breathing, I unknowingly threatened to cajole and disturb him with my medicines. His daughter was trying to tell me that he had already turned from life and the living. It was time to give to him one last "Ram Ram Sa, Oh Belaramji."

I discovered that he had chosen a deeper peace and dignity in dying that I had not yet come to understand.

7 My Father: "Can't We Have Some Peace?"

By James Campbell, Observer

James' father held in anger, which is typical of Peace Seekers. But then, rarely, they may explode like a volcano when they just can't hold it in any longer.

My father grew up in a fairly privileged family in South Bend, Indiana. His father (born 1849) was a math teacher, later a state senator, then co-founder of a local bank, and eventually started the Campbell Box and Tag Company in 1893. His mother was sort of delicate and my father catered to her needs since her husband was so busy.

My father started attending Wabash College in 1904 but dropped out after a couple of years because he was "playing too much billiards." He soon went to work for his father at the box company, eventually became president, and sold the company in 1959 at age seventy-five. He lived with his parents until his first marriage in 1928 at forty-three. After his wife and child died in childbirth in 1929 he had a mausoleum built for them. He married my mother (Dr. Ruth Rasmussen Campbell in Story #6 of Chapter 1 in 1933; she was from a Danish immigrant family and was a resident in pathology. His anger was audible early in the morning (he got up around 5:30 a.m.). We could all hear him seething as we were lying in our beds (not in the same room), which made me feel that he held in a lot of anger. My mother was the ultimate disciplinarian. Sometimes what he said didn't count, but I usually obeyed him.

My father had many friends and was socially prominent in South Bend, although in a quiet way. He was active in the Methodist Church but sort of in the background. He taught Sunday school for a while.

He belonged to the Great Books Society and read a lot of good books (but sometimes fell asleep reading them). He didn't express opinions often, was quite passive, and had a Victorian temperament; Dad hated vulgar language or any mention of sex.

He had slowed down considerably for two years prior but still could walk with a cane. One icy February day, he fell down the steps and became somewhat disoriented thereafter. He died one month later at age eighty-seven in a nursing home, where he had kept referring to the orderlies as "perverts." I think he was a Peace Seeker with a Perfectionist wing, probably a social subtype.

8 A Very Quiet Man

By Jill Owsley Fanning, Questioner

Barney Guss' ability to mediate is typical of Peace Seekers.

> *Our heart is normally benevolent allowing us to move ahead freely without the need to "Think about what's right." – David Bennett*

Barney Guss lived on the Tulalip Reservation on the Washington coast north of Seattle. He was the hereditary chief of the Snoqualmie people, an unrecognized tribe that was dying out. He had been a man with the gift of public speaking who was always expected to say inspiring words at public events and ceremonies.

When I knew him, he was very old and sleepy but still shared his words of encouragement when asked.

He was almost ninety when he died. People came from miles around to honor this quiet man who was everybody's friend. They said, "He was a peaceful man and brought us together, like he's doing now."

He had been a long-time member of the Indian Shaker Church of the Pacific Northwest. They are clean, strict, and devout in their practice, they dress in blue and white for their meetings, ring bells instead of beating drums, and they do rituals three times instead of four (the usual number for native Americans).

I got the phone call one evening after Barney had been in the hospital for a day or two. "You'd better come up to Everett Hospital soon. Barney is expected to leave us tonight." He had gone into a coma that morning. When I arrived, several of his relatives and good Shaker people dressed in white were sitting around his bed drinking coffee, eating donuts, and sharing light conversation and amusing stories. At ten minutes before 3:00 a.m., the nurse came in for a random check. When she left, the people stood and began to sing a Shaker song softly. They continued to sing prayerfully and quietly until 3:05 when the nurse came back and pronounced Barney dead. Barney had left at 3:00 a.m., the proper time for good Shaker people and respected elders to die. There was a profound sense of happiness and peace in the room. The family was weeping softly but smiling and joyful.

How did he know it was 3:00 a.m. and he was supposed to leave his body at that time when he was in a coma? The Shakers had come. They had prayed him on his way.

9 Love in Passing

By Bertha Reilly, Peace Seeker hospice worker, about her client

Bertha has the ability to merge with her client, whether listening to his stories or in the quiet of his dying hours.

The Enneagram of Death by Elizabeth Wagele

Be like water—flow. – Sylvie Nienhuis

They sat on the low wall facing the declining sun.
He said, "I could have three months
   or even six no one really knows."
She bowed her head knowing he had
   a week or two at the most.
She said nothing
Just noting his dreams flitting away
   at the edge of the reality that was so hard to touch.
Yet she knew he touched it.
But nonetheless he allowed his dreams to float
   before him into the sunshine.
His hair was growing back a little.
A soft downy fuzz covering
   the bald radiated head.
His eyes were sunken
   dark lines of black fatigue underscored the sockets.
Yet he was peaceful.
His worn body no longer fought the unwished for disease.
Acceptance had come.
"Still" he said
"I think I have done everything I wanted to do."
She touched and held his hand
   and they were silent.
There was nothing left to say but the mingling of their breaths in the
   afternoon air.
They stood up
   and walked slowly back into the hospice.
His weakness leaning on her strong body.

When she came the next day
He could no longer talk to her.
During the night
   he had slipped into a light coma.
She sat by the bed
   and stroked his hand and spoke soft comforting words to him.
How well he had lived his last few days of love and acceptance
And how she would not forget.
His breathing slowed and deepened, his eyes flickered open.
And she knew he was still there
Although he had now truly started on that long journey from where he

would never come back.
It seemed like he even tried to speak to her
    but no words came from the weakness of his body.
And so he died.

Still sometimes she goes to sit on that low wall
And thinks of Thomas
    how they sat there on the day before he died.
Such a brief time they knew each other.
    Yet she knows there were gifts he gave her as yet untold.
She hopes she gave him what she could.

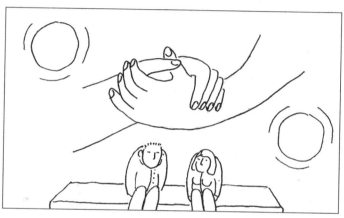

10 Dying of Picks (Almost)

By Joyce Dowling, Peace Seeker

Joyce was facing death but her wishes were humble—to do everyday things with her family, which expresses the Everyman aspect of the Peace Seeker.

There are times in one's life, as they say, if they don't kill you, they make you stronger.

On October 10, 2007, my ear exploded with the worst earache ever.

The emergency doctor put me on a treatment for an ear infection. In three days a different doctor put me on different antibiotics and decongestants and referred me to an ear, nose, and throat doctor (ENT) who added nose drops. My ear still ached, though the pain no longer made me cry. The ENT put a tube in my ear to drain the fluid.

A week later, the ENT calmly said it was TMJ (temporomandibular jaw joint disorder), with no explanation for the wrong diagnosis. He gave me a booklet and a prescription that didn't help much. Beside the intense pain, I now heard a loud constant ringing: tinnitus. I was going crazy. A neurologist took loads of tests and was concerned that I had no reflexes in my extremities. I tried new medications from my regular doctor, who also recommended a dentist. In desperation I went to a chiropractor, who relieved some tension from my shoulders and neck and promised some relief from the jaw pain and tinnitus in a few weeks, which didn't happen. The dentist fit me with a mouthpiece to take the pressure off my ear while I slept and said I'd probably have to wear it for the rest of my life. I studied about TMJ. My crooked jaw was probably causing fluid to be pushed in my ear and pinching a nerve to start the ringing.

No one could stop the pain or ringing so I decided not to think about it, which worked when I was concentrating deeply. I couldn't sleep, however, so I worked until I dropped.

Soon I received a call to substitute teach full-time in an elementary school for the deaf. I quickly said yes to keep busy. I only slept about five hours each night but I felt better and I was enjoying my work and loving life again. I was brought up a Unitarian and was taught I was in charge of my life—even my death. So I tried to heal myself and it was working. Even though I had a terrible ringing and the pressure on my ears swelled the right half of my face, I felt great! I was still helping others by teaching special needs kids, active in the racial justice work and managing the web site at my church, on the board of my county civic federation, singing in the church choir, giving online love advice, and helping several other organizations with their web sites.

One day my car got rear-ended. It shook me up, but everyone was fine so I hurried on to work. Near the end of the day, an official came in to observe our teaching and I pulled out a science experiment—teaching the kids about sound. While I was getting out a tuning fork and containers filled with water, the assistant, who can't hear, was explaining in American Sign Language what sounds were like and how they could feel the vibrations. We were in sync and the kids seemed to understand and enjoy the experiment: making water splash with vibrations from the tuning fork. The director called me into her office after the kids left. When I tried to write some ideas down for her, it appeared like gibberish. Driving home that day, I thought about how I had been so over-tired lately. The stress was taking a toll. I could feel my mind slipping away.

When I arrived home, no one was there, but I was paranoid that my husband would be upset with me when he saw me in that condition. He knew I wasn't taking care of myself, especially getting sleep. I wanted to write him a note before he arrived to explain but I saw him coming home with our son so I scribbled it quickly, which also ended up being gibberish. I was in the throes of a nervous breakdown but didn't know it. I ended up in the hospital psychiatric ward and was given an MRI. They started me on some medications to help with the ringing in my ears and my sleep. Before I left the hospital, they told me there was a problem with the MRI and I needed to make an appointment with the neurosurgeon.

At home I had a relaxing celebration with my daughter and my mother-in-law. My husband and son were doting on me, too. No more hard work and lots of sleep. I got a clean bill of health to go back to work, but the director of the school thought the assistant could teach the kids by herself. The medication and compresses on my jaw helped and the mouthpiece was slowly helping my TMJ. Finally, to my amazement, they told me I have a shrunken brain. Fluid was in my skull where my brain should have been.

I went to my regular doctor and he said, "Picks," before telling me that I needed some neurological tests to rule it out. We found out Picks is a severe neurological disorder in a group of rare diseases known as frontotemporal dementia (FTD). It could kill in mere months or I could have one of the other diseases that would extend the dementia even longer. Early Alzheimer's is one of the FTDs.

I joined an online support group and heard sad stories of the terrible process of those diseases from caretakers, widows, and widowers. It is similar to what the boy had in one of my favorite movies, *Lorenzo's Oil*. My husband tried to reassure me that we did not *know* it was Picks, but we had been married long enough for me to see he was doubtful. I could understand how a person in pain could think of suicide or a caretaker could think of putting a loved one out of her misery. I felt bad for my family and all the good life I would miss.

When I took tests at the University in Washington, DC, the student doctor thought my MRI was so interesting that he kept it. I was sent to another neurologist for further tests. In the mean time, I heard from the FTD forum about a specialist in Baltimore. Waiting for the appointment, I had a great life and didn't want to change it. I wanted to see the people I loved the most, go thrift shopping with my daughter and mother-in-law, and play with my granddaughter.

I'd already cut down on the volunteer responsibilities that I loved. My church was there for me. I especially liked singing in the choir, teaching children sign language, and being a small part of a faith organization trying to make the world a better place. What could be better than that!

My loving husband of thirty plus years was there for me, too, and I knew he'd be there to the end. Though he never let on, I learned later that he was starting to withdraw because he didn't want to think about the hurt of losing me. I also found out that the first neurologist who had taken an MRI had seen the recessed brain and had chosen not to say anything. When I asked why, he said, "Why bother if you can't do anything about it?" What a philosophy!

The neurologist in Virginia thought it wasn't likely I had an FTD; with that much brain loss my tests shouldn't have turned out so well unless the symptoms from the degeneration were caught at a very early stage. The real test was with the doctor at John Hopkins who had a special computer program to look at the digital images of my brain.

I went through the same neurological tests for the fourth time in half a year with the same results: no noticeable signs of degeneration of my brain function. He then analyzed the imagery on his computer and said I definitely did NOT have an FTD because my brain tissue was healthy. For all they knew, I was born that way, but he told me that I should have another MRI in eighteen months to make sure. I wasn't going to experience a horrible lingering death any time soon.

I had been ready to go if it was my time. Now I live every day as if it could be the last. I never go to bed or leave someone feeling bad. We have to work out any tiff or let it go if it doesn't make a difference in the scheme of things— and not much does. But I was happy it looked like I had many more healthy years of living. I was getting used to the TMJ and tinnitus and in comparison to some friends' arthritis or cancer treatment, I was doing great.

Longevity runs in my family with women living to their nineties. I better take care of myself if I don't want to live many of those years with osteoporosis like my grandmothers did. They both got depressed but I don't expect to; even if I out-live my husband and children, I see myself as much more than a wife and mother. My church community helps me do that. Even if I move, there are Unitarian Universalists and like-hearted people everywhere. With the Internet connecting me to them, I feel like I have friends everywhere. Life is great now. I'm more aware of the inevitability of death, but I've learned that I can deal with it.

11 About Peace Seekers

Peace Seekers have a positive outlook, dislike conflict, understand many points of view, and consequently are good at helping others get along together, like Barney Guss. Many have an affinity for nature and might wonder something like, "How many have gone before and will go after me?" Peace Seekers relate to the Everyman in themselves, ordinary individuals leading ordinary lives. They often espouse the concept of the unity of all things.

The Peace Seeker's arrows point to the Questioner, a model for loyalty and skepticism, and the Achiever, a model for being energetic and getting things done. Joyce Dowling seems to have a connection to her Questioner arrow—especially when she wonders about what possibilities her old age might bring. When James Campbell describes the story of his lover's brain tumor, we find out Peace Seeker Real is something of a chameleon; this suggests his connection to his Achiever arrow. Achievers sometimes reinvent new personas for themselves.

Real may have a Perfectionist wing, judging from his moments of being overly critical. Peace Seekers with Asserter wings are notable for being more confronting than most other Peace Seekers.

The agenda of most Peace Seekers is to remain calm. I've often heard Peace Seekers say they look more laid back than they feel. When others see their easygoing manner, they tend to relax, which in turn calms the Peace Seekers.

Peace Seekers tend to be down to earth and humble. When Joyce thought she might be dying soon, she wanted to see the people she loved the most, go thrift shopping with her daughter and mother-in-law, and play with her granddaughter rather than indulge herself in an extravagant dream.

Peace Seekers are sometimes thought of as "self-forgetting." They don't always know what they want or how they feel so they tend to go along with whomever they're with. This in turn can lead to resentment, which they are slow to notice.

Grieving

Peace Seekers are normally loving and supportive of others in grieving situations. Some might space out in order to avoid their own painful feelings, however. Since starting and stopping can both be difficult due to their inertia, some may take a long time to feel their loss. Most would like to say—and feel, "I'm fine, everything is okay, don't worry," as Tom Purcell's father did in Tom's dream.

Shadow

The shadow for Peace Seekers is the warring side of themselves and others, the anger they go out of their way to avoid. James Campbell's father may have been projecting his anger onto the orderlies in his nursing home when he called them perverts.

Shadow elements show up in the arrows. Among other things, the Questioner arrow represents nervousness and fear. The Achiever arrow can represent high ambition or social climbing. Mary Bast speaks of the shock of recovering from cancer: "We can begin to take charge of our fate when we're able to talk about our feelings, absorb the reality of our circumstances, and move into action."

The nine types of people

Learning the nine types' points of view helps individuals find balance, acceptance, and wholeness. The Enneagram is valuable both in facing an immediate crisis and in long-range growth.

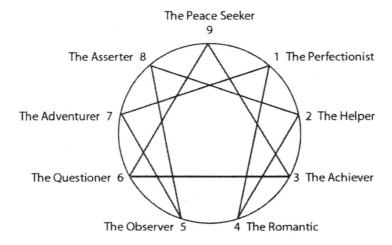

Afterword

Now that you've read these stories about how different Enneagram types have coped with dying and faced their fear of death, here's an example that illustrates what a difference the acceptance of death can make in a person's life. May all these examples—be they vulnerable, open, strong or brave—accompany you on your journey.

My relationship with death experiences is that I can sit with someone who is dying without the anxiety I notice others having. When my beloved grandmother died, I made sure I was there at the moment of her death, while other relatives fled. I sat with her body until the mortuary came. It is a sacred thing and an honor to me to be present with another through this time.
      – Leslie Maycroft, Helper, strong Achiever wing

I think that if people started thinking about death sooner they'd make fewer foolish mistakes. – Dmitri Shoshtakovich

About the Author

Elizabeth Wagele (pronounced "Way'glee") attended the University of California at Berkeley majoring in music and music composition. She has co-written *The Enneagram Made Easy, Are You My Type, Am I Yours?*, and *The Career Within You*. She also wrote *Finding the Birthday Cake, The Happy Introvert, The Enneagram of Parenting*, and *The Beethoven Enneagram* CD on which she performs the piano. She and her husband Gus live in Berkeley CA where they raised four children.

Wagele Cartoons and Books: http://www.wagele.com
Psychology Today Blog: http://bit.ly/psychtdy
Enneagram Blog: http://ewagele.wordpress.com
The Happy Introvert on You Tube: http://bit.ly/HapInt
The Creative Enneagram on You Tube: http://bit.ly/y37z2f

About the International Enneagram Association

Like any vibrant, dynamic organization, the IEA continues to evolve as the needs of our members evolve.

Our vision *a world where the Enneagram is widely understood and constructively used* remains unchanged but our mission, the way the IEA will help bring that vision to fruition, has changed. The IEA's board of directors voted to revise the IEA's mission statement to:

The IEA's mission is to help our members thrive through providing opportunities for:
- *Developing greater excellence in the use of the Enneagram*
- *Education in theory and application of the Enneagram*
- *Engagement with an international community of shared interest and diversified approach*

In the past, the IEA's mission has been to serve as a hub for developments in theory and application of the Enneagram. As popularity of the Enneagram spreads we see a larger need, a need driven by the changing demographics of our membership.

Essentially, our members fall into two broad categories:
- Those who use the Enneagram in their own personal work.
- Those who also use the Enneagram in their work with others in areas such as spirituality, psychology, education, the arts, or business.

The IEA will continue to provide the same (and even more) services that we always have to the first category of members. We are committed to: insightful and informative publications covering all the latest developments in Enneagram theory and application; an international conference and an increasing number of regional conferences that bring the finest Enneagram teachers in the world together under one roof; and providing an opportunity for local and global communion with fascinating, like-minded people.

The growth in the IEA's membership has been in the second category, people who use the Enneagram in their work with others. As people take the Enneagram out into the world, it is important to all of us that we do so constructively, in a manner that is ethical and beneficial to the individual. We see our mission as supporting and encouraging those efforts - serving the community of people publicly committed to a shared set of ethical standards and commitment to integrity in our practice.

The new mission statement changes little about the spirit of the organization, but it serves as a public declaration of intent. It will help the IEA's board of directors, other volunteers, and all of us, as members, better focus our energy and the organization's resources on the initiatives that matter the most.

Benefits of Membership

Membership in the IEA brings a variety of benefits. The more-tangible benefits are listed below, but it is easy to overlook the intangible benefits of membership. Membership in the IEA sends a signal to the world that you are part of an international community of practitioners committed to excellence in their personal and professional practices. It shows that you find value in fellowship with people who share your commitment to the development of wisdom, understanding, and compassion for self and others. And, it shows that you are committed to helping to bring about the IEA's vision of a world where the Enneagram is widely understood and constructively used.

Other member benefits include
- The IEA's quarterly Nine Points Magazine
- Discounted Registration to the Annual IEA Conference and some regional conferences
- Access to Member Only section of the IEA website, which includes:
  — Members Only directory
  — Enneagram symbols for download
  — Back issues of Nine Points Magazine available for download
- Discounts on books and many training programs
- IEA podcast interviews with leading Enneagram teachers

Professional members also receive
- A free copy of the annual *Enneagram Journal*
- Free listing of their services and events on the IEA website calendar
- Eligibility for IEA Professional Accreditation
- Eligibility to present at IEA conferences and events
- Eligibility for listing on IEA Speakers Bureau
- Listing in the "Find a Professional" directory on the website
- Invitation to attend the Professional Member reception at the annual IEA conference
- Eligibility to purchase an email blast sent to the IEA database

The International Enneagram Association brings together Enneagram professionals and aficionados from around the world. Be part of a global learning community by becoming a member of the IEA today!

Visit us at www.internationalenneagram.org

CPSIA information can be obtained at www.ICGtesting.com
Printed in the USA
LVOW01s1458060415

433472LV00005B/99/P

9 780985 786106